THE AMERICAN DREAM

THIS SIDE OF PARADISE *Scott and Zelda Fitzgerald on their honeymoon, 1920. The photo is a virtual compendium of American Dreams: house, car, beauty, youth, talent. (Photo from the collections of the Library of Congress)*

For Mary
with admiration and
gratitude for our
fruitful collaboration.

— Jim Cullen
2004

THE

AMERICAN DREAM

A Short History
of an Idea That Shaped a Nation

JIM CULLEN

OXFORD
UNIVERSITY PRESS

OXFORD

UNIVERSITY PRESS

Oxford New York

Auckland Bangkok Buenos Aires Cape Town Chennai
Dar es Salaam Delhi Hong Kong Istanbul Karachi Kolkata
Kuala Lumpur Madrid Melbourne Mexico City Mumbai Nairobi
São Paulo Shanghai Taipei Tokyo Toronto

First published by Oxford University Press, Inc., 2003
First issued as an Oxford University Press paperback, 2004
198 Madison Avenue, New York, New York 10016
www.oup.com

Oxford is a registered trademark of Oxford University Press

Library of Congress Cataloging-in Publication Data
Cullen, Jim, 1962–
The American dream : a short history of an idea
that shaped a nation / Jim Cullen.
p. cm.
Includes bibliographical references (p.) and index.
ISBN 0-19-515821-0 (cloth) ISBN 0-19-517325-2 (pbk)
1. United States—Civilization—Philosophy.
2. United States—Politics and government—Philosophy.
3. National characteristics, American.
4. Social values—United States. I. Title.
E169.1 .c837 2003 973—dc21 2002072340

Book design and composition by Mark McGarry, Texas Type & Book Works
Set in Monotype Baskerville

1 3 5 7 9 8 6 4 2

Printed in the United States of America

For My Children

You have to describe the country in terms of what you passionately hope it will become, as well as in terms of what you know it to be now. You have to be loyal to a dream country rather than to the one to which you wake up every morning. Unless such loyalty exists, the ideal has no chance of becoming actual.

—**Richard Rorty,** *Achieving Our Country,* 1998

CONTENTS

THE AMERICAN DREAM

INTRODUCTION: A DREAM COUNTRY

I have learned this, at least, from my experiment: that if one advances confidently in the direction of his dreams, and endeavors to live the life he has imagined, he will meet with a success unexpected in common hours.

—Henry David Thoreau, *Walden*, 1854

THAT TITLE WON'T WORK, James Truslow Adams was told. No one will pay three dollars for a book about a dream.

Adams, author of a series of popular books on American history—think of him as the David McCullough or Ken Burns of the 1930s—was seeking to broaden his literary horizons. A man with elite bloodlines dating back to the seventeenth century, when one of his ancestors came to Virginia as an indentured servant and ended up in the landowning class, Adams, born in 1878, had nevertheless grown up under relatively modest circumstances. (His father was an unsuccessful Wall Street broker.) After graduating from Brooklyn Polytechnic Institute in 1898 and earning a master's degree in philosophy at Yale in 1900, he went to work on Wall Street himself, making enough money to devote himself to writing. His local histories of Long Island brought him some renown and attracted the attention of presidential adviser Col. Edward M. House, who hired him to assemble data for the Paris Peace Conference following World War I, which he attended as a cartographer in the American delegation. After the war, Adams wrote his "New England trilogy"—which included the Pulitzer Prize–winning *The Founding of New England* (1921)—and gained scholarly recognition for *Provincial Society, 1690–1763* (1927), a volume in the highly regarded

"History of American Life" series edited by Dixon Ryan Fox and Arthur M. Schlesinger Sr., leading academic historians. He was now poised to become the premier popularizer of his day.

Adams wanted to write a one-volume history of the United States for the general reader, and his publisher, Little, Brown, agreed. As he noted in the preface, there was no shortage of such books. What he wanted to contribute was a broad interpretive sensibility that emphasized important historical themes. For Adams, no theme was more important than what he called

> that American dream of a better, richer, and happier life for all our citizens of every rank, which is the greatest contribution we have made to the thought and welfare of the world. That dream or hope has been present from the start. Ever since we became an independent nation, each generation has seen an uprising of ordinary Americans to save that dream from the forces which appeared to be overwhelming it.

Writing in the early years of the Great Depression—the book was published as *The Epic of America* in 1931—Adams sensed he was living on the cusp of such an uprising. "Possibly the greatest of these struggles lies just ahead of us at this present time—not a struggle of revolutionists against the established order, but of the ordinary man to hold fast to 'life, liberty, and the pursuit of happiness' which were vouchsafed to us in the past in vision and on parchment." As it turned out, Adams was deeply disillusioned by Franklin Roosevelt and his New Deal, feeling they represented a betrayal of American traditions of autonomy and a case of government collusion in the creation of a soulless, materialistic consumer society. Though he would remain popular for the rest of the decade, Adams was increasingly out of step with the temper of his times, and he died, disappointed with his country, in 1948.

In retrospect, it seems odd that Adams was talked out of his wish to call his most popular book *The American Dream*. While it's not clear whether he actually coined the term or appropriated it from someone else, his publisher's reluctance to use it suggests "American Dream" was not in widespread use elsewhere. In any event, Adams invoked it over thirty times in *The Epic of America,* and the phrase rapidly entered common parlance as a byword for what he thought his country was all about, not only in the United States but in the rest of the world. So in this regard it is notable that the edition of the book I happened to pluck off the shelf at the Harvard College library came from a 1941 edition stamped as the property of an army educational supervisor stationed in Europe: the American Dream had become a weapon in the fight against Hitler (and later Stalin). One can only wonder that there was once a moment when the words "American Dream" could be dismissed as obscure or unappealing.

Times change. When, in an early phase of this project, I typed those words into a library catalog, I got back over seven hundred titles: *Education and the American Dream; Tenants and the American Dream; Advertising the American Dream; The American Dream and the Popular Novel; The Endangered American Dream; Prisoners of the American Dream;* and so on. None of the books I looked at makes anything like a systematic attempt to define the term or trace its origins; its definition is virtually taken for granted. It's as if no one feels compelled to fix the meanings and uses of a term everyone presumably understands—which today appears to mean that in the United States anything is possible if you want it badly enough.

Actually, "American Dream" has long since moved beyond the relatively musty domain of print culture into the incandescent glow of the mass media, where it is enshrined as our national motto. Jubilant athletes declaim it following championship games. Aspiring politicians invoke it as the basis of their candidacies. Otherwise sober businessmen cite achieving it as the ultimate goal of their enterprises. The term seems like the most lofty as well as the most immediate component of an American identity, a birthright far more meaningful and compelling than terms like "democracy," "Constitution," or even "the United States."

The omnipresence of "the American Dream" stems from a widespread—though not universal—belief that the concept describes something very contemporary. At the same time, however, much of its vitality rests on a premise, which I share, that it is part of a long tradition. In this view, the Pilgrims may not have actually talked about the American Dream, but they would have understood the idea: after all, they lived it as people who imagined a destiny for themselves. So did the Founding Fathers. So did illiterate immigrants who could not speak English but intuitively expressed rhythms of the Dream with their hands and their hearts. What Alexis de Tocqueville called "the charm of anticipated success" in his classic *Democracy in America* seemed palpable to him not only in the 1830s but in his understanding of American history for two hundred years before that. And it still seems so almost two hundred years later.

In the twenty-first century, the American Dream remains a major element of our national identity, and yet national identity is itself marked by a sense of uncertainty that may well be greater than ever before. Over the course of human history, peoples have used any number of means to identify themselves: blood, religion, language, geography, a shared history, or some combination of these. (Japan comes to mind as an example that draws on all of them.) Yet the United States was essentially a creation of the collective imagination—inspired by the existence of a purportedly New World, realized in a Revolution that began with an explicitly articulated Declaration, and consolidated in the writing of a durable Constitution. And it is a nation that has been re-created as a deliberate act of conscious choice every time a person has landed on these shores. Explicit allegiance, not involuntary inheritance, is the theoretical basis of American identity.

To be sure, the United States has also benefited from some of the glue that holds together other nations. But at the turn of the century, some of that social cement is loosening. In some ways, large transnational institutions like corporations shape the lives of ordinary citizens far more than local government does. Economic and racial stratification have grown markedly, raising doubts about the breadth and depth of opportunity. And amid the greatest surge of immigration in our history, one that brings more people from more of the world than ever before, we don't always speak the same language. At a time like this, the American Dream becomes a kind of lingua franca, an idiom that everyone—from corporate executives to hip-hop artists—can presumably understand.

Indeed, one of the more remarkable things about the Dream is its hold on those one might think are most likely to be skeptical, even hostile, toward it. In her 1996 book *Facing Up to the American Dream,* political scientist Jennifer Hochschild compiles data suggesting that working-class black Americans, for example, believe in it with an intensity that baffles and even appalls more affluent African Americans, who see the dream as an opiate that lulls people into ignoring the structural barriers that prevent collective as well as personal advancement.

This book grows out of a belief that any attempt to assess the possibilities and limits of the American Dream requires a more thorough reckoning than we customarily give it. Such a reckoning begins with a recognition that the Dream is neither a reassuring verity nor an empty bromide but rather a complex idea with manifold implications that can cut different ways. Some of those implications involve the oft-over-looked costs of dreaming. The unfulfilled yearnings of Jimmy Stewart's character in *It's a Wonderful Life,* for example, are never quite erased by the movie's happy ending. The failure of countless social reforms in this country, which founder on the confidence of individual citizens that *they* will be the ones who overcome the odds and get rich, is one of the great themes of American politics. And we've all heard stories about celebrities who find themselves overwhelmed by the very success they so fiercely pursued—and attained. On the other hand, simply *having* a dream has sustained, even saved, lives that otherwise might not be deemed worth living.

The American Dream would have no drama or mystique if it were a self-evident falsehood or a scientifically demonstrable principle. Ambiguity is the very source of its mythic power, nowhere more so than among those striving for, but unsure whether they will reach, their goals. Yet resolution may not afford clarity, either. Those who fail may confront troubling, even unanswerable, questions: Do I blame myself? Bad luck? The unattainability of the objective? Such uncertainty may be no less haunting for the successful, who may also question the basis of their success – and its price.

Beyond such considerations, a reckoning with the Dream also involves acknowledging another important reality: that beyond an abstract belief in possibility, there is no *one* American Dream. Instead, there are many American *Dreams,* their appeal simultaneously resting on their variety and their specificity. What James Truslow Adams called in the epilogue of *The Epic of America* "that dream of a land in which life should be better and richer and fuller for every man" may be fine as far as it goes, but the devil is in the details: just what does "better and richer and fuller" *mean?*

The answers vary. Sometimes "better and richer and fuller" is defined in terms of money—in the contemporary United States, one could almost believe this is the *only* definition—but there are others. Religious transformation, political reform, educational attainment, sexual expression: the list is endless. These answers have not only been available at any given time; they have also changed over time and competed for the status of common sense.

This book explores a few varieties of the American Dream: their origins, their dynamics, their ongoing relevance. It does so by describing a series of specific American dreams in a loosely chronological, overlapping order. I begin with what I regard as the first great American Dream, that of small groups of English religious dissenters who traversed an ocean seeking a way of worshipping God as they saw fit. Their dream was one of manifold ironies, not the least of which involved their clearing a space for subsequent generations to come and pursue aspirations they would have found reprehensible—if they could comprehend them at all.

I then proceed to examine what I call the charter of the American Dream: the Declaration of Independence. This political manifesto was the cornerstone of the American Revolution, the justification for a small group of men to seize the reins of power from the British. But almost despite itself and the intentions of the men who signed it, the Declaration resonated far beyond such relatively narrow aims; my point is to show that notwithstanding the almost impossible remoteness (and ambiguity) surrounding its creation, the document has an immediacy and appeal that has coursed through the marrow of everyday life ever since.

From there, I turn to one of the most familiar American Dreams: that of upward mobility, a dream typically understood in terms of economic and/or social advancement. This too took root early. At the locus of this chapter is a man widely regarded as the greatest American: Abraham Lincoln. Though Lincoln's career is typically understood in terms of the ending of slavery or the preserving of the Union, I argue that for him both were means to a larger end: sustaining the American Dream. Lincoln's rise from obscurity to the pinnacle of American life—and, in particular, the remorseless clarity with which he finally came to understand the dream he embodied—makes him a uniquely compelling lens through which to understand the possibilities and limits of upward mobility.

Moving on to the post–Civil War era, specifically the notorious *Plessy v. Ferguson* Supreme Court decision of 1896, I discuss what I regard as one of the most noteworthy—and unsuccessful—of all American Dreams: the quest for equality, focusing specifically on the struggle of African Americans. This chapter culminates with the civil rights movement of the 1950s and 1960s, and especially the great civil rights leader Martin Luther King Jr. It was King's genius to define his struggle in terms of what a foreign observer once dubbed "the American Creed"— a series of shared ideals that, like the Declaration of Independence, helped define the American Dream in the popular imagination (and

made it difficult for his opponents to resist him). It was also his achievement to compellingly define that dream in terms of something more
than individual fulfillment.

I then look at the most widely realized American Dream: home
ownership. Once again, this is an old dream; I pay special attention to
the way it took shape in the years from the passage of the Homestead
Act (signed by Lincoln in 1862) to the flowering of suburbia in the second half of the twentieth century. The triumph of the suburban dream
has had consequences that have been both deeply reassuring and
deeply troubling.

Which brings me to my final American Dream. This is also a dream
of personal fulfillment, albeit of a very different kind than that of the
Puritans or Abraham Lincoln. Like the others, its roots go back to the
origins of American life, from the so-called adventurers seeking sudden
fortunes on the plantations of Virginia to the speculators mining their
prospects in western cities like Las Vegas. But nowhere does this dream
come more vividly into focus than in the culture of Hollywood—a semi-
mythic place where, unlike in the Dream of Upward Mobility, fame
and fortune were all the more compelling if achieved without obvious
effort. This is the most alluring and insidious of American Dreams, and
one that seems to have become predominant at the start of the twenty-
first century.

This by no means exhausts the list, of course. Indeed, as you read
you may note any number of omissions, even begin to map out addi-
tional varieties of the American Dream. If so, then the book will have
succeeded on some important level, as its goal is to be suggestive rather
than exhaustive.

As with many dreams that become a reality, much about this book
has turned out differently than I expected. (A project that began as a
history of American patriotism has turned into something else that
took much longer, and was much harder, to produce.) One of the
things I realized in writing it is that the American Dream is closely
bound up with freedom and that this book had willy-nilly become a
kind of exploration of that concept as well. For a while, I resisted this
tendency, in large measure because I believe freedom today has largely
become a slogan for marketers and conservative ideologues eager to
enlist it in their causes. (As members of some think tanks like to remind
us, the American Revolution was a tax revolt.) But it is now clearer to
me than ever before that freedom has meant many different, even con-

tradictory, things in American history—as when we're told, for example, that we protect out freedoms by surrendering our privacy or civil liberties. The pluralistic nature of freedom can be a source of frustration, but also a source of hope.

However variegated its applications—which include the freedom *to* commit as well as freedom *from* commitment—all notions of freedom rest on a sense of *agency*, the idea that individuals have control over the course of their lives. Agency, in turn, lies at the very core of the American Dream, the bedrock premise upon which all else depends. To paraphrase Henry David Thoreau, the Dream assumes that one *can* advance confidently in the direction of one's dreams to live out an imagined life. One of the greatest ironies—perhaps *the* greatest—of the American Dream is that its foundations were laid by people who specifically rejected a belief that they *did* have control over their destinies. In its broadest sense, you might say that the narrative arc of this book begins with people who denied their efforts could affect their fates, moves through successors who later declared independence to get that chance, to heirs who elaborated a gospel of self-help promising they could shape their fates with effort, and ends with people who long to achieve dreams without having to make any effort at all. This is, of course, a simplification, in part because all these types have been around at every point in the last four hundred years. But such an encapsulation does suggest the changing tenor of national life, and suggests too the variety, quantitative as well as qualitative, that has marked the history of the American Dream. I hope it also suggests the role a sense of humility can play in grappling with an idea that seems to envelop us as unmistakably as the air we breathe.

CHAPTER I

DREAM OF THE GOOD LIFE (I): THE PURITAN ENTERPRISE

FEW PEOPLE in American history have been as consistently disliked as the Puritans. To be sure, they have always had relatively rare, if prominent, champions (usually direct heirs). And they have often received grudging respect for their tenacity. But that's about as far as it goes. Some figures, like the Founding Fathers, quickly ascended into our pantheon of heroes; others, like leading Confederates of the Civil War, have had fluctuating reputations; still others, like the presidents of the late nineteenth century, rapidly fell into deserved obscurity. But the Puritans have had a consistently bad reputation that stands out like a scarlet letter in collective national memory.

There are a number of reasons for this. First, and most generally, the Puritans are widely regarded as very unpleasant people. Arthur Miller's 1953 play *The Crucible,* which used the Salem witch trials of the seventeenth century as a metaphor for the McCarthyite witch hunts of the twentieth century, remains a fixture of high school literature classes, providing millions of American schoolchildren their most vivid image of Puritanism. The word "puritanical" is still in wide usage in the early twenty-first century, usually as a synonym for intolerance, and knowledgeable observers at home and abroad have attributed American prurience and self-righteousness (typified, to many, by the sex scandal

surrounding another turn-of-the-century president), to the nation's
Puritan heritage. The American philosopher Richard Rorty has memorably summed up the prevailing contemporary view of the Puritans:
"self-flagellating sickies."

This is not a new idea. "We call you Puritans," an English clergy-
man wrote in the early seventeenth century, "not because you are purer
than other men . . . but because you think yourselves to be purer."
Later American writers like Nathaniel Hawthorne and H. L. Mencken
saw the Puritans as the source of most defects in American society.
Hawthorne, writing more than two hundred years after his own Puritan ancestors arrived, was obsessed with them, indicting them (in his
ironic, elliptical way) in his stories and novels. A far less ambivalent
Mencken had few compunctions about using sarcasm. In one of his
typically merciless epigrams, he defined Puritanism as "the haunting
fear that someone, somewhere, may be happy."

Recent scholarly trends have emphasized the degree to which the
Puritans were part of a broad wave of early modern European conquest in a hemisphere that was neither "discovered," "new," or even a
"world." In such a context, the important point is that the Puritans not
only made it difficult for the people who lived *among* them; they made it
impossible for anyone to live *alongside* them. In the succinct words of a
literary critic in the 1980s, the Puritans were people "who massacred
Indians and established the self-righteous religion and politics that

PURE LEGEND *An 1806 engraving of
Massachusetts founder John Winthrop.
Winthrop's American Dream was a communitarian one: "We must delight in each
other, make others' condition our own,
rejoice together, mourn together, labor and
suffer together," he reputedly said in his
famous address "A Model of Christian
Charity," delivered before the Puritans
arrived in Massachusetts. (Photo from the
collections of the Library of Congress)*

determined American ideology." Of course, they were not alone in this regard. From the Spaniards who enslaved natives (and imported Africans) to the British who sold disease-riddled blankets to Indians in North America, genocide was at best an incidental and at worst an avowedly embraced practice of European societies in the place they named "America." But if the Puritans were no worse than their contemporaries, there's little reason to think they were any better, as their track record in the Pequot (1637–38), King Philip's (1675–76), and other wars attests. One does not have to sentimentalize the Indians—who, in many cases, gave as good as they got—to nevertheless conclude that the lives of generations of Americans were only made possible by the slaughter of countless innocents.

And yet I admire them greatly. This attachment is in some degree irrational, tethered to some of the fondest memories of my early adulthood, like driving by white clapboard churches in Maine. But there's a firmer foundation for my feelings, too. To begin explaining why, I'll echo an heir of people the Puritans and others enslaved: they had a dream. In and of itself, that's not enough: so did Adolf Hitler. Nevertheless, the Puritans' dream, however strange and even repellent, was an exceptionally powerful one that had tremendous consequences, most of them unintended. In a palpable sense, it is only because of their dream that those Americans who followed had theirs, and only because of their ambitions that later Americans had the terms and standards by which they justly condemned the Puritans.

They had a dream. You don't have to love it, but you'll never really understand what it means to be an American of any creed, color, or gender if you don't try to imagine the shape of that dream—and what happened when they tried to realize it.

The myth of America, if it persists at all, has always rested on a precarious foundation. It is precisely its fragility, not its audacity—the perpetual worry of its believers, not their arrogance—that has made it something different (dare we say, something better?) than just another version of nationalist pomp.

—Andrew Delbanco, *The Puritan Ordeal* (1989)

"Puritanism" is one of those words—like "racism," or "democracy," or "feminist"—whose meaning is often far more clear in the minds of those who speak or write them than those who hear or read them. Any social label associated, as "Puritan" often is, with figures ranging from Plymouth Colony founder William Bradford to U.S. Founding Father John Adams *has* to be a little vague (237 years separated Bradford's birth in 1589 and Adams's death in 1826). Indeed, some of the most important writers on early American history have given up on the word entirely.

Yet elasticity has its uses. Noted Puritan scholar David Hall, who believes that "the term 'Puritanism' is so lacking in precision that I have tried to do without it," follows his disclaimer with a good umbrella definition. "In general," he writes, "the term may be understood as referring to a tendency within the Church of England to practice stricter 'discipline,' as in limiting access to the Lord's Supper." *Discipline* was the key. With its connotations of sustained inquiry (like the study of history), an attractive capacity for deferred gratification (like an athlete in training), or a punitive approach to regulating behavior (like an authoritarian police officer), the concept of discipline went to the very heart of the Puritan experience. Of course, any number of other people were disciplined about their religion and much else, but relatively few Catholics, Buddhists, or atheistic workaholics lived within, or in the context of, the Anglo-American Church of England (also known as the Anglican Church) in the centuries following the Protestant Reformation.

Defined this way, the Puritan experience, like its membership, was varied and really *did* encompass people ranging from William Bradford to John Adams. It was useful to say so when one considered, for example, the characteristics that made New England culture distinctive in American life—like, for example, its relative receptivity to a government role in social and economic life when compared to other regions in what eventually became the United States. Yet texturing that assertion was also important: Adams could only be called Puritan in the loosest sense of the term (such as when compared with his less morally rigorous friend, fellow Founding Father Thomas Jefferson); as an organized religious movement, Puritanism was on its last theological legs by the time Adams was born in 1735. And Bradford wasn't exactly a Puritan either, because he and his fellows who arrived on the *Mayflower* in December of 1620—popularly known as the Pilgrims—were, in the language of the time, "Separatists" who avowedly broke from an Anglican Church they viewed as corrupt beyond redemption, even as they shared many of the assumptions and practices of those who did not make that break.

One got closer to the heart of Puritanism with the founders of Massachusetts Bay Colony, who came to New England in 1630. *These* Puritans were—in theory, anyway—"*non*separating" members of the Church of England, who hoped its members back home would finally come to their senses, acknowledge their mistakes, and reform it on (more disciplined) Puritan lines. In practice, however, Massachusetts Puritans, like their friendly rival Pilgrims, wanted to get as far away from England and its Church as possible, and their particular brand of congregation-based organization eventually became a separate church in its own right in the increasingly sprawling world of early modern Protestantism.

Viewed in this light, the Massachusetts Puritans were actually moderates compared to the separatist Pilgrims and more radical sects like Quakers and Anabaptists, who had even less respect for traditional organized religion than the Puritans did. Indeed, one can visualize seventeenth-century Christianity on a spectrum, placing the nonseparating Puritans in the middle, with the Anglican and Catholic churches on one side and the Pilgrims and Quakers on the other. Thinking of the Puritans as middling figures departs from the traditional view of them as extremists, but doing so gives one a more accurate sense of their place in their American world.

Amid all the various abstruse concepts that complicate discussions of sixteenth- and seventeenth-century Puritanism—episcopacies and presbyteries, Arminians and Antinomians, covenants of grace and covenants of works—the irreducible foundation of *all* varieties of Protestantism was this: a belief that the world was a corrupt place, but one that could be reformed. *How* it could be reformed, of course, was another question, one that provoked all kinds of squabbling. But that it *could* be reformed has been central, a belief—actually, there were times it was an aggressive assertion—that distinguished sixteenth- and seventeenth-century Protestantism from Roman Catholicism (which did reactively reform itself by its own lights, though never enough for Protestants skeptical of its emphasis on institutional authority). This faith in reform became the central legacy of American Protestantism and the cornerstone of what became the American Dream. Things—religious and otherwise—could be different.

For the first generation of American Puritans, reform meant starting over, building a new society of believers for themselves and their children. Actually, this possibility had first been glimpsed in the sixteenth century by Sir Thomas More, a man who persecuted English Protestants before himself becoming a martyr at the hands of Henry VIII, who decided they had the right idea after all and founded a Protestant sect of his own, the Church of England. In his classic work *Utopia*, first published in 1516, More imagined a place—inspired by the discovery of a previously unknown hemisphere, in which he had a keen interest—where the opportunity to create a new society would lead to religious freedom and a communitarian approach toward property. More's Utopia was a relatively abstract thought experiment, but in the following century more pragmatic utopians, who weren't much more happy with the Church of England than More himself was, moved toward actually acting on such impulses. These Separatists initially tried to achieve their goals more modestly by leaving England for Holland, where a successful struggle to achieve independence from Spanish Catholic rule inspired the belief that perhaps here was a true holy land. Yet here too they were disappointed. The most far-sighted of these Separatists "began both deeply to apprehend their present dangers [of moral corruption] and wisely to foresee the future and think of timely remedy," their future governor, William Bradford, later recorded in *Of Plymouth Plantation*. "In the agitation of their thoughts, and much discourse of things hereabout, they began to incline to this conclusion: of removal to some other place." Writing almost a hundred years later, the Puritan minister Solomon Stoddard added that they "would not have left England merely for their own quietness; but they were afraid that their children would be corrupted there." From the very beginning, then, a notion that one's children might have a better life has been a core component of the American Dream.

The place that later became the United States has been called "the Promised Land" by innumerable people in the past four hundred years, many of them Jews, but it's important to emphasize here that the Pilgrims who crossed the Atlantic Ocean in 1620 really did believe themselves to be literal and figurative descendants of the tribes who wandered in the desert for forty years after leaving Egypt and founded the nation of Israel. In trying to convince Separatists back home to leave England, Robert Cushman, author of *Reasons and Considerations Touching the Lawfulness of Removing out of England into the Parts of America* (1622), argued that for them there had been no "land or any possession now, like unto the possession which the Jews had in Canaan, being legally holy and appropriated unto a holy people, the seed of Abraham." But British North America, Cushman said, would change all that. After all, there was no one there but heathen Indians who could be converted; "to them we may go, their land is empty."

Those Indians surely viewed the matter a little differently. But compared to later immigrants who arrived to find teeming citizens and a multiracial society, the Pilgrims and Puritans came to what seemed to them an impossibly remote place. In his *Dissertation on the Canon and the Feudal Law* (1765), a political pamphlet that fanned the flames of the American Revolution, John Adams imaginatively evoked the new world they confronted:

> Recollect their amazing fortitude, their bitter sufferings—the hunger, the nakedness, the cold, which they patiently endured—the severe labors of clearing their grounds, building their houses, raising their provisions, amidst dangers from wild beasts and savage men, before they had time or money or materials for commerce. Recollect the civil and religious principles and hopes and expectations which constantly supported and carried them through all the hardships with patience and resignation. Let us recollect it was liberty, the hope of liberty, for themselves and us and ours, which conquered all discouragements, dangers, and trials.

Principles, hope, and liberty were powerful attractions, and would remain so for subsequent generations who came here from all over the world. But it's worth remembering that unlike many of those who followed, the Pilgrims were not immigrants with nothing to lose. Without minimizing the challenges faced by many of the teeming masses who arrived under the gaze of the Statue of Liberty, these immigrants were relatively well educated people who in many cases had substantial financial resources at their disposal, making their decision to leave everything behind all the more striking. This sense of worldly prosperity was even more true of the Puritans who arrived in Massachusetts Bay in 1630. They were certainly not the first people of means who threw away their security for the sake of an idea; figures ranging from Saint Francis to Vladimir Lenin have done similarly. But the scope of the Puritan enterprise, both in its collective nature and its logistical complications, was amazing. Here, truly, were some astonishingly committed people, people who were all the more so for *not* being solitary geniuses, battle-hardened soldiers, impoverished peasants, or unwilling slaves.

So it was that some people with a strong sense of religious mission founded a new world they hoped would become a model for the old one. Their confidence—in themselves, in their sense of mission for their children, and in a God they believed was on their side—impelled them with ruthless zeal to gamble everything for the sake of a vision. In the process, they accomplished the core task in the achievement of any American Dream: they became masters of their own destiny.

But a good Puritan would never put it that way.

The Puritans were gifted—or cursed—with an overwhelming realization of an inexorable power at work not only in nature but in themselves, which they called God; whatever may have been the factors in their society and their experience that so sharpened their sense of awareness, the acuteness and poignancy of the awareness are phenomena which psychology will recognize though it cannot explain, and which history must take into account.

—**Perry Miller,** *The New England Mind:*
The Seventeenth Century, **1939**

The Puritans descended from the Calvinist branch of Protestantism, which meant that they were predestinarians: they believed individuals' fates were sealed from the moment they were born, and there was absolutely nothing they could do to affect their ultimate salvation or damnation. But they could not know for sure where they were actually headed and so had to live their lives hoping for signs that things would turn out for the best.

This psychology is alien to a modern Western mindset. Contemporary Americans in particular are typically contractual: being a good person isn't easy but seems like a reasonable investment, if, not in immediate or even earthly payback, then perhaps in an afterlife, one will have racked up enough points on a moral scorecard to get into heaven (a forgiving God giving the benefit of any doubt). But if the matter is already decided before one is even born, then what's the point? One might as well indulge every instinct, since it won't affect the outcome.

Of course, one does not have to be a Calvinist to point out that such logic misses the point. In theory one *could* live a life of amoral excess, but even articulating a *desire* to do so would not seem like an especially encouraging sign one was on the right track. Nor does God necessarily think like an accountant who keeps a careful set of books. (The Puritans were fond of comparing God to an indulgent landlord ready to forgive regular lapses on the rent—but not a cavalier attitude—from his spiritually impoverished tenants.) Calvinism may or may not have been a compelling element in some Protestant denominations, but our reaction to it may reveal more about the world we live in than the one they did.

In any case, the historical record is reasonably clear that in theory—and in widespread, though probably not universal, practice—Puritans followed a Calvinist line. To at least some extent, this was a response to one of the most important reasons for the Protestant Reformation in the first place: the Roman Catholic practice of selling indulgences whereby the rich could buy forgiveness of their sins. What made this so repellent was not so much what might bother someone today—a kind of class inequality that suggested salvation went to the highest bidder—but rather a suggestion that any human being could exercise prerogatives that belonged to God alone. For a committed Puritan, it was offensive to maintain that an ordinary sinner could somehow exercise the levers of destiny—more offensive, even, than garden-variety Catholic corruption, like priests who had neither the training nor inclination to actually minister to the people, or those who declined to even say mass at all (except perhaps for the dead landlord whose estate paid their income).

Perhaps you sense a tension, even a contradiction, here. On the one hand, the Puritans believed and acted as if a person could make a difference in making the world a better place—indeed, had an obligation to do so. On the other, they believed they were powerless to do anything but follow the dictates of God's inscrutable will. Here, it seems, is the worst of all possible worlds: accountability without power. The Puritans were haunted by questions: how do I know? How do I know that I really am sanctified and will thus have a place in heaven? How do I know that my beloved dead are at peace? And when there are conflicts, as there so often are, between contesting versions of what is truly right, how will I know which way to follow? Maybe they would hear an inner voice. But could they trust it? And if there was only silence, what would that mean? To ask these kinds of questions is to begin to imagine the sheer anxiety involved in Puritanism.

Like other people who have inhabited worlds governed by difficult, even contradictory, ideas, some Puritans negotiated their way through life by trying to find a middle ground on their new native soil. For them, this middle ground was known as the doctrine of preparationism. It was out of the question that one could actively affect one's fate through specific actions; this constituted a heretical "doctrine of works" embraced by Catholics, Protestants influenced by Dutch theologian Jacobus Arminius, and the much-hated William Laud, the Bishop of London who persecuted Puritans in the name of the Church of England. On the other hand, to live a life without knowledge of, or power to affect, who was saved—a doctrine known as the "covenant of grace"—was for many Puritans too much to bear. Preparationism softened the covenant of grace by suggesting that there were steps one could take to get in a proper frame of mind so that one could be fully receptive to sanctification if it were forthcoming. If this sounds a little fuzzy, that's because it undoubtedly was; even with the elaborate sequencing and terminology of preparationist doctrine—which must surely have confused, if not exasperated, many a lay Puritan—the line between preparationism and a doctrine of works seems gossamer thin. Indeed, one faction of Puritans specifically rejected the notion of preparationism as a slipshod compromise with the doctrine of works. (On the other hand, as Andrew Delbanco has pointed out, preparationism may well have increased rather than allayed anxiety, because it effectively ratcheted up expectations that Puritans *would* prepare rather than passively wait.)

Notwithstanding the widespread, and generally accurate, perception that the Puritans were mavericks in the world of early modern Protestantism, the doctrine of preparationism was an important indication of their instinctive moderation. It was evident, too, in the way Massachusetts Bay Puritans contrasted with the Separatists of Plymouth by not formally reneging on their ties to the Church of England. And it was evident again in their less than wholly intimate relationship with the Puritans in the English Civil War of the 1640s, a war that threatened the colonial "errand into the wilderness" because a reformed England would make a *New* England superfluous. That such pragmatism—some might say cynicism—could coexist with their rigorous theology suggested that these were flesh-and-blood people who lived lives that were very different than, and yet comparable to, our own. They made compromises in pursuit of what they wanted, and what they wanted often caused them a good deal of grief, whether they got it or not.

But what, exactly, *did* they want? And what happened when they tried to turn their dream into reality?

It appeared as if New England was a region given up to the dreams of fancy and the unrestrained experiments of innovators.

—**Alexis de Tocqueville, *Democracy in America*, 1835**

They wanted freedom—any high school history textbook will tell you that. They *themselves* would tell you that. But they didn't define it the way we typically do today. In fact, insofar as they did understand freedom as we do, they considered it monstrous. "There is twofold liberty—natural (I mean as our nature is now corrupt) and civil or federal," Massachusetts Bay founder John Winthrop explained in 1645. "The first is common to man with beasts and other creatures. By this, man as he stands into relation to man, hath the liberty to do as he lists." This kind of freedom "makes men grow more evil, and in time to be worse than brute beasts." True freedom, on the other hand, "is maintained and exercised in a way of subjection to authority." Freedom involved a willing surrender to the will of the Lord, a choice to defer to Godly clerical and civil authorities that ruled in His name. Oppression, by contrast, involved having to live with—having to *tolerate*—self-evidently corrupt sects (like the Anglican Church back home, which was virtually as bad as the Roman Catholicism it supposedly reformed) and complacent rulers (like Queen Elizabeth I, whose noncommittal, split-the-difference approach to theology seemed more a matter of dispiriting indifference than anything else). To cast off such tawdriness and sloth: *that* was freedom.

The free new world of their dreams was to be a place of, by, and for the Puritans. There would be other people around; the best shipwrights, for example, weren't necessarily true believers, and there was always the possibility of Indians to convert, visitors to entertain, or even colonial officials to appease. But the leaders of the Plymouth and Massachusetts Bay colonies planned to be in charge in both sacred and secular realms—which, while separate, were nevertheless intertwined. No one could join their churches without giving convincing testimony of their religious commitment, that is, without "conversion." And no one could vote in secular matters who was not a member of the church.

Religious toleration was out of the question; these people had not come all this way to accept the indolence, conflict, or obvious evil that had marred the Holland and England they had left. From now on, they would cut through all the clutter and cacophony: no more ornate iconography in churches; no more decadent amusements like plays and gambling; no more idolatrous distractions like Christmas celebrations. Long-standing convictions could finally become the law of the land.

This all sounds rather severe. But toleration was not a fixture of religious life in many places in the Western world of that time, and to the extent pluralism was present, it was as much a function of the irrelevance of religion as a principled embrace of diversity. And while Puritan stringency regarding recreation was notable even for the time, there was never any suggestion that pleasures like laughter, drinking, and sex were impermissible, only that they had a clear time and place. Moreover, the Puritans were unusual, even unique, for the degree to which popular participation in civic life was widespread; while it was not really a democracy as we would understand the word—there were far too many gender, racial, economic, and religious constraints on political participation—New England really did represent the leading edge of changes that would transform Western life in the eighteenth and nineteenth centuries. The most important manifestation of this embryonic democratic impulse was the Mayflower Compact, a document binding the Pilgrims to frame and obey "just and equal laws" that they signed even before they landed. The signal institution in subsequent Pilgrim and Puritan life was the town meeting, in which members of a community could vote on matters of concern to them and elect representatives to voice their concerns to the colony as a whole.

Yet to focus too much on the procedural dimension of New England would be to lose sight of what these people were really after. And that was a sense of *community*: not a philosophical or legal framework so much as a series of deep emotional and affective bonds that connected people who had a shared sense of what their lives were about. Freedom was a means to that end. There is, of course, a paradox here, because so much of their faith was premised on the fate of the solitary soul, but the very intensity of Puritan individualism makes the need for some compensating dimension all the more important. If the Puritans were essentially alone in the world, they nevertheless wished to be alone together.

This longing for intimacy dominates one of the great early addresses of American history, John Winthrop's "A Model of Christian Charity." Winthrop, one of the organizers of the Massachusetts Bay Company, was chosen by the company to govern the colony, a post he was subsequently elected to twelve times. While on board the *Arbella*, one of four ships that carried about seven hundred immigrants across the Atlantic Ocean, he delivered a lay sermon. Though its precise content is not certain (it was not published in his lifetime), the sermon captures both the world the Puritans sought—and the world they inhabited.

In some ways, "A Model of Christian Charity" was a document of hard-headed realism. "God Almighty in his holy and wise providence hath so disposed the condition of mankind, as in all times some must be rich, some poor, some high and eminent in power and duty, others mean and in subjection," Winthrop began. God, he explained, ordered these differences "for the preservation and good of the whole" and exhorted the Puritans to maintain that order. Never a fan of democracy—he held out for as long as he could to prevent the election of representatives to the general court, even though the colony's charter explicitly called for it—Winthrop, like most Puritan leaders, affirmed sacred and secular hierarchy in government.

And yet the heart of the sermon was a call for interdependence, even equality, for all Puritans in the eyes of God. "No man is made more honorable than another or more wealthy, etc., out of any particular and singular respect to himself, but for the glory of his creator and the common good of the creature, man," he asserted. Comparing the colony to a body with different organs that work in complementary effort to sustain it, Winthrop invoked a communitarian vision of American life: "We must delight in each other, make others' condition our own, rejoice together, mourn together, labor and suffer together, always having before our eyes our commission and community in the work, our community as members of the same body."

Such soaring hopes coexisted with mundane, even gnawing, realities. At first glance, one of the more surprising things about "A Model of Christian Charity" was the amount of space it devoted to financial matters. In the highly structured interrogative style typical of Puritan sermons, Winthrop posed a series of questions (How should one determine how much money to give to charity? What rules should govern lending?) that he goes on to answer in some detail. For a century after

Max Weber's classic study *The Protestant Ethic and the Spirit of Capitalism*
in 1918, associations between Puritans and their money were common,
and rightly so. But what was sometimes overlooked was the intense
ambivalence, even hostility, the Puritans felt toward a market economy
even as they plunged into it. Winthrop was only one of many landholders in the late sixteenth and early seventeenth centuries to be impaled
on the horns of a painful dilemma: inflationary pressures for rising
rents conflicted with feudal injunctions to deal paternalistically with
tenants. Some made the transition to the new economy; others lost
their fortunes to their overseers. Winthrop was one of a few who dealt
with the problem by fleeing to America. In this context, a call for communitarian cooperation was less a cheap sentiment than a utopian
vision.

Moreover, the threat of failure loomed large over "A Model of
Christian Charity." Winthrop's clarion call for a "city upon a hill" has
been cited as a source of inspiration by later Americans, notably
Ronald Reagan. Yet in the context of his sermon, the city Winthrop
imagined was perhaps less a shining example than a potential object of
ridicule. "The eyes of all people are upon us, so that if we shall deal
falsely with our God in this work we have undertaken, and so cause
him to withdraw his present help from us, we shall be made a story and
a by-word through the world," Winthrop said. "We shall open the
mouths of enemies to speak evil of the ways of God, and all professors
for God's sake. We shall shame the faces of many of God's worthy servants, and cause their prayers to be turned into curses upon us till we
be consumed out of the good land whither we are agoing."

Such was the mix of hope and fear, of looking ahead and looking
over their shoulders, that characterized the Puritan migration. On bal-
ance, their utopian impulses overrode their conservative ones: they
made the journey. Perry Miller, the historian who more than any other
imaginatively projected himself into the mind of the Puritans, called
them "cosmic optimists"—a strange phrase in light of the dour image
of the Puritans, but one that finally explains how they marshaled the
energy to act on their imaginations. But only in appreciating just how
hard it was—not simply in terms of the physical privations but in terms
of the emotional and intellectual doubts that haunted them—can we
appreciate the audacity of their strange American Dream.

Perhaps inevitably, things didn't turn out as planned.

"Are these the men that erst at my command
Forsook their ancient seats and native soile,
To follow Me into a desart land,
Contemning all the travell and the toile,
Whose love was such to purest ordinances
As made them set at nought their fair inheritances?"

—Michael Wigglesworth,
"God's Controversy with New England," 1662

From the start, things began to go astray. More accurately, *people* began to go astray—not so much in a spiritual sense (though some surely said and felt so) as in a literal one: the Puritans diffused over a much wider area than a compact city and ended up in plains and valleys as well as upon hills. The Pilgrims were supposed to land in Virginia; instead they anchored at the tip of Cape Cod, eventually settled further west in Plymouth, and spread out from there ("for now as their stocks increased, and the increase vendible, there was no longer any holding them together, but now they must of necessity go to their own great lots," William Bradford reported). The Puritans of Massachusetts were even more itinerant. Their first encampment was at the present-day town of Salem, then at Charlestown, then a scattering across Watertown, Roxbury, Dorchester, Medford, and Saugus before concentrating in the peninsula known as Shawmut, which was ultimately named "Boston" for the port city in East Anglia, the wellspring of the Puritan movement. By 1634 settlers were leaving Massachusetts Bay altogether and moving into New Haven and Hartford, laying the foundations for what would ultimately become Connecticut. Puritans also infiltrated New Hampshire, overwhelming the Anglican population there. The lust for land, the fear of contagious disease, and, one surmises, a desire for freedom from the burden of community impelled this dispersal, which leaders like Winthrop regularly lamented. But expressions of regret, however sincere, did little to concentrate the spread of people who would go on to show a seemingly inexhaustible appetite for frontiers.

The problem with pursuing dreams, even shared ones, is that not everyone sees them in quite the same ways. The course of events in New England was shaped not only by material conditions and timeless human impulses (like greed) but also by aspirations that pulled people apart in literal as well as figurative ways. Although the precise reasons are unclear, it appears that theological and/or political factors impelled Thomas Hooker, a minister at Newtowne (later Cambridge), to take one hundred members of his congregation to Hartford in 1636. Some historians believe that rivalry with fellow minister John Cotton was a consideration; others believe Hooker's faith in more democratic governance clashed with Winthrop's beliefs on the matter. In any event, it is clear that even the relatively homogeneous world of the Puritans was marked by factions and sectarianism.

Much of the conflict in Massachusetts centered on just how far to take basic philosophical tenets of Puritanism. This issue was particularly pressing, because the unwillingness to break publicly with the Anglican Church engendered compromises that the Separatists of Plymouth, for example, did not make. Some Puritans considered this an unacceptable form of hypocrisy.

The most famous of these malcontents was Roger Williams. Williams came to Massachusetts in 1631, a generally well liked figure with strong ministerial credentials. But his refusal to serve as pastor for a Boston congregation because it had not severed its ties with the Church of England was only the first of a series of declarations—among them assertions that the Puritans had acted illegally in acquiring land from Indians—that at first worried and finally infuriated colonial officials, who banished him from the colony in 1636. Williams fled to what became known as Rhode Island, for which he received a charter, over Massachusetts's objections, in 1644, and helped lay the foundations for what became the Baptist Church in America. Rhode Island has been remembered as a haven of toleration, an achievement for which Williams deservedly gets credit. It's worth noting, however, that the impetus for Williams's ministry was less an embrace of pluralism for its own sake than a refusal to allow what he regarded as the pollution of his religious practice; temperamentally he belonged, in effect, to a congregation of one.

One of the most serious challenges to the Puritan project was the so-called Antinomian crisis of the mid-1630s, the event that more than any other suggested the practical limits of Puritan ideology. Antinomians insisted that since no one knew who was saved, no one—not even ministers—could have authority over the individual conscience. At the heart of the Antinomian movement was a disgust with formulaic Puritan religious practices, which critics charged were lapsing into empty rituals—or a heretical "doctrine of works" that contradicted the core

Calvinist principle that individuals could not affect their salvation. Instead, the Antinomians called for a rigorous, but deeply personal, approach to piety grounded in a more pure form of Puritanism.

Taken to its logical conclusions, however, Antinomianism had deeply subversive implications for Massachusetts. It would only be a matter of time before an individual's beliefs would lead to the rejection of all outside authority, since just about any law, sacred or secular, could be perceived as trampling on a personal conscience. Any form of collective governance would be impossible. What to some might seem like an American Dream of religious freedom was to others a nightmarish prescription for anarchy.

Antinomianism was no marginal faction in early Massachusetts. While few openly pressed the doctrine to its extremes, sympathizers included the ministers John Cotton and John Wheelwright, as well as Henry Vane, a prominent Englishman who arrived in Massachusetts in 1635 and was elected governor in 1636. The most vocal proponent of the creed was Anne Hutchinson, the wife of a wealthy merchant, whose controversial views on the subject led to her trial for "traducing the ministers and their ministry." The surviving transcript shows her to be an agile defendant, able to invoke scripture with the best of her male adversaries. But when she claimed that she knew scripture was correct because God had spoken to her directly about its veracity, her opponents branded her a heretic and had her banished from the colony. She and her followers fled to Rhode Island and ultimately to New York, where she was killed by Indians near the parkway that now bears her name.

For nearly four centuries, the Antinomian controversy has eluded those who tried to untangle motives and events that remain shrouded in mystery. The Puritans themselves seemed haunted by the affair, referring to it repeatedly in their journals and memoirs. They and later observers have viewed the Puritans' subsequent history as a long gradual slide away from an ultimately untenable doctrine of grace toward a more practical doctrine of works. And the Hutchinson affair continued to generate heat into the twentieth century. One writer in the 1930s referred to Hutchinson's trial as "a legal travesty"; in his 1958 biography of John Winthrop, Edmund Morgan described her and her fellow travelers as guilty of "seventeenth-century nihilism." Feminist scholars considered it no coincidence that a woman ended up as the scapegoat of the affair, and still others warned of the dangers of trying to impose twenty-first-century categories on a seventeenth-century consciousness. Whatever one concluded, one fact was unmistakably clear: despite an unusual degree of social homogeneity, the Puritans were unable to create a harmonious community in their new home, succumbing to all too human foibles as well as highly specific, even technical, intellectual disagreements (the two often overlapping).

Ironically, even apparent *consensus* created problems for the Puritans. New England prospered throughout the 1630s, as a steady arrival of disaffected English settlers found refuge and developed the local as well as international economy of the region. But the onset of the English Civil War, a war waged and won by Oliver Cromwell's Puritans, created multiple problems for New England in the 1640s. Wartime disruptions precipitated an economic recession, as the stream of new arrivals and the flow of goods slowed to a trickle. This ebbing also engendered a psychological trauma: once an alternative beacon for discouraged English Puritans, New England now seemed irrelevant at best—and a self-indulgent sideline at worst—to some on *both* sides of the Atlantic. Cromwell's ascension to dictatorship in the 1650s also revealed previously hidden fissures within Puritanism. In England, a fierce debate broke out between those Puritans who wanted discussion and rule-making between congregations to be led by ministers of particular congregations in an egalitarian manner (i.e., a congregational approach) and those with a slightly more hierarchical approach, who thought such governance should be conducted by more powerful bishops in the name of groups of congregations, or presbyteries (hence the eventual emergence of a separate Presbyterian Church). All Puritans rejoiced at the execution of the much-hated Archbishop Laud, but in some ways it was easier maintaining independence from avowedly hostile British authorities than from a supposedly friendly Puritan dictatorship seeking to centralize its administration and wary of New England's independence. (Cromwell himself described Massachusetts as "a poor, cold and useless place.") Perhaps fortuitously, Cromwell's death in 1658 was followed by the restoration of the Stuart monarchy in 1660, and the New England Puritans were again, at least theoretically, ruled by hostile, but highly inefficient and distracted, crypto-Catholic kings. For a little while longer, anyway, they were situated where they were happiest: as a largely autonomous set of communities on the Atlantic rim of a global empire.

Indeed, the problems I'm describing here—with Roger Williams

and toleration, Anne Hutchinson and Antinomianism, Oliver Cromwell and his revolution—are essentially political disputes that most
directly affected those in, or near, positions of power. That's not to say
the issues argued over were unreal, or that they didn't affect ordinary
people in palpable ways. But the fact remains that as the months
became years and the years became decades, the Puritans truly took
root in America. Even their much-lamented relations with Indians
weren't all that bad. Between the end of the Pequot War in 1638 and
the beginning of King Philip's War in 1675, there were almost four
decades of relatively peaceful coexistence between the two races. Many
of those who survived the initial adversity built houses, founded
churches, started schools, and lived to see their children have children.
America became their home—the only one they ever knew. The dream
had once been the creation of a new world. Now the task was to sustain
and extend it. By any standard, then or now, this was a tremendous
accomplishment.

And yet that accomplishment was in some ways oppressive. As the
first generation of Puritans died off and their children took their place,
a persistent mantra seems to run through the Puritans' copious com-
mentaries: we are not the men our fathers were. The very strenuous-
ness of their literary forms—particularly their election day sermons and
a form of vitrolic preaching known as the jeremiad—testifies to their
difficulty in maintaining the white-hot intensity of the founders. Poets
like Michael Wigglesworth, in his widely reprinted "Day of Doom"
and "God's Controversy with New England," looked to portents like
droughts (in apparent violation of the covenant of grace, which denied
that God would give such signs) and saw them as warnings. One imag-
ines that there was a less dramatic, but probably more widespread,
sense of melancholy over the limits of the Puritans' achievements and
the failure of ideals to meet up with realities.

Faced with this prospect, many Puritans did what most people do
when ideals and realities seem irreconcilable: they compromised. This
approach was on vivid display in the debate over the so-called Halfway
Covenant of 1662, over how to handle the church membership of children. The founders had been clear, even emphatic, about who could
become full members of a congregation: only those who had rendered
convincing testimony of their spiritual conversion from sin to grace.
Almost by definition, children were incapable of doing so. Case closed,
said some Puritans. Others, however, could not bear the thought of

denying their children what they themselves most cherished. Under the pressure of such sentiment, Congregationalists developed a doctrine whereby children could be provisionally accepted into the church, pending a later confirmation-type experience. Such was but one example of how the Puritans were pulled, seemingly inexorably, away from the covenant of grace toward the very practices of the churches they most hated.

Another way of dealing with unrealized dreams was a conscious rededication to original ideals. As late as the 1740s, amid the swirling eddies of religious revivals known as the First Great Awakening, ministers like Jonathan Edwards (1703–58) sought to shape, channel, and temper newer, more works-based tendencies in American Protestantism by calling on the faithful to embrace a tough-minded, but psychically satisfying, pursuit of spiritual rigor. Edward's classic sermon "Sinners in the Hands of an Angry God" is to religious literature what Frank Sinatra's version of "My Way" is to popular music: a signature expression of a particular cast of mind (and one that was ebbing at the very moment of its most crystalline expression). But Edwards was dismissed by his congregation in 1750, an indication of exhaustion and impatience with a century of Puritanism.

And yet the energy, the personality of Puritanism survived even when its founding ideals were discarded. The utilitarian aphorisms that characterized the writing of Edwards's contemporary, the Boston-born Benjamin Franklin, were bracing precisely because they inverted, satirized, or reconfigured Puritan ideology. "So convenient a thing it is to be a *reasonable* creature, since it enables one to make a reason for everything one has a mind to do," the founder of *Poor Richard's Almanac* wrote in his 1758 *Autobiography*. The line was simultaneously a subtle jab at the Puritan tendency to scrutinize (and rationalize) behavior, a (glib) acknowledgment of a common psychological pattern, and, perhaps, an implicit admission of Franklin's own fall from Calvinist grace (he had by this point long since given up Puritan Boston for a Quaker-dominated, but increasingly secular, Philadelphia). Once a form of distraction or comfort while awaiting the implacable hand of fate, becoming healthy, wealthy, and wise had gone beyond an instrument of salvation into being a practical end in its own right. This emphasis—some might say mania—for self-improvement, cut loose from its original Calvinist moorings, remains a recognizable trait in the American character and is considered an indispensable means for the achievement of any American Dream.

It was clear that by the end of the seventeenth century, the original Puritan vision no longer held sway in New England or anywhere else. Outside influences—whether Quakers subject to persecution by Puritans seeking to preserve their homogeneity, or Anglicans who could not be pushed around so easily—became increasingly important in shaping provincial life. More obvious social dislocations also played a role. Years in coming, the outbreak of King Philip's War (named after a Native American leader whose very name suggests the degree of intercultural contact between Indians and whites) proved to be a debacle in New England, where not even the combined forces of the Massachusetts, Plymouth, Hartford, and New Haven colonies were able to prevent the destruction of dozens of New England towns. The colonists ultimately prevailed. But in the aftermath of their costly victory—adjusted for population, the bloodiest war ever fought on American soil—the Stuart monarchy resolved finally to do something about its unruly subjects, and King Charles II named his brother James, the duke of York, to govern a vast territory that stretched from Manhattan to Maine. Finally, over half a century after they arrived, the Puritans were brought to heel. New Haven and Hartford were combined into Connecticut; Plymouth was folded into its dominant neighbor of Massachusetts. The latter's luck had not altogether run out; no sooner had a royal delegation arrived in New England than the Stuarts themselves were toppled in the Glorious Revolution of 1688 that brought the Dutch William of Orange and his English Mary to the British throne.

Yet the New England Way never quite recovered. William III and his wife were both committed Protestants, effectively ending a century and a half of religious struggle in Britain. But for precisely that reason, the Puritan insistence on a narrowly defined religious orthodoxy was regarded as needlessly divisive. New Englanders were told in no uncertain terms they could no longer persecute religious minorities with impunity.

Instead, the region must resemble other parts of British North America, whether it took as its model the casual Anglicanism that dominated Virginia or the heterogeneity that characterized Middle Atlantic colonies like New York. The Act of Toleration of 1690, which established the new order, did guarantee the Puritans the same rights as

Englishmen back home. But the price was high: it forced them not only to accept self-evident reprobates like Gortonists (who denied the Holy Trinity) or Anabaptists (who rejected any form of state church) but also to recognize that the Puritans *themselves* were nothing more than a dissident sect within a now firmly established Anglican Church that would never, as they once hoped, reform itself in their own image.

Perhaps, as the great Puritan historian Perry Miller suggested, it was a sense of brittle bitterness over such defeats that provoked the Puritans into one of the most notorious episodes of their checkered history: the Salem witch trials of 1692, an event that has lastingly stained their reputations. Twenty people were executed in the wake of the trials, which took place after a group of young girls became hysterical while playing at magic and were described as bewitched. (Tolerating religious diversity was one thing, but tolerating Satan was another.) Once again, this was a prismatic historical event that has been subject to multiple interpretations: sexual anxiety, economic distress, psychological trauma, and (especially) political hysteria.

It was, surely, all these things. But Miller's point—I mean historian Perry Miller, but playwright Arthur Miller applies as well—that the witch trials represented a grotesque effort to recapture a sense of lost cohesion, a lingering longing for communion curdled into a dictatorship of false virtue, remains salient. If the dispersal of the original Puritans suggested the degree to which the dreams of individuals compromised collective aspirations, the trials suggested the way in which collective fears could crush individual lives. More than three centuries later, the American Dream still straddles—perhaps it's more accurate to say it *blurs*— the tension between one and many, a tension we still all too often fail to recognize, let alone resolve.

Amid the changes, even reverses, the Puritans tried to forge a usable past for those who followed. Cotton Mather's 1702 history of the Puritans, *Magnalia Christi Americana* ("The Great Achievements of Christ in America") begins on a triumphal note that rarely wavers: "I write of the wonders of Christian religion, flying from the depravations of Europe to the American strand; and, assisted by the holy author of that religion, I do, with all conscience of truth itself, report the wonderful displays of His infinite power, wisdom, goodness and faithfulness, wherewith his divine providence hath irradiated an Indian wilderness." The point of this was to suggest all that had been, and still was being, accomplished, to celebrate as well as goad. Yet try as he might to affirm an unbroken history, Mather—grandson of Massachusetts founders Richard Mather and John Cotton, and son of the powerful Increase Mather—could not help but realize he was not the man his forefathers were. (If nothing else, his many clerical, educational, and political enemies were there to remind him, for example, of his silence during the Salem witch trials and his subsequent defense of the judges.) As an early twentieth-century historian once wrote of Mather, "Essentially a conservative, he was always torn between allegiance to inherited ideals and realization that a newer day demanded new standards." A reluctant Mather was forced to realize that dreams are a difficult business. Not only must they compete with other dreams, but they are mortal, whether realized or not. Other dreams—better dreams?—were taking root in the very garden the Puritans had cleared and tilled.

There is no object that we see, no action that we do, no good that we enjoy, no evil that we feel or fear, but we may make some spiritual advantage of all; and he that makes such improvement is wise as well as pious.

—Anne Bradstreet,
"Meditations Divine and Moral" I (undated)

The basic outline of the Puritans' history in the century after their arrival in New England seems like one damning episode after another. Arrogance, querulousness, hypocrisy, and even murder followed them wherever they went. Here was a people who affirmed the primacy of the individual conscience yet demanded religious orthodoxy. Who denied knowledge of salvation but devised doctrines, like preparationism, that resembled the very practices they most severely condemned when practiced by others. And who claimed to want to convert Indians, only to destroy them. Most fundamentally, their dream of a city on a hill became an empire on a continent, largely peopled by Americans who would have appalled them in their diversity and secularity.

In the end, though, it's their dream—the fact of it, the degree of good faith, however incomplete, that animated it and the degree to which it was realized—that despite all that has happened partially redeems them. The Puritans were not the first people to have a dream, even in North America. Virginia was founded before New England,

and its founders also had a dream: to get rich. They might not achieve it with gold, the way the Spaniards did in Mexico and Peru, but tobacco was a possibility (so was attacking Spanish shipping). The Puritans wanted to get rich too, and as a number of observers pointed out, their temperament was exceptionally well suited to an emerging capitalist world order. But Puritanism was not finally about money. For all its focus on the afterlife, it was also about making the world a better, more holy, place. Even among themselves, Puritans disagreed about how to do this, and many of their best intentions did indeed pave a road to hell. Yet it is also true that some of the most important reforms in American life, from the end of slavery to the creation of the nation's great universities, derived from conceptions of community and morality central to the Puritan worldview. In the Puritans one could find refuge in the faith that one of the most important things that makes us human—the capacity for ideas—might actually be a basis for living one's life, not as a matter of brute self-interest or of self-abnegation from worldly concerns but rather as a possibility that one can simultaneously be intellectually and emotionally engaged with contemporary life even as one always remembers that something lies beyond it. Hence the Puritan injunction to "live in the world, but not of it." This is an extraordinarily difficult thing to do. But it is precisely the willingness to do something difficult, painful, unintentionally mischievous, or finally impossible that gives purpose to individual lives, both as they are lived and as they are remembered.

The Puritans, of course, weren't the only ones to try. The Quakers, for example, followed some early forays into New England—where they would do unforgivable things like allow women to preach—by forming their own far more tolerant colony under the leadership of the remarkable William Penn, who founded Pennsylvania in 1682. And though it isn't exactly our idea of paradise now, the governorship of William Berkeley of Virginia (1642–76) helped transform a primitive Virginia colony into a highly elaborate slave society that captured the imagination of successive generations of southerners. In the centuries that followed, countless groups of Americans—from the Mormons who founded Utah in the 1840s to the hippies who founded communes in the 1960s—made their own efforts to found cities on hills, valleys, or plains. Hope sprang eternal in a promised land that straddled a continent.

CHAPTER 2

DREAM CHARTER:
THE DECLARATION OF INDEPENDENCE

THE WIGS, THE BREECHES, the unsmiling faces in formal portraits: for those of us who drink coffee at Starbucks, surf the World Wide Web, or stand at automatic teller machines that give us currency featuring those portraits, the American Revolution might well have occurred on another planet. There are places—for many Americans, they're thousands of miles away—that preserve battlefields and remind tourists what actually happened in the 1770s and 1780s. But even for those who visit them, the Revolutionary past is compartmentalized, an interlude in another time and place more likely to be accessed via resort hotels and interstate highways than classrooms or textbooks.

This isn't quite as true of other eras in American history. As already suggested, the Puritans remain vivid precisely because they're so irritating. And the Civil War, though it began a mere seventy-eight years after the Revolution—a lifetime for a hardy soul of those days—seems much more recent. There are a number of reasons why this would be so. The Civil War covered a much larger geographic territory, from the mountains of eastern to the deserts of western North America. Moreover, the documentary record is much fuller, particularly with regard to photography. The personalities of the Civil War era are more familiar; Ulysses S. Grant's unkempt candor seems decisively more familiar than

SELF-EVIDENT APPEAL *The William Stone engraving (1823) of the Declaration of Independence. Though the original document has faded, most of us have "life, liberty, and the pursuit of happiness" wired into our consciousness as the source code of the American Dream. (Courtesy of the National Archives and Records Administration)*

George Washington's Olympian detachment, even if Washington's detachment was difficult for him to maintain. (We have a hard time understanding why someone would even *want* to be that formal.) Most of us know Abraham Lincoln had a sense of humor, even if his portraits are unsmiling, and his expressive face and words attest to an inner life that seems oddly absent in the public visage of Thomas Jefferson. (One can sympathize with those twentieth-century historians who had a hard time believing that the mature Jefferson fathered children with one of his slaves: it was hard to imagine him having sex with *anybody*.)

But the Civil War seems more recent than the Revolution mostly because its legacy is so much more apparent. The Civil War's outcome not only made places like Starbucks possible but also determined who *went* there—a much more varied demographic mix than would have been likely had the Confederacy won the conflict. Nor would the national highway system, assuming it was built, have been as expansive in the event of a Confederate victory. But the Civil War lives on not so much in what has been resolved but in questions and issues that continue to have currency in our national life, particularly in regard to the role of the federal government and the temper of American race relations.

For the most part, the Revolution lacks this relevance. As far as I can tell, there is little nostalgia on either side of the Atlantic for the time when England's thirteen American colonies were part of Great Britain. Most of us walk around with some sense of the grievances that sparked the conflict—taxes on tea, something about stamps—but the list is hard to keep straight because it is essentially trivial. To be sure, taxation remains a hot button in American life, and conservatives are fond of invoking colonial resistance as a principled precedent for their own hostility to government spending. But this seems like a bit of a stretch for most of us, if not in logic, then across a chasm of time.

There is one aspect of the Revolution, however, that is anything but remote: the Declaration of Independence. Far more than simply the centerpiece of any notion of American historical and cultural literacy, the kind of document virtually all of us are taught in school, the Declaration actually shapes the way we live our lives—not always well or consciously, mind you, but powerfully nonetheless.

Maybe saying that the Declaration of Independence is central in contemporary American life seems odd, since few of us have actually read the entire document. And those of us who have can't help but notice that this manifesto, like so much else about the American Revolution, is remote, even tedious. Most of the Declaration is a long list of grievances that only some familiarity with late eighteenth-century Anglo-American history could make intelligible—complaints about royal administration of the colonial courts, the quartering of British troops, etc. This is mostly the latter part of the Declaration. Its opening is a very different affair; indeed, virtually all of us can recite at least part of it from memory before trailing off into forgetfulness and ignorance: "When in the course of human events . . ."

The key to the Declaration, the part that survives in collective memory and which underwrites the American Dream, is the opening clauses of the second paragraph: "We hold these Truths to be self-evident, that all Men are created equal, that they are endowed by their Creator with certain unalienable Rights, that among these are Life, Liberty, and the Pursuit of Happiness." These words speak to us. It's not only that they laid the foundations for sweeping social movements like the struggle to end slavery, and thus created a recognizably modern United States. These words actually structure the minutiae of everyday existence: where we go to school, who we marry, what we buy. In other times and places, people have made such decisions on the basis of the greater glory of God, the security of their nation, or obligations to their ancestors. We usually don't, and on those relatively rare occasions when we do, there is a powerful perception that such decisions are atypical, even foolish. (The literature of immigration, for example, is animated by precisely such tensions over schooling, marriage, and consumerism.) The fact that we have such an explicit basis for our actions—most vividly "the pursuit of happiness," a phrase that more than any other defines the American Dream, treating happiness as a concrete and realizable objective—obscures the degree to which, in the larger scheme of history, our notion of common sense would have been viewed as neither especially common nor sensible, even by earlier Americans like the Puritans.

Of course, not all of us *do* view the Declaration as common sense, exactly. We recognize, even if we haven't subjected them to close scrutiny, that the grandiloquent phrases of the Declaration can seem pretty threadbare. What's more than a little surprising is how the ways even less privileged and more jaded Americans take it for granted far beyond the confines of bucolic college campuses, and the way people who might not have anything else in common—the self-satisfied business executive, the desperately poor urban athlete, the angry activist for gay rights—will nevertheless embrace it instinctively even as they differ on just what it means.

Nowhere is the immediacy of the Declaration—and its relationship to the American Dream—more obvious than in contemporary advertising. I don't mean that the very concept of advertising emphasizes individual agency and personal fulfillment, just as the Declaration and the American Dream do. I mean that the Declaration is implicitly and explicitly invoked all the time—"life, liberty, and as much entertainment as is digitally possible," in the words of one recent radio advertisement. Such invocations are significant because advertisers are not in the business of questioning existing social and political arrangements; they accept the status quo and try to align what they sell with what they think their audience already believes. They wouldn't use patriotic rhetoric if they didn't think it would work. As a look through any general-interest magazine will readily show, however, the appeal of such rhetoric is, well, self-evident.

The Declaration can be manipulated in these and other ways because it rests on premises with which we all (sometimes unthinkingly) agree. And yet what we agree *to* can become slippery, if not depressing. "Life" once seemed clear enough, at least until debates about abortion, genetic engineering, and cloning muddied those waters.

The meaning of liberty, by contrast, sometimes seems all too clear: a celebration of the right to buy—if you've got the cash or credit. And the pursuit of happiness—is it simply the acquisition of creature comforts? Even advertisers would say surely not. ("There are some things that money can't buy," goes one slogan, acknowledging the limits of corporate power as the prelude for the key assertion: "For everything else, there's MasterCard.") Yet we Americans often act as if we believe there really *isn't* anything money can't buy.

The very prestige of the Declaration and its rhetoric, a sense that there's something high-minded and timeless about it, makes account executives, political candidates, and real estate agents so apt to borrow its power. Ironically, though, such invocations increasingly engender cynicism even as Americans succumb, in ever greater numbers, to a notion that life, liberty, and the pursuit of happiness are a matter of individual fulfillment and ease, not striving and hard work.

Many Americans, disappointed if not appalled by such hucksterism and laziness, fear that the once-grandiloquent cadences of the Declaration are now empty slogans and that the American Dream has lost its luster and may even be dying. In this view, the Founding Fathers who framed the Declaration and waged the Revolution were men of principle who would be appalled by the way their ideals have been unthinkingly taken for granted and trivialized. Actually, I *do* think the Founders would not be entirely happy about what had become of their country by 2000. But then, many weren't entirely happy about what had become of their country by 1800, and obituaries for the American Dream date back to the mid-seventeenth century, when ministers regularly lamented in their jeremiads that the latter-day Puritans were not the men their fathers were. Modern-day market capitalism has certainly put a distinctive spin on the Declaration of Independence, but dismay or even disgust with the state of the nation is often at least as much a psychological phenomenon as it is a historical one.

Indeed, the flip side to the sense of hope that goes to the core of the Declaration and the Dream is a sense of fear that its promises are on the verge of being, or actually have been, lost. To return for a moment to the Civil War: one way to understand the white southern decision to secede from the Union is to see it as motivated by dread—that an American Dream based on a particular way of life was being eroded by growing northern power, and the only way to preserve that way of life was to pull out while there was still least a chance to do so. Whether or not this assessment was correct—the outcome of the war suggests the South left too late to secede successfully—white southern hopes for independence were inextricably bound up in fears of losing freedom (including the freedom to buy and sell slaves).

The American Revolution, and the Declaration of Independence that is its living legacy, were marked by a similar sense of hope and fear, of dreams for the future rooted in the conditions of the past. They are also marked by deep ambiguities, ambiguities that are perhaps the only real constant in the centuries they have been remembered (and forgotten). If we are today less than wholly satisfied with the state of the Declaration as it is commonly understood, we are likely to be even less satisfied by how it was understood by the men who created it. Actually, a sense of dissatisfaction, a belief that the nation we inhabit isn't quite right—but *could* be—represents its most important legacy.

Objects of the most stupendous magnitude, measures in which the lives and liberties of millions, born and unborn are most essentially interested, are now before us.

**—John Adams, arguing for
American independence, July 1, 1776**

Simply put, the American Dream of the Founding Fathers was freedom. But to put it simply is also to put it a little misleadingly. For one thing, these people did not understand the term in quite the way the Puritans, for instance, did. For another, it took them a very long time to realize that achieving freedom *was* their dream, because in some important respects freedom was not a dream at all but rather a living reality.

To begin with that reality: by the time the Declaration of Independence was introduced in Congress in 1776, much of what would become the United States had already been inhabited by British and other European colonists for well over 150 years. This long strip of land running from modern-day Maine to Georgia was a land of enormous contrasts. While New England was a region of small towns and farms, the South was dominated by large plantations. The middle colonies, particularly the commercial centers of New York and Philadelphia, were relatively densely populated places of enormous racial and ethnic diversity. Yet such differences were ultimately less important than some crucial similarities. Though not universal, Protestant religion was one. The English language was another.

The most important similarity of all, though, is that these were among the most lightly governed people on earth. To some extent, this was a matter of simple logistics: given the global span of the British empire, it simply wasn't possible to micromanage people three thousand or more miles away, particularly when it took weeks, if not months, for imperial communication to cross the Atlantic. That's not to say Britain didn't try to supervise her North American possessions, and even succeeded, to some extent: a thick bureaucracy managed maritime trade and traffic, and in cultural and economic terms, the colonies were more oriented toward London than they were to each other. But even in England, the relative lack of supervision was viewed as less a necessary evil than a positive good. A relatively minimalist approach to the colonies had proved cheap and profitable; by some estimates they accounted for about a third of Britain's economy on the eve of the Revolution, principally as a source of raw materials and a market for finished products. Hence British prime minister Robert Walpole's maxim *"quieta non movere,"* which in an American context boiled down to a policy of benign neglect.

By the mid-eighteenth century, however, such a policy was becoming increasingly difficult to maintain. International jockeying with France and Spain for global supremacy led to a series of wars fought across the globe. In North America, the most important of these was the Seven Years' War of 1755–63, which, after a series of losses, culminated in a resounding British victory. Given the choice during protracted peace negotiations between pursuing extremely profitable slave plantations in the Caribbean or evicting the French entirely from North America, the British finally opted for, and got, the latter. In waging and winning a global war, they gained supremacy over a continent—and were saddled with gargantuan bills.

This is where the standard narratives of the American Revolution typically begin. The British, laboring under a mountain of debt, thought it only natural that the colonists help bear the cost of the war and their future protection. This is why, beginning in 1764, Parliament placed a series of taxes on commodities and began enforcing old taxes, like a 1733 duty on molasses, that had been honored more in the breach than the observance. To each of these acts, the colonists reacted with growing concern, hostility, and resistance, leading the British to back down on most of the particulars even as they became increasingly determined to insist on their right to collect such revenue in the first place. The colonists, in turn, became increasingly determined to deny Parliament had that right.

That's a rather abbreviated summary of how the American Revolution came about. Like all such summaries, it omits a lot in the name of other objectives. The main thing it omits is confusion: the uncertainties and even contradictions that surrounded a decade-long process that led to a desire for political independence only at the very last stages of that process. The colonists were virtually unanimous that having to buy stamps to prove they paid a tax for everything from tea to newspapers was wrong. But the *basis* of that opposition, the reason *why* it was wrong, remained varied and murky for a very long time—even after war was actually under way.

The struggle to justify resistance to British rule was conducted in one of the primary forms of popular culture in the eighteenth century: political pamphlets. In a blizzard of paper that blew back and forth as well as up and down the Anglo-American world, late eighteenth-century writers like John Adams, Thomas Jefferson, Alexander Hamilton, and others sought to galvanize intercolonial support. Was Britain wrong because Parliament, which had the right to regulate trade between the colonies *as a whole* and the mother country, didn't have the right to impose taxes *on individual* colonies, which had always handled that themselves? Or was it because Parliament, which could impose taxes to regulate trade, could not do so simply to make money for the government? Or was the problem more fundamental—that there could be no taxation without American representation in Parliament? But did Parliament have any business governing the colonies in the first place?

One did not have to be a member of Britain's House of Lords to look upon some of these questions with skepticism; many Britons responded to them, often with questions of their own. Can you really distinguish between an internal and external tax, or gauge whether its motivation is for regulation or revenue? they asked. Other questions were answered more decisively: No, the colonies are not represented in Parliament, but then neither are some parts of England. Parliament, in any case, governs the whole empire, and the colonies in particular are "virtually" represented, just as Englishmen in many other places are.

See: that's the point, still other voices responded. We *are* Englishmen, and as such share the legacy of the Magna Carta of 1215, the Civil War of 1642–46, and (especially) the Glorious Revolution of 1688. Englishmen at home wouldn't allow a standing army. So why, given that the French are now gone, is one being stationed in the colonies—at our expense? Maybe you wouldn't *need* to tax us so heavily if you didn't saddle us with things we don't want in the first place!

Well, maybe if you didn't do stupid things like aggravate the Indians in the West, riot in the streets of Boston, or throw tea in that city's harbor, the army wouldn't be as necessary. Honestly, given all we've done for you in creating and defending the colonies, one might think you children of the Empire would be more grateful—

Children! Grateful for what? Why do you think we came here in the first place—because everything was wonderful at home? And just who was defending whom in that last war? *You're* the ones who are dependent, and you don't even realize it! Well, you're about to learn the hard way when we refuse to buy the goods you're so anxious to sell your "children . . ." *

You get the idea: multiple arguments and multiple responses, often talking past each other and shifting ground rather than boring in on one specific point. In any event, whatever the particular issue or principle in question, the colonists almost always couched their arguments in precedents: this is the way it was before, so this is the way it should be now. To which the British government essentially replied: no, *this* is the way it was before, and that's why what you're worried about isn't really some big change. Not until the publication of Thomas Paine's *Common Sense* in January of 1776 did any leading figure seriously consider anything like a rejection of history as a guide and simply say: let's leave. Until then, freedom was not a goal to be *gained*; it was a cherished possession the colonists wanted to prevent being *lost*.

Were they right to be so anxious, so militant? Even after reading multiple accounts of the Revolution, it's hard to know. Perhaps more to the point, it may be hard to *care*. Here again, the Civil War furnishes a useful comparison. Although it wasn't the only or even primary cause, the slavery issue—however garbled *that* debate—has always led me to identify with the Northern states fighting to preserve the Union. At the same time, many Americans, invoking a variety of justifications, continue to have strong Confederate sympathies. Slavery was a matter of some moment in the Revolution, too. But it was never at issue to the same extent; a collective agreement was reached that for the moment, at least, "freedom" was to be a relative and racially limited term. Moreover, there was no other controversy in the Revolution that seemed to have the same degree of moral clarity about it. I'm glad about the way the Revolution turned out. But like a sports team that wins a game on a

* I am, of course, paraphrasing the arguments. But the actual exchanges weren't all that far from what I've rendered here. "Will these Americans, children planted by our care, nourished up by our indulgence until they are grown to a degree of opulence, and protected by our arms, will they grudge to contribute their mite to relieve us from under the heavy weight of that burden which we lie under?" asked Parliamentarian (and future prime minister) Charles Townshend during a debate over the much detested Stamp Act of 1765. To which French and Indian War veteran Isaac Barré replied, "Planted by *your* care? No! Your oppressions planted them in America. . . . They nourished by *your* indulgence? They grew up by your neglect of them. They protected by *your* arms? They have nobly taken up arms in your defense." The seams of division between the two sides were thus already apparent a decade before the Revolution actually began.

disputed call or technicality, I feel a twinge of unease along with relief and pleasure about the outcome.

In point of fact, that outcome was at least as much a matter of the outcome of a series of battles that were fought between 1775 and 1781 than any abstruse arguments about taxation, administration, or the social conditions of British colonists in the preceding 175 years. Indeed, the search for intellectual causation in any struggle can sometimes overlook the degree of contingency in human affairs, or the degree to which all too human impulses (like greed) motivate people more decisively than historically specific opinions (like Adam Smith's assertion, published the same year as the Declaration of Independence, that a free market economy works better than a mercantilist economy). Cutting through a Gordian knot of scholarly argument, historian Theodore Draper succinctly summarizes the Revolution in his aptly titled 1996 book *A Struggle for Power*. "In the end," Draper concludes, "the Revolution was a struggle for power—between the power the British wanted to exercise over the Americans and the power the Americans wished to exercise over themselves." Draper dutifully traces the often complicated sequence of events and controversies over sugar, stamps, tea, and the like but shows it was the British themselves who, along with a few prescient Frenchmen, recognized as early as the seventeenth century that the colonies were destined to pull away from the Mother Country. It is *this* kind of common sense, far more than the musings of Thomas Paine, that explained the Revolution. "The Declaration of Independence put it bluntly—the Americans in 1776 wanted nothing more than to assume a 'separate and equal station' among 'the powers of the earth,'" he writes, quoting the document directly.

The problem for the Founders and their heirs is that this isn't all the Declaration said. It also said a bunch of things that may well have been wishful thinking—like the equality of men, the requirement of consent on the part of the governed, above all the legitimacy of happiness as a personal objective—that nevertheless were taken seriously by a lot of people in a position to make trouble then and ever since. It's important to note here that the Declaration of Independence was by no means a work of blazing originality. As John Adams wrote forty-six years later, there was "not an idea in it, but what had been hackneyed in Congress two years before." Jefferson himself agreed. In an 1823 letter to his protégé James Madison, he explained that he "did not consider it my charge to invent new ideas altogether, and to offer no sentiment which had never been expressed before." John Locke's invocation of "life, liberty and the pursuit of property," from his 1689 *Second Treatise on Government,* was only the most obvious example. Jefferson, of course, tweaked that locution by replacing the last phrase with "the pursuit of happiness."

Yet this phrase was not exactly new, either. Indeed, there is frequent talk of happiness in late eighteenth-century politics. Back in 1765, the New York General Assembly passed a resolution asserting that the levying of taxes "must be the grand Principle of every free State. Without such a right vested in themselves, exclusive of all others, there can be no Liberty, no Happiness, no Security." In his 1776 "Declaration of Rights for Virginia," an important source for Jefferson's Declaration, George Mason wrote of "the enjoyment of life and liberty, with the means of acquiring and possessing property, and pursuing and obtaining happiness and safety." Phrases like these made clear the true nature of Jefferson's (and his editors') accomplishment: a certain economy and zing in "life, liberty, and the pursuit of happiness" that help explain why it's so widely remembered—and cherished.

But the alchemy of such phrases was more subtle than that. Somehow, the Declaration of Independence changed the course of history—by which I mean it reversed the flow of time. *Before* July of 1776, the American Revolution had been justified in terms of preserving 150 years of relative autonomy threatened by England's need for revenue. *After* July of 1776, though, the Revolution was increasingly viewed in terms of the future changes it would justify. In the much-quoted words of Benjamin Rush, "The war is over, but this is far from being the case with the American Revolution. On the contrary, nothing but the first act of the great drama is closed." And the Declaration, which asserted presumably timeless truths, nevertheless came to function, in the words of Pauline Maier, as "a moral standard by which the day-to-day policies and practices of the nation could be judged." Freedom had been a reality; now it was a dream.

"May it be to the world what I believe it will be to some parts sooner, others later, but finally to all, the signal for arousing men to burst the chains under which monkish ignorance and superstition has persuaded them to bind themselves, and to achieve the blessings and security of self-government."

—Thomas Jefferson on the Declaration of Independence, 1826

The Founding Fathers typically defined freedom in terms of its oppo-site: slavery. When they used the term "slavery," however, they weren't referring to the peculiar institution whereby many of the Founding Fathers themselves bought and sold African Americans as property; they referred to what they felt Great Britain was doing to their lives and livelihoods. "Remember officers and soldiers, that you are Freemen, fighting for the blessings of Liberty—that Slavery will be your portion, and that of your posterity, if you do not acquit yourselves like men," George Washington told his troops on Long Island in July 1776.

This unself-conscious comparison between freedom and slavery was a fixture of the newspaper and pamphlet literature of the time. "We are taxed without our consent expressed by ourselves or our representa-tives," wrote John Dickinson in his highly influential 1765 pamphlet *Let-ters from a Farmer in Pennsylvania*. "We are therefore—SLAVES." Others echoed the charge. "I speak it with grief—I speak it with anguish—Britons are our oppressors: I speak it with shame—I speak it with indig-nation—*we are slaves,*" the Massachusetts revolutionary Josiah Quincy wrote in 1774. Another Massachusetts work from the same year bore the more pithy title *The Misery and Duty of an Enslav'd People*. The misery was slavery; the duty, revolt.

From a modern standpoint, it's difficult to take these claims and fears seriously. Relative to a lot of other people in the world, these British subjects had it pretty good, and it's almost impossible to imagine them ending up really *enslaved*—the way these colonists actually com-modified those Americans with African ancestry. But you don't have to be a modern-day cynic to make such an observation: a lot of people at the time did, too. "How is it that we hear the loudest yelps for liberty among the drivers of negroes?" asked the famed British essayist Samuel Johnson in 1775.

Nor were such comments limited to critics of the rebels. "Would anyone believe that I am the master of slaves of my own purchase!" Patrick Henry—best known for his slogan "Give me liberty or give me death"—wrote in a letter of 1773. "I am drawn here by the general inconvenience of living here without them. I will not, I can not justify it." Henry hoped that "a time will come when an opportunity will be offered to abolish this lamentable evil."

As the Founding Fathers realized—some of them fearfully—the attainment of their dream could encourage others to pursue theirs. This realization that they might be opening a Pandora's Box loomed large over the drafting and discussion of the Declaration of Independence. Certainly it was on Jefferson's mind. As a member of Virginia's House of Burgesses, Jefferson repeatedly broached abolition of the slave trade—which, given the insuperable opposition to the measure, the commercial implications of driving up the value of slaves that were already in America, and Jefferson's lifelong wish that he could simply make African Americans go away, was more a symbolic gesture than a proposal that could be expected to be taken seriously. A similar sense of mixed motives and bad faith animated Jefferson's draft of the Declaration. His bill of particulars against George III, which included accusations of "cutting off our Trade with all Parts of the World" and "imposing taxes on us without our consent," culminated in a final charge that begins as follows: "He has waged cruel war against human nature itself, violating it's [*sic*] most sacred rights of life & liberty in the persons of a distant people, who never offended him, captivating and carrying them into slavery in another hemisphere, or to incur miserable death in their transportation thither." It takes no great leap of imagination to suspect that friends *and* foes of bondage found this indictment problematic, if not embarrassing. Most of it was cut or revised. What remains is much more oblique: "He has excited domestic Insurrections amongst us, and has endeavored to bring on the Inhabitants of our Frontiers, the merciless Indian Savages, whose known Rule of Warfare, is an undisguised Destruction, of all Ages, Sexes, and Conditions." The slave issue has been expanded (and diffused) to encompass racial violence generally among all people. Britain's alliances with Indians here is obvious; the reference to slavery, in case you missed it, is the "domestic insurrections." Perhaps Dr. Johnson got it wrong: it's euphemism, not patriotism, that's the last refuge of scoundrels.

One of the strongest indications that recognition of the contradictions surrounding a slaveholders' revolution for freedom was not simply a later imposition of future attitudes on past realities can be gauged by the sudden quickening interest in ending slavery that accompanied the American Revolution. The first antislavery society in the United States was established within days of the Battles of Lexington and Concord in 1775. Slavery was abolished in Vermont in 1777, Massachusetts in 1780, and New Hampshire in 1784, while Connecticut, Rhode Island, and Pennsylvania adopted plans of gradual emancipation. By 1804 every northern state had made some provision for ending slavery. More important, many *southern* states explored colonization, voluntary manumission, and even outright emancipation. In the decade following the Declaration of Independence, every state but South Carolina and Georgia prohibited or heavily taxed the slave trade, which was outlawed in 1808 under the provisions of the U.S. Constitution. Indeed, undoubtedly out of shame, the word "slavery" appears nowhere in the document.

Slavery wasn't the only example of the Declaration bringing alternative dreams into focus. Students of women's history are fond of quoting Abigail Adams's admonition to her husband to "remember the ladies" while he was on the committee to draft the document. But it is John's exasperated response no less than his wife's prescience that is revealing here: "We have been told that our struggle has loosened the bonds of government everywhere; that children and apprentices were disobedient; that schools and colleges were grown turbulent; that Indians slighted their guardians, and negroes grew insolent to their masters."

Indeed, Adams himself had been stung by the very forces he was in the process of unleashing during a religious controversy at the first Continental Congress of 1774. The roots of the problem went back to 1759, when the Church of England opened a mission in Cambridge, Massachusetts. The Congregationalists (that is, the church of the Puritans, to which Adams himself belonged) objected that it was wrong for England to establish an official state religion there supported by local taxes. Yet by the 1770s a series of other churches was pointing out that the *Congregationalists* were the established church in Massachusetts, imposing taxes on Baptists, Quakers, and others. Invited by a group of Philadelphians to attend an interdenominational meeting, Adams and the Massachusetts congressional delegation found themselves ambushed by Quakers and Baptists concerned about the discrepancy between the way "in which liberty in general is now beheld" and the way Baptists were treated in Massachusetts. An embarrassed Adams, emphasizing that he had no authority to act on behalf of his church, tried to explain that Congregationalism in Massachusetts was barely established (in fact one could apply for an exemption from taxes). Thirty years later, still sore from the experience, he attributed it to the machinations of a wily Quaker—in Adams's words, an "artful Jesuit"—who was simply trying to make him look bad.

Perhaps the most significant example of the Revolution's logic being pressed against its leaders—significant because it helped convince them to hold a convention that trimmed back some of the grand promises of the Declaration into a far more legalistic Constitution—was Shays's Rebellion. By the 1780s a combination of excessive land taxation, high legal costs, and economic depression led about a third of all male heads of households to be sued for debt. The state legislatures, dominated by mercantile interests, demanded payment in hard currency. During the spring and summer of 1786, groups of disaffected western Massachusetts farmers responded by mustering militia companies and closing down the courts that were throwing them in jail, just as they had done during the Revolution. (Were not debt and depression a denial of life, liberty, and the pursuit of happiness?) They emphasized the continuity between that struggle and this one by using liberty trees and liberty poles, the same symbols they had employed a decade before. Similar events were recorded throughout New England and were in large measure repeated in western Pennsylvania during the Whiskey Rebellion of 1794, an uprising against a deeply unpopular tax on alcohol.

The Founders did not necessarily capitulate to such challenges. (Indeed, Washington eagerly marched at the head of the militia called to crush the Whiskey Rebellion, which melted away before the troops arrived.) The process was typically more subtle, however. Even as changes in race relations and other issues continued, the pace of reform slowed, then stopped. There was not enough shame to prevent the three-fifths clause from being inserted into the Constitution, which literally made (male) slaves less than full men but allowed southern whites to count them for purposes of representation in Congress—just one of many ways slaves' bodies were used against them. Fear of insurrection, technological innovation in cotton farming, and narrow self-interest held the nation's ideals at bay. As Theodore Draper might say, it was a struggle for power, and those who had won it were not going to give it up easily.

It would be misleading, however, to simply view subsequent American history as a contest between the soaring ideals of the Founders and the cynical realities that checked them. There was, in fact, a coherent rationale at the heart of their actions, a rationale that framed the society they aspired to create: a republic. Perhaps the best way to explain what a republic was to them is to name what it wasn't: an aristocracy or democracy. On the one hand, the Founding Fathers wanted to overthrow what they regarded as a corrupt system of government run by people who had no other qualification for office than having been born into a particular family. On the other, they were terrified of what they called "mob rule" and people governing for no other reason than crudely personifying a popular point of view. The happy medium for them was a *natural* aristocracy: people of demonstrated talent and virtue *earning* the right to represent the people.* No less than the natural aristocrats themselves, a republic required the masses to be sufficiently moral and wise to *recognize* talent when they saw it and to willingly invest their collective power in such people. As part of an ongoing project to earn and inculcate trust, the Founders were willing to use democratic means, like elections, to realize their republican ends—but only among people they felt confident were capable of exercising such morality and wisdom. Jefferson, for example, thought farmers with small holdings to be ideal citizens. But whether by nature or nurture, it was clear to them that many of the people who lived in the United States—slaves, women, Indians—lacked this virtue, and that is why they were excluded from what became a democratic republic.

So you see, there is *a* logic to their American Dream. It wasn't exactly *our* logic two hundred years later, but it made a kind of sense. When the Declaration of Independence proclaimed that all *men* are created equal, the writers of that document really *did* mean men, by their lights: not females, not some black- or yellow-skinned "savage," but civilized white males (a.k.a. "men"). *All* those people were created equal—an assertion notable for both its inclusiveness relative to what came before and its exclusivity relative to what followed. Whether or not others, like slaves, were also created equal in terms of a theoretical capability for republican government was a matter of some uncertainty (and less debate). It was the obvious common ground, in any case, not the ambiguity of those on the boundaries, that was their focus.

In its eighteenth-century context, "equal" worked in a similar way. The Founding Fathers would be the last to argue that all men, much less all human beings, were born equal in physical, intellectual, or legal

* The term "natural aristocracy" is Jefferson's; in a letter to Adams, he wrote that "I agree with you that there is a natural aristocracy among men. The grounds of this are virtue and talents." Adams, ever the skeptic, expressed discomfort with any use of the term "aristocracy," writing back to Jefferson that "your distinction between the aristoi and the pseudo aristoi will not help the matter. I trust one as soon as the other with unlimited power." Yet while it is clear that Adams distrusted elite rule as much as mob rule, he clearly believed that the United States should be led by men of morality and talent—men like himself.

terms. But they believed all men (and perhaps some others) were born with what was commonly called "the moral sense," that is, an ability to tell right from wrong, good from bad. This notion of the moral sense and its fit in the larger republican dream was aptly described in metaphorical terms by Jefferson: "State a moral case to a ploughman and a professor; the former will decide it as well, and often better than the latter, because he has not been led astray by artificial rules." For Jefferson and others, the ploughman and the professor were equal in their ability to grasp the difference between right and wrong and to apprehend what can be done in a given situation. They were not equal in terms of their talents or achievements. The professor—who, in the purest of republican worlds, was a child of ploughmen (perhaps even a former ploughman himself)—was the best equipped to advise, organize, and execute policies. But professors were not to single-handedly decide what those policies should be. Professors should guide and represent the ploughmen, but it was they, not the professors, who would have final say in the voting booth, and if absolutely necessary, in revolution.

That was the theory—or, perhaps more accurately, that was the Dream. The world had never really worked that way before, and it hasn't exactly worked that way since, either. (It's probably no accident that only one actual professor, Woodrow Wilson, has ever been president of the United States; by the end of his tenure in 1921 he had exhausted and exasperated the American public with his high-handed, moralistic approach to governance.) But at least some American revolutionaries of 1776 considered their particular version of the Dream ideal.

Not all of them: the Declaration notwithstanding, they did not usually speak with one voice. Thomas Paine was a good deal more democratic than Jefferson; his post-Revolutionary rival, Alexander Hamilton, would have been quite happy with an aristocratically dominated monarchy. South Carolinian and Georgian planters were suspicious of anything that might disturb the racial status quo. Moreover, individual Founders could be ambivalent or ambiguous about their American Dream. Jefferson, for example, seemed to believe that African Americans really did have a moral sense and suspected their obvious inferiority was more environmental than racial, but he never came up with a fully coherent position on slavery—or the money to pay his debts so he could free his own slaves.

Moreover, even though we speak the same language as our Revolutionary forebears, the meanings of words we use have been subject to change and disagreement. Indeed, as a number of twentieth-century historians suggested, the very degree to which we comprehended—and were attracted to—words the Founders could obscure implications we would have found puzzling, even repugnant. Some people today, for example, might think "natural aristocracy" corresponds to what is commonly called "meritocracy." But Jefferson would probably have been confused, if not appalled, by the idea of a black woman at the University of Virginia as anything but a servant, and most of us would have found his plan for sorting and educating children—removing them from their parents, subjecting them to escalating batteries of tests, and promoting only those who show the most obvious promise—a little frightening. Other Jeffersonian ideas seem downright strange, like his and others' attempts to reduce happiness to a mathematical equation, or his suggestion, after much calculation of average life spans, that no contracts should be binding after twenty years. This was Jefferson in his "natural philosophic" or (pseudo-) scientific mode, and such opinions were by no means widespread in his time, any more than they are in ours. Instead, we associate him with more arresting propositions, like "the earth belongs to the living," which seem to extend a benevolent blessing across time. We might find his famous assertion that "the tree of liberty must be refreshed from time to time with the blood of patriots and tyrants" striking, even brave—until we consider the relative aridity, even chilliness, of such an assertion when we compare it to Patrick Henry's more passionate and engaged "Give me liberty or give me death!" (Henry, to his credit, did free his slaves by the time of his death.)

I could go on, emphasizing the gaps, flaws, or contemporary misunderstandings in the thought of Jefferson and other Founding Fathers, but the truth is that their American Dream and the suppositions that underlay it are largely beside the point. For the Dream would not unfold in quite the way they imagined. By the beginning of the new (nineteenth) century, it was unmistakably apparent that the People in whose name they secured the Revolution weren't much interested in virtue, natural aristocracy, and the rest—at least as the Founders defined them.

Some Founders wondered if they bothered to define such words at all. Shortly before his death in 1799, George Washington lamented that one of the emerging political factions could "set up a broomstick" as a candidate, call it "a true son of liberty," "Democrat," or "any other epi-

LOOSE LEGACY *Thomas Jefferson (by Rembrandt Peale). Future generations would invoke the Declaration of Independence for aims he would consider unfathomable, if not offensive. Yet Jefferson seemed to know this. "May it be to the world what I believe it will be to some parts sooner, others later, but finally to all, the signal for arousing men to burst the chains under which monkish ignorance and superstition has persuaded them to bind themselves," he wrote to planners of a fiftieth-anniversary celebration in 1826. (Photo from the collections of the Library of Congress)*

thet that will serve a purpose," and it would "command their votes in toto!" Even Jefferson, whose sunny optimism seemed to define American character, despaired for the future at the end of his life. "All, all dead," he wrote to an old friend in 1825, "and ourselves left alone amidst a new generation whom we know not, and who knows not us." This sense of neglect and mutual incomprehension was more than hyperbole or the crankiness of an old man who had lived too long. As barriers to political participation for white men dropped and opportunities for economic advancement beckoned, American ploughmen were paying less and less attention to professors. In fact, after an initial flurry of excitement when it was publicly read, the Declaration of Independence itself fell into relative obscurity in the 1780s and 1790s. "I See no disposition to celebrate or remember, or even Curiosity to enquire into the Characters, Actions, or Events of the Revolution," John Adams wrote to John Trumbull, painter of the Founding Fathers' portrait, in 1817. Actually, the Declaration and its creators were beginning a comeback even as Adams wrote, and his and Jefferson's death on the same day marked the beginnings of its ascent to a preeminence in American life. The democratizing tendencies of American life became apparent during Jefferson's two-term presidency—for which he was widely, though not always fairly, criticized by his opponents—but he, no less than the more obviously conservative John Adams, was discomfited by the raucous democratic culture typified by Andrew Jackson (who ultimately threw Adams's son out of the presidency). The Adams–Jefferson correspondence, which persisted almost to their deaths on July 4, 1826, is a document of two men awed, troubled, and finally amazed by what they had wrought.

In sum, the Declaration of Independence proved to be far bigger than the Founding Fathers. It was something they came to only fitfully, under real duress and with real reluctance, and it was a document whose ambiguities and implications they incompletely understood. Ultimately, it was the fact of the Declaration itself—the hardware, to use a twentieth-century metaphor—that proved far more important than the imperfect and perishable "software" of their particular republican dream. Its ongoing vitality and legitimacy would ultimately rest with others who inherited a machine whose circuitry would be repeatedly reconfigured and replaced for centuries to come.

Consider, for example, the following:

We hold these truths to be self-evident: that all men and women are created equal. (Seneca Falls Declaration, 1848)

Assembled upon the 116th anniversary of the Declaration of Independence, the People's Party of America, in their first national convention,
invoking upon their action the blessing of almighty God, puts forth, in
the name of the people of this country, the following preamble and declaration of principles. (American Populist Party platform, 1892)

I still have a dream. It is a dream deeply rooted in the American dream
that one day this nation will rise up and live out the true meaning of its
creed—we hold these truths to be self-evident, that all men are created
equal. (Martin Luther King Jr., 1963)

Each of these statements from important social movements—or, to put
it another way, each of these American Dreams—rested on the language, prestige, and confidence of the Declaration of Independence.
John Adams may have been present at the creation, but it was his wife
Abigail who sensed the possibilities of a movement that first stirred
after their deaths and finally flowered almost two centuries later. The
Populist movement of the late nineteenth century grew out of conditions comparable to those that sparked Shays's Rebellion but resulted
in many notable examples of peaceful economic collaboration that at
its best crossed racial lines and put forth proposals—among them voting, currency, and tax reforms—that later became law. And the civil
rights movement of the 1950s and 1960s made its most significant head-
way by calling attention to the yawning gap between the cherished
ideals of the Declaration and the appalling realities of American life.
Words alone could not win these battles, but they did allow them to be
fought—sometimes successfully.

Sometimes. Simply invoking the Declaration has never been
enough. Adams and his colleagues did not, in fact, remember the
ladies. It would not be until fifty-eight years after that embarrassing
meeting in Philadelphia that the Congregational Church was finally
disestablished in Massachusetts. And the Shays and Whiskey rebellions
were summarily put down with force. When push came to shove—and
there are many examples in American history where push really *did*
come to shove—frank assertions of power almost always mattered far
more than lofty assertions of freedom.

But then, as now, it usually didn't have to get that far. The real reason the legacy of the Declaration of Independence isn't a seamless, triumphant narrative of Progress has more to do with the wielding of words than the wielding of weapons (or, perhaps more accurately, the wielding of words as weapons). The Founding Fathers were never able to fix the definitions of terms like "life," "liberty," and the "pursuit of happiness" to their satisfaction, and no one since has, either. Life, liberty, and happiness for whom? The answer wasn't always obvious (Do Chinese-born immigrants really count? The answer, for decades, was no.), and we always had a lot of trouble recognizing, never mind actually addressing, direct conflicts.

"Liberty" in particular continued to be a sore topic. At different points in subsequent American history, powerful interests have succeeded in persuading key people and institutions—like the U.S. Supreme Court—that liberty means:

- the right of whites to own blacks (*Dred Scott v. Sanford,* 1857);
- the prerogative of an employer to enforce a contract with workers over any government provisions made for those workers *(Lochner v. New York,* 1905);
- the ability for the national government to prosecute those whose speech it decides represents "a clear and present danger" (*Schenk v. U.S.,* 1919).

Still, this has never been the whole story. Others in American history have argued, successfully, that liberty does not mean a person can own slaves, that in fact this is the antithesis of liberty (the Thirteenth Amendment, 1865). In the 1940s Franklin Roosevelt propounded "the Four Freedoms" that were the birthright of every American: freedom of speech, freedom of worship, freedom from want, and freedom from fear. The first two elicited little comment. (It had taken two hundred years, but now virtually everyone agreed at least theoretically on religious liberty, and even Supreme Court Justice Oliver Wendell Holmes, who followed the *Schenk* decision later the following year with his dissent in *United States v. Abrams,* offered a ringing defense of freedom of speech.)

The last two of the Four Freedoms proved to be too much for some, however, particularly those whose American Dreams were premised on acquiring as much as possible without having to share it with anyone else. It was for such people that in a 1947 speech Roosevelt's successor,

Harry Truman, dropped the "freedom from want and fear" and replaced it with "freedom of enterprise." Freedom of enterprise is an American Dream that has been present from the very beginning—liberation from Britain had very profitable implications for merchants like John Hancock and real estate speculators like George Washington—and at certain points in American history (the Gilded Age, the 1920s) has enjoyed special prominence. The closing decades of the twentieth century have been particularly notable in this regard, and a vast commercial infrastructure dedicated its considerable resources to persuading Americans to understand the Declaration of Independence in such terms. And that's more or less where we remain today: life, liberty, and as much entertainment as is digitally possible. For now.

If there is one constant in the Declaration of Independence, it lies in the way no version of the status quo is ever completely acceptable. It provides us with (often imperceptibly shifting) standards by which we measure success but simultaneously calls attention to the gap between what is and what we believe should be, a gap that defines our national experience. A piece of wishful thinking composed in haste, the Declaration was born and lives as the charter of the American Dream. It constitutes us.

CHAPTER 3

DREAM OF THE GOOD LIFE (II): UPWARD MOBILITY

THE DECLARATION OF INDEPENDENCE may be the charter of the American Dream, but between that abstract document and current reality are countless variations on the
pursuit of happiness: *e unum, pluribus.* Yet it is also true that among all
the possibilities, as variegated as any American who has ever lived, are
basic classes of dreams that rest on concepts whose meaning both tran-
scends a particular context and gets defined by that context. The Puritans dreamt of freedom; so did African Americans. Both understood
freedom to represent a loosening from coercive restraints, but the
nature of the restraints was very different. For the Puritans, they were
primarily spiritual; for African Americans, they were all too often literal
(which in turn could have major spiritual consequences).

Similarly, while the Puritans and many of their successors sought to
live good lives, the nature of "good" changed over time. In the nineteenth century in particular, the term began to take on a more obvious
secular orientation (though in its fondest formulations, moving up in
this world by no means precluded moving up in the next one). Hard
work was no longer a (hopefully useful) distraction from the dictates of
fate but rather an instrument of fate itself, a tool for self-realization.

Like the American Dream broadly construed, this one of the good
life exists in a series of variations. The most common form was cast in

terms of commercial success. For hundreds of years, American readers and writers have had tireless appetites for tales of poor boys (and, later, girls) who, with nothing but pluck and ingenuity, created financial empires that towered over the national imagination (and in some cases towered over the national landscape as well). The archetypal example of such a bootstrap-pulling figure is steel magnate Andrew Carnegie, whose regularly published capitalist sermons, culminating in his highly selective posthumous *Autobiography* (1920), are tiresome catalogs of implemented plans and surmounted challenges, all wrapped in a complacently moral tone. But there are other forms of mobility, too: tales of transformation through education, for example, or people with modest resources who triumphed in the arts, sports, or other realms of human aspiration.

And like other American Dreams, the power of this one lay in a sense of collective ownership: anyone can get ahead. An assertion of universal enfranchisement is routinely reaffirmed by this dream's boosters (the obsessive quality of their reaffirmations never quite leading them to raise troubling questions about the ongoing need for regular reassurance). Occasionally, it has been roundly condemned as an opiate of the people, usually by critics of American society who are dismissed as disgruntled, foreign, or both. Only rarely have the contours of this dream been seriously explored and tested in a sympathetic, but probing, way. But that could not happen until those contours had clearly emerged. It took a couple hundred years for the realities of American life to shape the Dream of Upward Mobility.

> *"If rascals knew the advantage of virtue,*
> *they would become honest men out of rascality."*
>
> **—Benjamin Franklin, ca. 1776**

The American Dream of the Pilgrims and Puritans may have been otherworldly, but earthly improvement was not necessarily antithetical to their plans. Indeed, in many cases it was an important component of them. Moreover, these people were frequently a minority even in the heart of New England, where the unchurched often played pivotal roles in actually making that society work.

Throughout the British colonies—as well as non-British colonies—

the prospect of moving up in the world was an avowed motive of virtually every Euroamerican (and even some non-Euroamericans). This
was particularly true of apprentices and indentured servants who
signed contracts to work, in many cases as virtual slaves, for fixed terms
in return for the price of passage. In the early years in particular, these
parvenus were given a payment in cash or supplies with which to make
an independent start in the world when their contracts ended. That
start might yield riches, but riches were not the sole measure of moving
up in the world. Economic self-sufficiency, a secure and esteemed pro-
fession (e.g., the ministry), the leisure to pursue a career in politics:
these among others were the yardsticks by which upward mobility was
measured.

In an important respect, however, the Dream of Upward Mobility,
particularly in the South, was actually *too* successful: it quickly became
apparent to those who employed servants that it was in fact quite
expensive to support them and that they could become dangerous com-
petition when they moved on. Better, they concluded, to invest in slaves,
who cost more initially but who had no payoff price and even rose in
value. (Indeed, the slave trade itself became a major means of upward
mobility for many colonists.) African Americans, who were only a tiny
fraction of Virginia's population in the mid-seventeenth century, represented almost half of it by the mid-eighteenth. And in parts of some
colonies, like South Carolina, they were well more than half. By the
time of the Revolution, slavery was legal in all the colonies, and indentured servitude was on the decline. Upward mobility remained possible,
but the terms had a decisively racial cast. For much of American history, then, upward mobility was understood, even defined, by a visible
alternative of immobility.

Nor was mobility necessarily honored even among Europeans and
their descendants. In many respects, colonial American society was still
structured along traditional English lines of deference and noblesse
oblige. Aristocrats had privileges other colonists did not, and commerce
itself was viewed as ungentlemanly by important segments of the
elite—even if, as with the case of plantation owners, it was increasingly
important to sustaining their stature. Nor was this social stability
defined and regulated solely by established authorities back in England.
Massachusetts, for example, remained a theocratic colony substantially
controlled by clergy well into the eighteenth century.

No one was more aware of this than Benjamin Franklin, born in

1706 in Cotton Mather's Boston. At the behest of his father, who could not afford much in the way of formal schooling for his youngest son, the twelve-year-old Franklin signed a nine-year contract for an apprenticeship with his older brother James to learn the printing trade. In 1723 James sought to engender controversy—and thus sell copies of his newspaper, *The New England Courant*—by attacking Mather's controversial promotion of smallpox vaccinations. It was at this point that sixteen-year-old Ben began writing pieces under the assumed identity of an old woman named Silence Dogood. (The name was derived from two of Mather's recently published works, *Silentarius* and *Bonifacius, or Essays to Do Good*.) In the pieces that followed—published by a delighted James Franklin, who eagerly awaited anonymous delivery of work from his unknown correspondent—young Ben poked fun at a series of sacred cows, including that bastion of Puritan orthodoxy, Harvard College, where students learned "little more than how to carry themselves hand-

MOVABLE TYPE *Benjamin Franklin in a pose designed to burnish his legend. More than any other Founding Father, he embodied the ideal of upward mobility. (Painted by Charles E. Mills. Photo from the collections of the Library of Congress)*

somely and enter a room genteely (which might as well be acquired at a dancing school) and from whence they return, after abundance of trouble and charge, as great blockheads as ever, only more proud and conceited." When James was jailed for his heresies, his brother continued running the paper in his absence, gaining still more experience—and increasingly chafing at the constraints James placed upon him. He ultimately broke his apprenticeship and fled to New York and ultimately to the new city of Philadelphia, where he began his ascent to international stature.

There is much that could be said—there is much that Franklin himself *did* say—about his rise, but for our purposes it is important to point out that the justification for all Franklin said and did rested on an emerging theological foundation that would support American culture for much of the next three hundred years. The original Puritan doctrine had strongly emphasized the degree to which men and women could not know what God intended for them and faith as the single most important instrument of their salvation. Yet by the early eighteenth century it was possible for a young man like Franklin to articulate a far more pragmatic—one might say self-serving—spiritual vision that emphasized the degree to which virtue and happiness were not only correlated but discernible and achievable. "I think opinions should be judged of by their influences and effects; and if a man holds none that make him less virtuous or more vicious, it may be concluded he holds none that are dangerous; which I hope is the case with me," he told his parents in 1738. If, then, acting on a belief in the efficacy of hard work yields affluence, then surely this is a sign of God's favor. Here, in effect, is an embrace of the old Catholic doctrine that works were more important than faith—except that the doctrine was now enlisted in the service of personal and social reform (which Franklin considered mutually reinforcing). A new form of common sense was emerging.

Franklin thus became the patron saint of doing well by doing good. In reading his writings, one is struck by the way he enlists old Puritan verities in the service of secular gain. "He that lies down with Dogs, shall rise up with fleas," his famous alter ego Poor Richard counseled in one of the sayings that were scattered throughout his annual almanacs (this one from 1733). "Lost time is never found again," he counseled in 1748. "'Tis against some Mens Principle to pay Interest, and seems against others Interest to pay the Principal," he observed in 1753. A series of such aphorisms strung together comprised "The Way to Wealth," the widely reprinted preface to his 1758 collection *Poor Richard Improved.*

Homilies like these help explain why Franklin has often been considered the prophet of American capitalism. Yet making money for him was always the means to a greater end: public service and notoriety (not necessarily in that order). He retired from the printing business as soon as he could do so comfortably and began his pioneering work on the nature of electricity as a man of leisured learning. He refused to take out a patent for the hugely popular wood stove he invented, because he believed that scientific knowledge should be freely shared and diffused. His philanthropic work, which included the creation of the first fire department, lending library, public hospital, and countless other municipal institutions in Philadelphia, gradually widened as he became involved in colonial affairs. His diplomatic work in France during the Revolution, and the prestige he lent to the Constitutional Convention of 1787 (he apparently slept through much of it), were capstones of a career that had been notably distinguished long before the Declaration of Independence, which he helped Jefferson draft. Here, truly, was the first American celebrity (and one quite ready to avail himself of celebrity's fruits).

Rarely, if ever, has any American been so upwardly mobile—or more clear about the basis and meaning of his success. "I conceived my becoming a member would enlarge my power of doing good," he wrote to a friend of his election to the Pennsylvania Assembly in 1751. "I would not however insinuate that my ambition was not flattered by all these promotions. It certainly was. For considering my low beginning they were great things to me."

And, somehow, great things were always beginning, and always overcoming false steps and setbacks along the way. An epitaph Franklin wrote for himself, probably in the late 1720s, brilliantly captures the essence of a worldly, yet deathless, American Dream in which sins and mistakes made along the way were merely "errata"—the spiritual equivalent of typographical errors—in a process of self-realization:

> The Body of
> B. Franklin,
> Printer;
> Like the Cover of an old Book,

> Its Contents torn out,
> And stript of its lettering and Gilding,
> Lies here, Food for Worms.
> But the Work shall not be totally lost:
> For it will, as he believ'd, appear once more,
> In a new & more perfect Edition
> Corrected and amended
> by the Author *

Franklin's American Dream was not universally admired by his contemporaries or heirs. John Adams, himself a man of relatively modest
beginnings who served with Franklin as ambassador to France during the
Revolution, was exasperated by what he termed his "continual discipa-
tion," dissipation which Adams felt grew out of Franklin's all too complacent view of himself and humanity in general. Mark Twain, who had
little patience for the pieties of either man, spent much of his career
repeatedly satirizing the sage of Philadelphia: "Never put off until tomorrow what you can do the day after tomorrow just as well," he wrote in an
1870 sketch, "The Late Benjamin Franklin." Yet the core components
of Franklin's dream as expressed in his writings—trust in the basic
decency of human beings, a belief that earthly and heavenly rewards are
broadly consonant, and, above all, a serene confidence that both can be
attained—reflected the core convictions of a great many Americans of
his time. Here, truly, was a Founding Father of the American Dream.

*What is so enchanting as the American Dream? To be possessed of that
Dream presupposes that, like St. Paul, one must be obedient to the vision
splendid."*

**–Edgar DeWitt Jones, *The Influence of Henry Clay
upon Abraham Lincoln*, 1952**

If anything, Franklin's core convictions were even more widely
embraced in the decades after his death in 1790. But they also under-

---

* Perhaps not surprisingly, Franklin later decided on a considerably simpler epigraph for
the headstone he ultimately shared with his wife: "Benjamin and Deborah Franklin
1790." (She died in 1774 while he was on a long sojourn in England.)

went a subtle but important shift in emphasis. The Founding Fathers wrote the charter for the American Dream with the Declaration of Independence, but they did so as a self-conscious elite—a so-called natural aristocracy who attained their eminence, as Franklin did, through merit. Yet this begged the question: just what constituted merit?

It was clear what merit wasn't: inherited privilege. But its positive parameters were changing. For Franklin and younger colleagues like Jefferson, merit was reasonably clear; it involved things like education, experience, and (especially) virtue. The ploughman and the professor were equal in their moral sense but not their abilities, and thus the ploughman would naturally defer to his betters unless and until he became a professor himself.

The willingness to accept this formulation ebbed in the succeeding generations. In the early decades of the nineteenth century, state after state made voting privileges less restrictive, opening the political system to a larger set of white men—white men who, on the whole, were not inclined to defer to their "betters," "natural" or otherwise. The hero of many of these people—the man who in many ways defined the American Dream of upward mobility in the first half of the nineteenth century—was Andrew Jackson.

Though Jackson was in fact the product of an elite bloodline—his grandfather was a wealthy weaver from a family of standing with Scotch-Irish roots—he was celebrated, not entirely incorrectly, as the quintessential embodiment of upward mobility. Jackson was born deep in the woods bordering North and South Carolina in 1767; his father, an immigrant, died before he was born. The boy, his mother, and brothers were taken under the care of two uncles in Charleston, where he learned to read and write (though there were questions about the degree of his literacy for his entire life, and Jackson once joked that he could never respect a man who only knew one way to spell a word). He was a child during the American Revolution, in which he served as a messenger and during which his mother and brothers died or were killed. After the war he became a lawyer, began speculating in land, slaves, and horses, and became the first U.S. Congressman from the new state of Tennessee in 1796.

Yet Jackson's chief distinction seemed to be his toughness, for which he was legendary. Quick to take a slight, he fought a series of duels, winning one despite being shot near the heart. (His adversary died

TAKING THE REINS *Andrew Jackson in his heyday. By the time he became president, modest beginnings were no longer a somewhat embarrassing obstacle to be overcome but rather the indispensable bedrock of distinction. (Painted by Thomas Sully, engraved by James B. Longacre. Photo from the collections of the Library of Congress)*

thinking he had missed.) Jackson also distinguished himself as a soldier, winning battles against Indians despite a shattered shoulder sustained during another duel, and was lionized for his 1815 victory over the British in the Battle of New Orleans during the War of 1812. The battle was fought after the United States and Britain had agreed on peace terms but before news of the agreement had reached the combatants. Yet this hardly mattered to his large—and, to established figures like Thomas Jefferson, to some degree frightening—following.

To a great degree, Jackson's appeal lay in the way in which he rejected the kinds of refinement that had once represented the apogee of achievement in the Dream of Upward Mobility. Modest beginnings were no longer a somewhat embarrassing obstacle to be overcome but rather the indispensable bedrock of distinction. An 1845 eulogy to Jackson spelled this out: "As we remember how the soil of poverty has sent up its harvest of great men, our Franklin, our Adams, our [Patrick] Henry, and our Jackson; let us rather say that, as in *the kingdom of geology* the everlasting granite, the underlying basis of all other formations is found in the deepest gulf, yet ever bursting upward from the abyss, towering aloft into the highest hills, and crowning the very pinnacles of the world." In other words, Jackson was great *because* he was poor. The Founding Fathers had been republicans; here, it seemed, was a model *democrat* (slaveholding and ruthlessness toward Indians notwithstanding). Jackson was not a natural aristocrat; he was nature's nobleman—and a man who, paradoxically, was destined for success because of his fierce will to succeed. Also paradoxical, perhaps, was the way this celebrated man of the people led with the dictatorial manner of a Scottish clansman who would brook no dissent, as later opponents, ranging from the chief justice of the Supreme Court, John Marshall, to his own vice president, John Calhoun, would learn to their chagrin.

In 1824 Jackson ran for president and won the most votes in a crowded field. But because he lacked a majority in the electoral college—an institution that had been set up precisely to function as a circuit-breaker to slow a surge of popular will—the election was decided by the House of Representatives. It was there that another candidate, Henry Clay of Kentucky, threw his support behind John Quincy Adams, son of John Adams and a man who seemed to many not simply the prototype of the now-outmoded model of natural aristocrat but a hereditary one, too. Adams, with Clay as his secretary of state, ran the country amid charges of a "corrupt bargain" between them. Four years later, Jackson ran again against Adams and defeated him handily. His 1829 inauguration, with its mob of cheese-eating, beer-drinking country bumpkins trampling the White House carpet, chilled the old order. Newspaper critics used the image of the jackass to ridicule him—which supporters appropriated as the icon of the new Democratic Party that coalesced around Jackson and survived into the twenty-first century.

"Old Hickory," as he was affectionately dubbed, was president between 1829 and 1837, but in a larger sense the ensuing decades were actually, in the words of Arthur Schlesinger Jr., "the age of Jackson." An American Heritage encyclopedia set on the presidents I was given as a child helps explain why this is so: "Andrew Jackson won the people's support for a variety of reasons, but perhaps most significantly because he embodied what was then, and what would remain long after, the American Dream. Born poor in a near-wilderness, he had forged success largely on his own, by his strength, his iron will, his exertions and convictions."

That American Dream was evolving. One of the most telling indications of its emerging grammar was a host of new words and phrases that entered the language around this time. "We are a nation of self-made men," Jackson's longtime antagonist Henry Clay said in a speech in 1832, coining a term that has remained in the national lexicon ever since. Clay, himself a man of modest beginnings, staked his political career on his upward mobility—though he was never quite mobile enough to reach the White House. (His fellow Whig William Henry Harrison was able to do so in a celebrated presidential campaign that made much of his own beginnings in a log cabin.) In his masterful two-volume study *Democracy in America*, Frenchman Alexis de Tocqueville invented the word "individualism" to describe a new sort of secular striving he observed in the United States and used the term "self-interest rightly understood"—a Franklinesque construction that emphasized the practical value of moral precepts like reciprocity and (temporary) self-denial—as the credo of American life.

The credo seemed justified by the facts—for white men, at least. Indeed, I daresay that in terms of upward mobility, there probably was never a better time to be one than the first half of the nineteenth century (though some, like Irishmen, clearly had a harder time than others). The factory system that would ultimately swallow the aspirations of so many Americans had not yet become widespread, and it is surely no accident that the people who created the most gigantic fortunes of the later nineteenth century—Andrew Carnegie, John D. Rockefeller, J. P. Morgan, among others—all reached adulthood by 1840.

Contemporary accounts of this period are likely to note that the limits that were placed on access to the Dream of Upward Mobility were at least as important as eligibility. Indians, of course, were excluded altogether; no one was more insistent on this point than Jackson himself, who mercilessly—and illegally—drove them out of Georgia to expand opportunities for whites there. Women were marginalized from the public sphere that was the natural home of upward mobility, and the existence of slavery both limited the arena of upward mobility and gave whites an economic and psychological gauge by which to measure themselves.

Yet even at this early date, the dream had appeal to outsiders. Some African Americans, who in the twentieth century could be as easily seduced by the charms of upward mobility as anyone else, showed a predilection for it in the nineteenth. Free black families in Boston and Philadelphia attained stature in their communities through sustained effort. Its pull could even be felt below the Mason-Dixon line. The escaped slave Frederick Douglass titled his 1845 biography *Narrative of the Life of Frederick Douglass, an American Slave, Written by Himself,* those last three words emphasizing the degree to which Douglass, in the teeth of great adversity, was very much a self-made man. His account, which traces an arc from dependency to autonomy, is one of the most vivid illustrations of the appeal of the Dream of Upward Mobility—which in his case was quite literal, as he escaped from Maryland to Massachusetts to become a free man.

Upward mobility also had metaphysical dimensions that Franklin himself, whose pragmatic cast of mind gave his life philosophy a superficial sheen, would scarcely appreciate. One figure who explored these dimensions was the Transcendentalist poet, essayist, and philosopher Ralph Waldo Emerson. Emerson was a rather singular figure even in his own day, a rarified intellectual who seemed the very antithesis of Andrew Jackson. But Emerson was every bit the disciple of self-realization that the hard-bitten Jackson was. The descendant of a long line of ministers, Emerson began his career in the pulpit of one of the first Puritan congregations before striking out on a literary career that brought him lasting renown. "Trust thyself: every heart vibrates to that iron string," he admonished the readers of his 1841 essay "Self-

Reliance." Emerson professed to have little interest in material gain, but he was as adamant as any successful businessman that applied effort could make one the master of one's own destiny. "In the Will work and acquire, and thou has chained the wheel of chance, and shall sit hereafter out of fear from her rotations," he wrote in the conclusion of "Self-Reliance." One could live without fear not because it was possible to control events but because it was possible to achieve *self*-control. "A political victory, a rise in rents, the recovery of your sick or the return of your absent friend, or some other favorable event raises your spirits, and you think good days are preparing for you. Do not believe it. Nothing can bring you peace but yourself. Nothing can bring you peace but the triumph of principles."

Despite the relatively pragmatic thrust of Emerson's metaphysics, however, few ordinary Americans of his time paid much attention, absorbed as they were with what seemed like more immediately achievable gains. (As Emerson's protégé Henry David Thoreau once observed, "Every man looks on his woodpile with a kind of affection.") And yet, as the most perceptive observers realized, the Dream of Upward Mobility exacted a subtle price all the more insidious for being virtually unrecognizable. "In America I saw the freest and most enlightened men placed in the happiest circumstances the world affords; and it seemed to me a cloud habitually hung on their brow," wrote Tocqueville, who saw the cost with detached clarity. Tocqueville attributed this furrowed brow to the social equality among those with access to the Dream. Because he is so incisive and eloquent, he's worth quoting at some length here:

> When all the privileges of birth and fortune are abolished, when all professions are accessible to all, and a man's own energies may place him at the top of any one of them, an easy and unbounded career seems open to his ambition and he will readily persuade himself that he is born to no common destinies. But this is an erroneous notion, which is corrected by daily experience. The same equality that allows every citizen to conceive these lofty hopes renders all the citizens less able to realize them; it circumscribes their powers on every side, while it gives freer scope to their desires. Not only are they themselves powerless, but they are met at every step by immense obstacles, which they did not at first perceive.

Tocqueville later elaborated more fully on those obstacles, explaining how they were inherent in the very nature of the Dream:

In a democratic society, as elsewhere, there is only a certain number of great fortunes to be made; and as the paths that lead to them are indiscriminately open to all, the progress must necessarily be slackened. As the candidates appear to be nearly alike, and as it is difficult to make a selection without infringing the principle of equality, which is the supreme law of democratic societies, the first idea which suggests itself is to make them all advance at the same rate and submit to the same trials. Thus, in proportion as men become more alike and the principle of equality is more peaceably and deeply infused into the institutions and manners of the country, the rules for advancement become more inflexible, advancement itself slower, the difficulty of arriving quickly at a certain height far greater. From hatred of privilege and the embarrassment of choosing, all men are at last forced, whatever may be their standard, to pass the same ordeal; all are indiscriminately subjected to a multitude of petty preliminary exercises, in which their youth is wasted and their imagination quenched, so that they despair of ever fully attaining what is held out to them; and when at length they are in a condition to perform any extraordinary acts, the taste for such things has forsaken them.

"Great and rapid elevation is therefore rare," Tocqueville concluded. "It forms an exception to the common rule; and it is the singularity of such occurrences that makes men forget how rarely they happen."

In his own day and long after, however, Tocqueville was a minority voice, and there can be little doubt that some of his acuity was a by-product of his outsider status. But if there was clear consensus on the legitimacy of the American Dream of Upward Mobility in the nineteenth century, there were nevertheless often bitter disputes about the best way to foster it. Those disputes were typically conducted in the realm of party politics. Indeed, political parties themselves—which the Founding Fathers dreaded, and which only took a recognizably modern form during the Jackson administration—became singularly effective vehicles for upward mobility, whether in terms of political offices, patronage to be distributed to friends, or the production of ideas and propaganda by a nascent media industry.

On one side of the divide were Democrats, led by Jackson and his political heirs, who believed in the Jeffersonian maxim that that which governs best governs least. Democrats viewed national government involvement in the nation's economic life as a dangerous invitation to corruption. Chartering a national bank, land grants to railroads, taxes on foreign products to make domestic industry more attractive: all risked giving unfair advantages to the few at the expense of the many, thus compromising the tenets of upward mobility.

Their opponents, the Whigs, believed that such efforts by the national government promoted the good of all. The central figure in Whig party politics and ideology was Henry Clay, who championed what he called "the American System," whereby high tariffs on foreign goods would promote northern industry by making domestic products comparatively cheaply, which in turn would foster strong demand for western foodstuffs and southern cotton to fuel an industrial revolution. In fact, Clay's very invocation of the self-made man was issued, perhaps paradoxically, in a speech asserting the need for such protective taxes to foster commercial growth.

Many southerners were dubious about this proposition. While there were a good number of southern Whigs until the 1850s (Clay himself was a slaveholder from Kentucky), the majority of them believed that getting manufactured goods cheaply from abroad was better than paying high tariffs, especially when such tariffs prompted foreign customers for their own commodities, notably cotton, to respond in kind. But the issue was more than just narrowly economic. The fact is that the Dream of Upward Mobility had less of a hold on the South than on the rest of the

MAKING THE MOLD *Henry Clay, circa 1850. The man who codified a so-called American System on internal improvements and who coined the term "self-made man," Clay was a role model for the young Abraham Lincoln, who called him "my beau ideal of a statesman." (Produced by Matthew Brady's studio. Photo from the collections of the Library of Congress)*

country. There the force of tradition, familial ties, and, above all, the force of slavery limited the appeal and efficacy of the self-made man. There was a place for such figures in southern mythology—men who began with virtually nothing did amass fortunes, as vividly depicted in later novels like William Faulkner's *Absalom, Absalom* and Margaret Mitchell's *Gone with the Wind*—but because of the contradictions involved, being "self-made" through slave labor was a wobblier construct.

Indeed, while slavery had been a powerful presence in American life for well over two centuries by 1850, it was increasingly considered a threat to the Dream of Upward Mobility by a small but growing number of people. These people did not necessarily have any direct economic interest in slavery—nor, for that matter, did they always care whether it was wrong. What concerned them most was the way the peculiar institution compromised their view of themselves and their country. Such people felt the legitimacy of both depended upon not having too great an ideological gap between what actually was and what the Declaration of Independence said should be. This was, however, a relatively subtle point of view and would have a hard time competing with the more visceral appeals to resentment and narrow self-interest that are the usual staples of political discourse. Fortunately, one of the men who took up this challenge was no ordinary politician—in part because he came as close as any American to actually being an authentically self-made man.

> *I happen temporarily to occupy this big White House. I am a living witness that any one of your children may look to come here as my father's child has. It is in order that each of you may have through this free government which we have enjoyed, an open field and a fair chance for your industry, enterprise, and intelligence; that you may all have equal privileges in the race of life, with all its desirable human aspirations. It is for this the struggle should be maintained, that we may not lose our birthright—not only for one, but for two or three years. The nation is worth fighting for, to secure such an inestimable jewel.*

**—Abraham Lincoln, speech to the 166th Ohio Regiment,
Washington, D.C., August 22, 1864**

In 1860, journalist John Locke Scripps of the *Chicago Tribune* proposed to write a campaign biography of Abraham Lincoln for the upcoming

DREAM CANDIDATE *Abraham Lincoln in 1860 (photographed by Alexander Hesler).*
"It is a great piece of folly to attempt to make anything out of my early life," he told a journal-
ist around the time this portrait was made—one of the great fibs of American political history.
Few people incarnated the American Dream more vividly; no one expressed its possibilities, and
limits, more powerfully. (Wm. B. Becker Collection/photographymuseum.com)

presidential campaign. But the candidate expressed skepticism about the project. "It is a great piece of folly to attempt to make anything out of my early life," Lincoln replied, in Scripps's recollection to Lincoln's law partner, William Herndon. "It can all be condensed into a single sentence, and that sentence you will find in Gray's Elegy, 'the short and simple annals of the poor.'" Lincoln was alluding to the once-famous 1750 poem "Elegy Written in a Country Churchyard," by the English poet Thomas Gray:

> *Let not ambition mock their useful toil;*
> *Their homely joys, and destiny obscure;*
> *Nor grandeur hear with disdainful smile,*
> *The short and simple annals of the poor.*

"That's my life, and that's all you or anyone else can make of it," Lincoln told Scripps.

This is untrue, and Lincoln knew it: there was a great deal to be made of his early life. The managers of his successful presidential campaign of 1860 relentlessly exploited his humble beginnings (though by the time he ran for president he was a wealthy lawyer) and gave Lincoln the nickname of "the Railsplitter," a moniker that emphasized his familiarity with manual labor. Lincoln's entire public persona—his homely looks and unkempt appearance, his celebrated sense of humor, the self-effacing modesty he repeatedly deployed while running for and holding office (evident in his remark to Scripps)—was leveraged on his modest beginnings and what he had made of them. Even his oratory eloquence derived its power from Lincoln's reputed poverty; it was made, and heard, as a testament to how democracy could elevate Everyman.

Such an understanding was possible because of Lincoln's great conviction in this regard and because the facts of the case, slim as they are, tend to support him. The only surviving child of his parents, he was born on February 12, 1809, in a log cabin in Hardin County, Kentucky. His ancestors apparently came to Hingham, Massachusetts, during the first wave of Puritan migration and in subsequent generations spread into Pennsylvania and Virginia. Lincoln's paternal grandfather, also Abraham Lincoln, was killed by Indians while clearing farm land. There is virtually no information on the family of Lincoln's mother, Nancy Hanks. She died when he was a child, though his stepmother,

Sarah Bush Johnston, raised him as one of her own brood, and the two seemed to regard each other with great affection (she outlived him).

Lincoln's father, Thomas, migrated first to Indiana—"it was a wild region, with many bears and other wild animals in the woods," his son told another newspaper biographer in 1859—and then to Illinois in search of land uncomplicated by disputes over legal titles (a sign, it should be said, that the Lincolns were not exactly impoverished, as Thomas Lincoln sought to own land, not rent it). "A[braham] though very young was large of age, and had an axe put into his hands at once," he wrote of his boyhood, "and from that till within his twentythird year, he was almost constantly handling that most useful instrument—less, of course, plowing and harvesting seasons." Lincoln had little in the way of a formal schooling; in his own words, there was "absolutely nothing to excite ambition for education" in the rural Midwest of the early nineteenth century. Still, he somehow learned to read and write, and "the little advance I now have upon this store of education, I have picked up from time to time under necessity."

When he was nineteen years old, Lincoln got his first chance to see the wider world: he and a friend made a flatboat trip down the Mississippi River to New Orleans with a cargo of farm produce. During the trip they had to fight off seven black men who tried to rob and kill them. Three years later, he made a second trip with a stepbrother and cousin; upon his return he settled in the village of New Salem, Illinois, where he had a brief, unsuccessful career as a dry goods merchant. He subsequently worked as a hired hand, a surveyor, and a local postmaster, all the while reading avidly and carefully. He also served in the Illinois militia during the Black Hawk War against the Creek Indians and took lifelong pride in the fact that he was elected captain.

This background became virtually his only credential when Lincoln made his first bid for public office in 1832, seeking to represent Sangamon County, where New Salem was located, in the state legislature. He finished eighth in a field of thirteen for four slots, "the only time I have ever been beaten by the people," he later explained in a rare boast that suggested the depth of his investment in democratic values.* What is most remarkable about the campaign, however, is the way in which it

---

* Lincoln lost in his 1858 attempt to represent Illinois in the U.S. Senate, but in that race the votes were actually made by electors in the state legislature, which was apportioned on the basis of an 1850 census that did not fully reflect his party's strength.

revealed the lineaments of a worldview that would remain stable for the remainder of Lincoln's life. Like other avowed Whigs—Lincoln considered Henry Clay "my beau ideal of a statesman"—he called for public investment in the nation's commercial infrastructure. "Time and experience have verified to a demonstration, the public utility of internal improvements," he asserted in a campaign speech. To that end, he advocated dredging, straightening, and other work to improve the navigation of the Sangamon River. (Railroads were still expensive, and he repeatedly expressed his concern for keeping down the costs of such improvements and the greed of usurious bankers.) He diffidently emphasized the value of education, stopping short of actually calling for public financing of mass literacy in what was a heavily Democratic region suspicious of such enterprises.

Lincoln also addressed the issue of his own motivations. "Every man is said to have his peculiar ambition," the twenty-three-year-old told the voters. "Whether it is true or not, I can say for one that I have no other so great as that of being truly esteemed of my fellow men. How far I shall succeed in gratifying this ambition, is yet to be developed. I am young and unknown to many of you. I was born and have ever remained in the most humble walks of life." It must have been apparent to everyone, however, that he didn't want to remain in a humble walk of life forever. He acknowledged the possibility of failure in the closing of his speech in a tone of melancholy, even self-pity, that would occasionally resurface throughout the rest of Lincoln's life. "If the good people in their wisdom shall see fit to keep me in the background, I have been too familiar with disappointments to be very much chagrined."

Though Lincoln lost that election, he ran again two years later, winning the first of four terms to the state legislature. He also began studying the law, which he received a license to practice in 1836, and embarked on a lucrative legal career. Lincoln's Whig politics were consonant with his rising affluence, and he was a staunch supporter of railroads, the state bank, and other instruments of an emerging capitalist system. His marriage to Mary Todd in 1842 was a significant step up on the social ladder. By his early thirties, then, Lincoln had already transformed himself from a poor country boy to the epitome of the Successful Young Man. His self-image, in turn, shaped his politics. Lincoln was a classic exponent of self-interest rightly understood: the system was working for him, as well it should—and he could support it in good conscience as long as it could work for others, too.

Well into middle age, Lincoln had a serene confidence in the Dream of Upward Mobility, and while he was consistently in favor of expanding opportunities in every direction (including the right of women to vote), he also thought it was possible to succeed with relatively little outside intervention. "It is a small matter whether you read *with* anybody or not," he told an aspiring lawyer in 1855—and, in much the same words, many who asked to study with him later. "I did not read with any one. Get the books, and read and study them till, you understand them in their principal features; and that is the main thing." The great thing about the United States is that where there was a will, there was a way. "Always bear in mind that your own resolution to succeed, is more important than any other one thing," Lincoln told this young man.

Of course, this was not true of everyone; all the resolution in the world would not help most slaves, for example. It's important to note here, however, that slavery was not a major factor in Lincoln's thinking at this stage of his life. Indeed, few people in Illinois considered it an issue. There was a vocal minority, typified by the abolitionist editor Elijah P. Lovejoy, who so enraged the residents of Alton, Illinois, with his demands to end slavery that he was shot and killed by an angry mob. But Lincoln was among those who tended to regard such people as part of a radical fringe more likely to create problems than solve them. Not that he approved of slavery. Lincoln attributed his father's frequent moves as attempts to escape it, and in a vivid 1855 letter to his once-close friend Joshua Speed (the two had drifted apart geographically as well as politically), he recalled an experience that shaped his personal feelings—strictly *as* personal feelings:

> I confess I hate to see the poor creatures hunted down and caught, and carried back to their stripes, and unrewarded toils; but I bite my lip and keep quiet. In 1841 you and I had together a tedious low-water trip, on a Steam Boat from Louisville to St. Louis. You may remember, as I well do, that from Louisville to the mouth of the Ohio there were, on board, ten or a dozen slaves, shackled together with irons. That sight was a continual torment to me; and I see something like it every time I touch the Ohio, or any other slave border. It is hardly fair for you to assume, that I have no interest in a thing which has, and continually exercises, the power of making me miserable. You ought rather to appreciate how much the great body of Northern people do crucify their feelings, in order to maintain their loyalty to the constitution and the Union.

Lincoln occasionally did make his objection to slavery a matter of public record. He was one of only six of eighty-three assemblymen to vote
against a resolution condemning abolitionists in 1837, though he and
another member made clear in a written proclamation of their own
that while slavery was both unjust and bad policy, "the promulgation of
abolition doctrines tends rather to increase than abate its evils." For
most of his career he was content to reiterate his feelings, express his
opposition to the spread of slavery any further, and emphasize his willingness to accept it wherever it already existed.

The real threat to the land of opportunity seemed to come from
elsewhere. In 1838 Lincoln delivered an address to the Young Men's
Lyceum of Springfield, Illinois, in which he expressed his worry that
some future tyrant, restless for distinction, would appeal to mob rule
and overthrow the democratic order. "Towering genius disdains a
beaten path," he explained. "It thirsts and burns for distinction; and, if
possible, will have it, whether at the expense of emancipating slaves or
enslaving freemen." The only bulwark against this possibility, he
argued, was making the Declaration of Independence and Constitution "the *political religion* of the nation," inculcating a reverence for the
Union. But on what basis was this reverence to be justified? Lincoln
never quite said. Indeed, it was only as his career progressed that he
began to clarify the basis of this civic religion.

In 1846 Lincoln was elected to the U.S. Congress. He got there as
part of a rather unusual bargain he struck with two fellow Whigs that
each would run for one term uncontested by the others. Lincoln was
the third of the three to successfully win the seat, which he occupied
between 1847 and 1849. The principal political issue of the day was the
Mexican War. Lincoln, like many Whigs, was opposed to it, believing
that the United States had essentially provoked the conflict without
cause and that the Democratic president, James K. Polk, was subvert-
ing the Constitution in the manner in which he conducted it. At the
same time, Lincoln voted in favor of sending supplies to support American troops, reasoning that they should not suffer for the administration's errors—and perhaps that such a stance would afford him political
cover for expressing skepticism over a popular and successful conflict.
His stance is reminiscent of one taken by some politicians during a
much less popular and less successful conflict, the Vietnam War. In that
case, some argued the war was wrong even as they expressed support
for the troops. It wasn't an especially effective formula for them, nor

was it for Lincoln. Democrats regained the seat in the following congressional election, and for the next decade Lincoln was on the defensive for his posture toward the war.

Actually, in the years that followed, it appeared Lincoln's political career was over. Had he died in, say, 1853, he would have been little more than a historical footnote, albeit one exemplifying the possibilities of upward mobility for white men of modest means. Beginning in 1854, however, he began a gradual, but decisive, reemergence, which, when complete, would not only mark the ultimate ascent in national life, but provide him with the means to articulate the parameters of a powerful, though not omnipotent, American Dream.

This progress by which the poor, honest, industrious, and resolute man raises himself, that he may work on his own account, and hire somebody else, is that improvement in condition that human nature is entitled to, is that improvement that is intended to be secured by those institutions under which we live, is the great principle for which this government was formed.

**—Abraham Lincoln, speech in Cincinnati, Ohio,
September 17, 1859**

Slavery forced the issue. It was a subject virtually no white man wanted to fight over. This was true in 1787, when the word was pointedly omitted from the U.S. Constitution, in which a number of compromises were made, and it was true thirty years later, when the admission of Missouri as a state engendered arguments over whether it would have slaves or not. The famed Missouri Compromise of 1820 admitted the state with slavery but drew a line across the American territory: all states subsequently admitted below that line would have slaves; all states above it would not.

And that pretty much allowed everyone to get back to business. Southern congressmen imposed a "gag order" that kept the subject from coming up as a matter of public policy in the Capitol, and while its very word "gag" suggests tension, it was a rule in which most northerners duly acquiesced, whether in sympathy, indifference, or a calculation that consent was ultimately more profitable than argument. To be sure, there were always a few diehards like John Quincy Adams, who left the White House in 1829 and was elected to the House of Representatives, where he insisted on making a moral issue of slavery whenever he could. For everybody else, the real issues in the country were over the best means for promoting upward mobility for whites, like how to finance the building of transcontinental railroads, or deciding whether or not immigrants should be allowed to come here and pursue upward mobility themselves.

But slavery managed to come in through the back door. The problem can be traced back to the very issue that gave Lincoln trouble: the Mexican War. He opposed it on principle, but that rapidly became a moot point. Far less moot was a proposal made by the Pennsylvania congressman David Wilmot that slavery be excluded from all territory conquered from Mexico. With that nation virtually prostrate by the end of 1847, the question of how much of it to take, and in what form, became very much a burning issue.

It's important to note that at this stage of the game it wasn't exactly a matter of the South wanting Mexico and the North not wanting it. Some southerners wanted no part of a creole nation that would dilute its European blood further; some northerners wanted more U.S. territory in any form it might take. But in the ensuing years, opinions hardened along increasingly sectional lines. The regions became increasingly suspicious of each other, and the Whig Party, which had previously been national and which had elected two presidents, collapsed in the South and dwindled up North.

This was tragic to many, not for racial reasons but because it made it difficult to accomplish things that in theory had little to do with slavery. A very good example of this was the building of the transcontinental railroad, one of whose major champions was Stephen A. Douglas. Like Lincoln, the Vermont-born Douglas had grown up in Illinois and came up through the state legislature—Lincoln as a Whig, Douglas as a Democrat. Unlike him, Douglas ascended rapidly through his party's ranks and as U.S. senator was a major figure in national politics. It was Douglas who, in collaboration with the mortally ailing Henry Clay, shepherded through a series of provisions in the so-called Compromise of 1850.

In the years that followed, Douglas repeatedly asserted he didn't care whether slavery was voted up or voted down in new states. (In fact, this was not exactly true; Douglas was generally antislavery.) But he cared very deeply about the chartering of transcontinental railroads, and in 1854 he hoped the first one or ones would run through Illinois or

Michigan, where he had invested heavily in real estate. In order to get Congress to go along with his plan, he knew he was going to have to offer southern congressmen some incentive, especially because some political and business leaders wanted that line to run through Texas. It appears Douglas thought he could get his railroad bill passed by offering a bill stipulating that residents of the northern territories of Kansas and Nebraska, through which new railroads were likely to run, could decide for themselves whether to allow slavery when they became states. Actually, he originally tried to be vague on this point until southern senators pushed him into making it explicit by actually repealing the old line created by the Missouri Compromise.

Douglas's proposal—known as "popular sovereignty"—proved explosively controversial. Proponents argued for its simplicity; opponents argued it sounded more straightforward than it really was, since nothing could stop slaves from moving in *before* Kansas or Nebraska became a state. (Imagine a community trying to decide whether it was going to be alcohol-free *after* drinkers, liquor stores, and bars were already settled there.) Douglas shepherded the Kansas-Nebraska Act into law in 1854, but the price was disastrous: he split his own Democratic Party and, in rendering the Missouri Compromise dead, handed his opponents the issue they used to create a new party. Ironically, Douglas's subsequent railroad bill—which for him was a major, if not *the* major, reason for the Kansas-Nebraska Act in the first place—could not get through Congress. (Lincoln signed it when he became president.)

The new political party Douglas inadvertently helped spawn called itself Republican, in self-conscious homage to the ideology of the Founders. Its membership was a hybrid of old Whigs, nativists opposed to allowing immigrants into the country, and disaffected Democrats united in their distaste for slavery (and African Americans generally). Lincoln joined two years after it formed, and the strength of the speeches he gave opposing the Kansas-Nebraska Act helped him become its nominee to run against Douglas when he came up for reelection in 1858.

Lincoln was appalled by the doctrine of popular sovereignty. He had always viewed slavery as a necessary evil, and he believed that the Founding Fathers had as well. And he believed, as he believed they did, that it would eventually die out. But now it seemed that slavery was getting new protection and even being affirmed as a positive good. Moreover, in its 1857 decision *Dred Scott v. Sandford*, the U.S. Supreme Court ruled not only that slaves were property, not citizens, and thus had no rights, but also that the rights of whites included owning, moving, and retrieving such property wherever they pleased—and compelling others to respect those rights. Freedom meant the right of some people to own others. Slavery was not receding; it wasn't even holding its own. Instead, it seemed to be becoming more powerful.

Why did this matter so much to Lincoln? This brings us to the crux of the matter. Lincoln was not opposed to slavery because he cared very much about *slaves*. He was opposed because he cared very, very deeply about *whites* (and unlike some of his fellow Republicans, he cared about *all* whites). Slavery was bad for *them*. And it was bad because it contaminated and, if left unchecked, would eventually destroy the American Dream in which he believed so deeply.

How did slavery corrode Lincoln's American Dream? In two important ways. The first was economic. The presence of slavery impeded upward mobility not only of African Americans but also of European Americans, because the slave economy narrowed the prospects of men without the ever-greater amounts of capital necessary to invest in slaves. So, for example, a small farmer who employed hired hands for wages was at a distinct competitive disadvantage compared with a large plantation owner who paid his slaves nothing (and whose slaves had children who then also became assets of the plantation owner). Slavery hurt not just that small farmer but his hired hands as well, who would be viewed as too expensive relative to slaves; indeed, it was the relatively high cost of indentured servants that had led to the introduction of slavery into the southern economy in the first place. Of course, one could also claim that the factory owner who paid his workers a pittance—and who, moreover, didn't even have to pay for the upkeep on his workers—was as bad as any plantation owner, if not worse. This was the frequent riposte of slave owners, and the emerging factory system in the Northeast in particular gave force to the charge. But Lincoln lived in a time and place where it was still possible to believe, as he put it, that "there is no such thing as a man who is a hired laborer, of necessity, remaining in his early condition." He went on to render his understanding of the matter:

A young man finds himself of an age to be dismissed from parental control; he has for his capital nothing but his two strong hands that God has given him, a heart willing to labor, and a freedom to choose the mode of his work and the manner of his employer; he has got no soil nor shop, and he avails himself of the opportunity of hiring himself to some man who has capital to pay him a fair day's wages for a fair day's work. He is benefited by availing himself of that privilege. He works industriously, he behaves soberly, and the result of a year or two's labor is a surplus of capital. Now he buys land on his own hook; he settles, marries, begets sons and daughters, and in course of time he too has enough capital to hire some new beginner.

Lincoln regarded this a description of reality, and an attractive one it was. Virtue and reward are locked in a symbiotic embrace; it seems like a description of heaven on earth. Of course, he wasn't alone in subscribing to what was known as "free labor ideology": the seeds of Franklin's vision were bearing fruit. To be sure, plenty of people in Lincoln's time regarded it as sentimental nonsense. Conversely, however, there were plenty of people *after* Lincoln's time—too many people after Lincoln's time, truth be told—who did not.

For Lincoln, the dangers associated with upward mobility were not its internal tensions and contradictions but rather threats from those who could prevent it from fully taking root. Unlike the dreams of many of his contemporaries, Lincoln's was an expansive one; indeed, its very legitimacy depended upon its expansiveness. In the last of seven celebrated public debates he held with Douglas throughout Illinois, he explained why it was important to keep slavery from spreading—for whites' sake:

Now irrespective of the moral aspect as to whether there is a right or wrong in enslaving a negro, I am still in favor of our new Territories being in such a condition that white men may find a home—may find some spot where they can better their condition—where they can settle upon new soil and better their condition in life. I am in favor of this not merely (I say it here as I have elsewhere) for our own people who are born amongst us, but as an outlet for *free white people everywhere*, the world over—in which Hans and Baptiste and Patrick, and all other men from all the world, may find new homes and better their conditions in life.

If, as Lincoln feared, new slave states were formed, the Hanses, Baptistes, and Patricks of the world would not be inclined to come here—or would be defeated by the slave system when they did.

Yet even more than the economic problem posed by slavery, what might be termed its psychological implications troubled Lincoln. He began thinking this through in some notes he made to himself around the time of the Kansas-Nebraska Act. "If A. can prove, however conclusively, that he may, of right, enslave B.—why not B. snatch the same argument, and prove equally that he may enslave A.?" he asked. One answer might be on the basis of color, but if so, Lincoln noted, than one could theoretically be enslaved by anyone with skin fairer than his own. And if the basis of slavery was intellectual capacity, did not a person have a right to enslave anyone with less? In the years that followed, Lincoln explored such questions publicly and privately, eventually distilling his own position into three simple sentences: "As I would not be a *slave*, I would not be a *master*. This expresses my idea of democracy. Whatever differs from this, to the extent of the difference, is no democracy."

And democracy, it almost went without saying, was for Lincoln the greatest form of government. He realized this was not something everyone took for granted. "Most *governments* have been based, practically, on the denial of equal rights to men, as I have, in part, stated them," he wrote in notes to himself in 1854. "*Ours* began by *affirming* those rights. *They* said, some men are too *ignorant* and *vicious* to share in government . . . .We proposed to give *all* a chance; and we expected the weak to grow stronger, the ignorant, wiser; and all better, and happier together. We made the experiment, and the fruit is before us."

What scared Lincoln was that slavery weakened this affirmation of democracy and inculcated bad moral and political habits. The end result would be the very thing he talked about two decades earlier in his Young Men's Lyceum Address. In an 1858 speech during his Senate campaign, he articulated these fears again but framed them this time in terms of a slavery issue that now dominated his, and the nation's, consciousness. In language of rare moral power and emotional urgency, Lincoln addressed those whose hatred of African Americans he found not only appalling but truly dangerous:

> Now, when by all these means [e.g., popular sovereignty, the *Dred Scott* decision, etc.] you have succeeded in dehumanizing the negro; when you have put him down, and made it forever impossible for him to be but as the beasts of the field; when you have extinguished his soul, and placed him where the ray of hope is blown out in the darkness like that which

broods over the spirits of the damned; are you quite sure the demon
which you have roused *will not turn and rend you?*

"What constitutes the bulwark of our own liberty and independence?"
Lincoln asked. Was it the nation's impregnable coastline, its army or
navy? No. "All of them may be turned against our liberties, without
making us stronger or weaker for the struggle," he explained. Instead,

> our reliance is in the love of liberty which God has planted in our bos-
> oms. Our defense is in the preservation of the spirit which prizes liberty
> as the heritage of all men, in all lands, everywhere. Destroy this spirit,
> and you have planted the seeds of despotism around your own doors.
> Familiarize yourselves with the chains of bondage, and you are prepar-
> ing your own limbs to wear them. Accustomed to trample on the rights
> of those around you, you have lost the genius for independence, and
> become the fit subjects of the first cunning tyrant who rises.

In short, the great weapon in the preservation of the American Dream
was the "political religion" he spoke of in 1838.

This religion was codified in sacred scripture that functioned as a
guide to action: the Declaration of Independence, a document that
gained new significance for Lincoln in the 1850s. As he would later
explain, "I have never had a feeling politically that did not spring from
the sentiments embodied in the Declaration of Independence." In the
resounding affirmation of life, liberty, and the pursuit of happiness, he
clearly recognized what he called "the sheet anchor" of American identity. Lincoln took this affirmation very seriously. And because he did, he
could not help but feel that blacks, no less than whites, were entitled to it.

This was, however, a more complex matter than I'm making it
sound, and his understanding of the Declaration was by no means universal. For starters, any assertion that slaves were included in the Declaration of Independence must confront the obvious fact that the
Founding Fathers themselves were slaveholders. Yet for Lincoln this was
less a matter of hypocrisy than an intractable problem that defied
immediate resolution. "They found the institution here," he told the
crowd at the sixth Lincoln-Douglas debate. "They did not make it so,
but they left it so because they knew no way to get rid of it at that
time." The Founders' silence about slavery in the Constitution and
their determination to keep slavery from the territories testified to their

confidence that slavery would eventually fade out. They could live with it because they knew it would ultimately die—something that the Kansas-Nebraska Act suddenly threw into question, because it was now possible that slavery could grow stronger rather than weaker. And by throwing the death of slavery into doubt, people like Stephen Douglas—who repeatedly asserted he didn't care whether slavery died or not—were really throwing the Declaration of Independence into doubt. "This declared indifference, but as I must think, covert real zeal for the spread of slavery, I can not but hate," he said in an 1854 speech on the Kansas-Nebraska Act. "I hate it because of the monstrous injustice of slavery itself. I hate it because it deprives our republican example of its just influence in the world—enables the enemies of free institutions, with plausibility, to taunt us as hypocrites."

Lincoln saw himself as a patriotic conservative, a man seeking to defend an understanding of American identity that was now being actively challenged by slaveholders and their apologists. His opponents, by contrast, saw him as a closet radical, a fellow traveler with the abolitionists, who foolishly seemed to think that slaves deserved freedom because the Declaration said, in a passing rhetorical flourish, that all men were created equal. Lincoln considered this ridiculous. ("Negro equality! Fudge!!" he once wrote in exasperation over the rhetoric of his enemies.) *Freedom*, he repeatedly asserted, was not the same thing as *equality*. "Certainly the negro is not our equal in color—perhaps not in many other respects; still, in the right to put into his mouth the bread his own hands have earned, he is the equal of every other man, white or black," he told a crowd in Springfield at the beginning of his Senate campaign in 1858. "In pointing out that more has been given to you, you can not be justified in taking away the little which has been given to him. All I ask for the negro is that if you do not like him, let him alone. If God gave him but little, that little let him enjoy."

Lincoln made this request out of a sense of decency, but again, he was thinking of whites at least as much as blacks. At the end of his final debate with Douglas, he framed the slavery issue in moral terms—and in terms of self-interest. The whole campaign, Lincoln asserted, came down to one simple disagreement: he thought slavery was wrong, and Douglas did not.

> That is the real issue. That is the issue that will continue in this country when these poor tongues of Judge Douglas and myself shall be silent. It is the eternal struggle between these two principles—right and wrong—

throughout the world. They are the two principles that have stood face to face from the beginning of time; and will ever continue to struggle. It is the same principle in whatever shape that says, "You work and toil and earn bread, and I'll eat it." No matter in what shape it comes, whether from the mouth of a king who seeks to bestride the people of his own nation and live by the fruit of their labor, or from one race of men as an apology for enslaving another race, it is the same principle.

The Declaration of Independence, Lincoln believed, was a resounding rejection of this kingly logic where upward mobility on the part of those who actually produced the wealth was impossible. What the Declaration's authors "meant it to be, thank God, it is now proving itself, a stumbling block to those who in after times might seek to turn a free people back into hateful paths of despotism," he explained in a speech on the *Dred Scott* decision. For Lincoln, the Declaration affirmed the truth that the Good Life was good not only for the people enjoying the fruits of their labor but also good in the sense of doing so in a morally legitimate way. This was the essence of the Dream of Upward Mobility as he understood it.

Plenty of Lincoln's contemporaries believed he had a highly exaggerated notion of the Declaration of Independence—in terms of what it actually promised, and even whether it was all that important in American history and life in the first place. Stephen Douglas asserted repeatedly that he was second to no one in his reverence for the Founders and the Declaration. But he simply understood it differently than Lincoln did. The plain fact, Douglas explained, was that the United States was created as a white man's country with slavery in every one of the original thirteen colonies. "I say unto you, my fellow citizens, that in my opinion the signers of the Declaration had no reference to the negro whatever when they declared all men are created equal," he told the crowd at the third Lincoln-Douglas debate. "They desired to express by that phrase, white men, and had no reference either to the negro, the savage Indian, the Fejee, the Malay, or any other inferior and degraded race, when they spoke of the equality of men." This did not necessarily mean that African Americans should be slaves, Douglas added. But it didn't mean they *shouldn't* be, either.

Some politicians went much farther than this. Many southerners, of course, *did* think the inferiority of African Americans meant that they should be slaves, at least as much for their own good as that of their paternalistic masters. "No, sir," Virginian John Tyler replied to the notion that all men are created equal. "The principle, although lovely and beautiful, cannot obliterate those distinctions in society which society itself engenders and gives birth to." And even some northerners agreed. After U.S. Senator John Pettit of Indiana called the Declaration "a self-evident lie" in the halls of Congress, Lincoln argued that "he only did what consistency and candor require all other Nebraska men [i.e., those who supported the act] to do. Of the forty odd [pro] Nebraska Senators who sat present and heard him, no one rebuked him." Even Massachusetts senator Rufus Choate, an old-line Whig who considered slavery morally wrong, nevertheless considered the affirmations of natural rights in the Declaration as little more than "glittering and sounding generalities."

And such glittering generalities were hardly as compelling as some of the other emotions Lincoln's opponents could tap. Today, amid routine complaints that politics is now a dreary if not ugly affair, the Lincoln-Douglas debates are often cited as examples of how politics had once been high-minded. No one who actually has read the debates, however, could really make this statement after trudging through the repetition and race-baiting that run through them. Take, for example, this elegantly executed appeal to hate by Douglas in the second debate:

I have reason to recollect that some people in this country think that [escaped slave and abolitionist activist] Fred[erick]Douglass is a very good man. The last time I came here to make a speech, while talking from the stand with you, people of Freeport, as I am doing to-day, I saw a carriage, and a magnificent one it was, drive up and take a position on the outside of the crowd; a beautiful young lady was sitting on the box seat, whilst Fred. Douglass and her mother reclined inside, and the owner of the carriage acted as driver. ["Laughter, cheers, cries of right, what have you to say against it, &tc," reported the *Chicago Tribune*.] I saw this in your own town. ["What of it?"] All I have to say of it is this, that if you, Black Republicans, think that the negro ought to be on a social equality with your wives and daughters, and ride in a carriage with your wife, whilst you drive the team, you have a perfect right to do so. ["Good, good," and cheers, mingled with hooting and cries of "white, white."] I am told that one of Fred. Douglass' kinsmen, another rich black negro, is now traveling in this part of the State making speeches for his friend Lincoln as the champion of black men. ["White men, white men" and "What have you got to say against it? That's right, &tc"]

All I have to say on that subject is that those of you who believe that the negro is your equal and ought to be on an equality with you socially, politically, and legally; have a right to entertain those opinions, and will of course vote for Mr. Lincoln. ["Down with the negro," "o, no, &tc."]

Race, class, even sexual resentment are all stoked here, in rhetoric skillfully veiled in a tone of reasonableness and humor. This was the face of evil, circa 1858.

Lincoln was not without resources of his own in this regard. In the next debate, he noted that Douglas and his compatriots seemed to be quite interested in, even obsessed with, African Americans—African-American women in particular. Lincoln noted that he, like every other Euro-American he had ever known, believed it was impossible for whites and blacks to live as equals; he was "in favor of having the superior position assigned to the white race." But he still thought slavery was wrong. And he noted, "I do not understand that because I do not want a negro woman for a slave I must necessarily want her for a wife." (This to cheers and laughter.)

Still, it was an uphill battle for Lincoln. And at the end of the day, he lost: in the election of 1858, Democrats kept control of the state legislature and reelected Douglas to the Senate. Had Lincoln died then, he would have merited somewhat more mention than eight years earlier, because the race had received national attention. But once again, he seemed to have come up short. "I am glad I made the great race," he wrote in a letter a month after the election. "It gave me a hearing on the great and durable question of the age, and though I now sink out of view, and shall be forgotten, I believe I have made some marks which will tell for the cause of civil liberty long after I am gone." (One hears some whistling in the dark here, and perhaps some self-pity, too.)

Actually, even before he ever ran for the Senate against Douglas, Lincoln had done some thinking about what larger purpose, if any, there was in his personal ambition. In a note he made to himself around the end of 1856, Lincoln compared himself directly with his longtime antagonist. "With *me*, the race of ambition has been a failure—a flat failure; with *him* it has been one of splendid success. His name fills the nation; and is not unknown, even, in foreign lands." Still, while Lincoln frankly conceded admiration, if not envy, for Douglas, mere fame would not be enough. Douglas's indifference on the slavery question compromised the appeal of his eminence. If, by contrast, Lincoln could attain his fame so that "the oppressed of my species, might have shared with me in the elevation, I would rather stand on that eminence, than wear the richest crown that ever pressed on monarch's brow." Attaining upward mobility for oneself was great; but attaining upward mobility with and for others was greater.

Two years later, Lincoln was still grappling privately with such questions – and the possibility that a distant social goal could in fact be more important than personal success.

> I have never professed an indifference to the honors of official station; and were I to do so now, I should only make myself ridiculous. Yet I have never failed—do not now fail—to remember that in the republican cause there is a higher aim than that of mere office. I have not allowed myself to forget that the abolition of the Slave-trade by Great Britain, was agitated a hundred years before it was a final success; that the measure had it's [*sic*] open fire-eating opponents; it's stealthy "don't care" opponents; it's dollar and cent opponents; it's inferior race opponents; its negro equality opponents; and its religion and good order opponents; that all these opponents got offices, and the adversaries got none. But I have also remembered that though they blazed, like tallow-candles for a century, at last they flickered in the socket, died out, and were remembered no more, even by the smell.

There were more important things, Lincoln realized, than jobs, money, or fame. "Remembering these things I can not but regard it as possible that the higher object of this contest may not be completely attained within the term of my natural life." But Lincoln was not ready to drop his ambitions and become an abolitionist. A Senate seat beckoned.

He could not have anticipated the degree to which he himself ultimately became an instrument of that higher object of his speculations.

In giving freedom to the slave, we assure freedom to the free.

—Lincoln, annual message to Congress, December 1, 1862

"Senator Douglas is of world-wide renown," Lincoln told a crowd in Springfield, Illinois, in July of 1858. "All the anxious politicians of his party, or who have been of his party for years past, have been looking upon him as certainly, at no distant day, to be the President of the United States." Lincoln himself was another story. "On the contrary, nobody has ever expected me to be President. In my poor, lean, lank, face, nobody has ever seen that any cabbages were sprouting out."

In the aftermath of the campaign, however, the possibility of harvesting cabbages began to seem a little less ridiculous. "I must, in all candor, say I do not think myself fit for the Presidency," he responded to such a suggestion in April of 1859. He did so again two months later in a letter to a former congressman who also broached the subject. This was only politic; even if Lincoln were interested in the post, it would hardly have been appropriate for anyone, let alone a figure of marginally national status, to say so. Yet by the end of the year a Lincoln candidacy was a conceivable, if hardly likely, possibility.

Chance has always played a large role for even the most promising of presidential candidates, and in 1860 Lincoln needed more luck than most. True, the positions he staked out in the Senate campaign were unusual for their clarity and cogency in Republican circles, and the fact that he came from the crucial battleground state of Illinois boosted his prospects. (Indeed, his candidacy was initially justified as a way to lock up, and thus have the power to deliver, Illinois delegates for other candidates.) But intelligence and geography were limited assets at best, and there were figures in the party with far greater experience and stature. Yet Lincoln's lack of prominence ultimately became the most important factor in his favor, particularly since the figures of the greatest notoriety also attracted the most fierce opposition. "My name is new in the field; and I suppose I am not the *first* choice of a very great many. Our policy, then, is to give no offence to the others—leave them in a mood to come to us, if they shall be compelled to give up their first love." This, in effect, is what happened, as it often did in nineteenth-century presidential elections, and Lincoln became the Republican nominee in 1860.

But he could never have won the election without the help of Stephen Douglas, who, appalled by the way popular sovereignty actually played out in Kansas—that is, by armed gangs attacking each other and the passage of a proslavery constitution there amid widespread electoral fraud—denounced those, like the incumbent president, who condoned the outcome. The Democratic Party divided into two parts, with Douglas winning the nomination of its northern half and a future Confederate general taking the other. Still another electoral sliver nominated an old southern Whig, whose constituency was mostly the states of the upper South. Lincoln won the four-man race with less than 40 percent of the electorate, virtually all of it in the North. The American Dream of Upward Mobility seemed to have been realized in its purest form: a poor boy born in a log cabin had been elected the president of the United States. But his very election seemed to portend the end of those United States, and with it the dream of the boy. The South would not abide the results, and the war came.

The Civil War was a huge personal and political vortex for Lincoln, in which he was forced to consider all kinds of matters—notably military strategy—that had never previously concerned him. Yet despite the burdens and distractions that preoccupied him, he never lost sight of his American Dream. Indeed, the war proved important for it in two important respects.

The first is that for Abraham Lincoln, the war was an opportunity to reaffirm the nation's commitment to the Dream of Upward Mobility. This is work he began even before taking office. In February of 1861 Lincoln made a train tour from Springfield to Washington, giving speeches along the way. There was a reluctant quality to many of these speeches—he wanted to say as little as possible about the war situation before he was in a position to do anything about it—but there was one theme he repeated throughout the trip: the American Dream of Upward Mobility as both a beautiful promise and a moral imperative. "I hold that while man exists, it is his duty to improve not only his own condition, but to assist in ameliorating mankind," he told a crowd of Germans in Cincinnati, reaffirming his support of immigration. He reiterated this idea a little over a week later in Philadelphia. "I have often inquired of myself, what great principle or idea it was that kept this Confederacy together," he told a gathering at Independence Hall, site of the signing of the Declaration of Independence. "It was not the mere matter of the separation of the colonies from the mother land; but something in that Declaration giving liberty, not alone to the people of this country, but hope to the world for all future time. It was that which gave promise that in due time the weights should be lifted from the shoulders of all men, and that *all* should have an equal chance." As president, Lincoln was, as he put it in Indianapolis, "an accidental instrument, temporary, and to serve but a limited time." But while he was in office it was his job to embody the Dream. As he said in Philadelphia, "If this country cannot be saved without giving up that principle—I was about to say I would rather be assassinated on the spot than to surrender it."

In the months and years that followed—culminating in the assassination he seemed to chillingly predict—he grappled with the two great and pressing questions of the era: would the Union be saved? And: what would become of slavery? Then and since, the attention paid to these two questions has obscured the degree to which both were in effect two aspects of a larger question: how do we sustain the American Dream?

As far as Union versus slavery went, Lincoln was unambiguously clear about his own priorities. "My paramount object in this struggle *is* to save the Union, and is *not* either to save or to destroy slavery," he told newspaper editor Horace Greeley in August of 1862. "If I could save the Union without freeing *any* slave I would do it, and if I could save it by freeing *all* the slaves I would do it; and if I could save it by freeing some and leaving others alone I would also do that."

In fact, Lincoln already had a plan he would announce the following month: the Emancipation Proclamation, which, issued in Lincoln's constitutional capacity as commander-in-chief, freed slaves in rebelling states strictly on the basis of military exigency. In one sense, this was little more than a symbolic gesture, since Lincoln was in effect freeing slaves precisely where he had no actual power to do so. But as he and others recognized, he was setting a process in motion that would destroy slavery altogether. The very timing of the proclamation was designed in a successful public relations bid to prevent foreign intervention in the war, and it fostered desertions on the part of slaves who now had the prospect of freedom. The Emancipation Proclamation was also reinforced by Lincoln's support for a constitutional amendment to end slavery everywhere, which was passed by loyal states and signed by the President, who was reelected in 1864, at the very end of his first term of office. A long-standing goal—what for others was actually a separate long-standing American Dream—had finally been realized. Years before, when he began his Senate bid, Lincoln had declared, "A house divided cannot stand. I believe that this Government cannot endure permanently half slave and half free." Now, the house was reunited on the basis he favored. This was a tremendous achievement.

And yet, during his first presidential campaign, Lincoln had repeatedly expressed a sentiment that was arresting in its inversion of the familiar truism that might makes right. Instead, he asked, in a formulation rendered most memorably in a famous speech in New York, "Let us have faith that *right* makes *might*." His course in ending slavery seemed to fulfill this prescription: doing the right thing (abolishing slavery) helped secure the cause (saving the Union). Or, to put it another way, he did well by doing good.

There has always been something about this that has left me a little uneasy. "If slavery is not wrong, nothing is wrong," Lincoln wrote in 1864, and yet for his entire political life, the fight against slavery was simply a means, not an end. The end, presumably, was Union. But why was Union so important? Would two, or many, United States have been such an awful thing? Alexander Stephens, the vice president of the rebelling Confederacy, who served in Congress with Lincoln back in the 1840s and was friendly with him long afterward, later wrote that for Lincoln, "the Union with him, in sentiment, rose to the sublimity of religious mysticism." There's a sense of bemusement, even exasperation, in Stephens's observation with which one can sympathize.

What is ultimately apparent, however, is that Union was not an end any more than abolition was. It, too, was a means. The true end was the American Dream, a goal that sometimes seemed submerged but would nevertheless resurface again and again throughout the war. Take, for example, this passage from Lincoln's address to a special session of Congress held on July 4, 1861, on the brink of the first great battles:

> This is essentially a People's contest. On the one side of the Union, it is a struggle for maintaining in the world, that form, and substance of government, whose leading object is, to elevate the condition of men—to lift artificial weights from all shoulders—to clear the paths of laudable pursuit for all—to afford all, an unfettered start, and a fair chance, in the race of life. Yielding to partial, and temporary measures [like the presence of slavery in 1776] from necessity, this is the leading object of the government for those whose existence we contend.

The following year, in his annual message to Congress, Lincoln followed up his issuance of the Emancipation Proclamation by making a formal request for a constitutional amendment to end slavery altogether. In giving freedom to the slave, he explained, the government assured freedom to the free. In so doing, lawmakers would preserve what Lincoln called "the last, best hope of earth," a place where upward mobility would thrive without hypocrisy or the challenge of alternative ideologies that would subvert it.

But not all of Lincoln's invocations of the American Dream were made at the level of formal oratory in great halls. "This government must be preserved in spite of the acts of any man or set of men. It is worth your every effort," he told a group of soldiers returning from the front on their way home to Ohio in 1864. "Nowhere in the world is presented a government of so much liberty and equality. To the humblest and poorest among us are held out the highest privileges and positions. The present moment finds me at the White House, yet there is as good a chance for your children as there was for my father's." (So much for Lincoln's claim that it would be a "great piece of folly" to make anything of his early life.)

Perhaps you agree that the American Dream—a specific American Dream of Upward Mobility that fused earthly goals and heavenly means—is a more coherent, even attractive, justification for Lincoln's life and behavior than mere Union. But if you do, you might well share a sense that it somehow isn't quite adequate, either. It is surely an attractive vision. But it just doesn't quite seem enough when one considers the deaths of hundreds of thousands of soldiers, or the almost cavalier attitude Lincoln had toward African Americans themselves.

Which brings me to my second point about the impact of the Civil War on Lincoln: it revised—maybe a better term would be "chastened"—his notion of the American Dream. The principal form this chastening took was a growing skepticism over one of the key premises of the American Dream of Upward Mobility from the time of Benjamin Franklin: the ability to shape one's destiny. Perhaps, Lincoln was increasingly inclined to speculate, there was an invisible hand with objectives far removed from things like success in the marketplace. "In the present civil war it is quite possible that God's purpose is something different from the purpose of either party," he noted to himself sometime during the late summer of 1862, on the eve of the Emancipation Proclamation. "I am almost ready to say this is true—that God wills this contest."

Almost, but not quite. Actually, the really remarkable thing here is not Lincoln's reluctance to give up his sense of human agency (that would come) but rather that God would be playing such a large role in his private deliberations. Lincoln routinely mentioned the Almighty in his speeches, showed deep knowledge of the Bible, and had strong moral values regarding issues like slavery. But he belonged to no church, never attended services regularly, and during his campaign for Congress in 1846 was attacked by his opponent, an evangelical Methodist minister, for his religious infidelity. The charge was serious enough for Lincoln to publish a response, in which he asserted that "I do not think I could myself, be brought to support a man for office, whom I knew to be an open enemy of, and scoffer at, religion." (As Gore Vidal, an often caustic skeptic about virtually everyone except Lincoln, points out in an introduction to an edition of Lincoln writings, "the key word, of course, is 'open.'") Yet in that same statement, Lincoln also said that "in early life I was inclined to believe in what I understand is called the 'Doctrine of Necessity'—that is, that the human mind is impelled to action, or held to rest by some power, over which the mind itself has no control; and I have sometimes (with one, two or three, but never publicly) tried to maintain this opinion in argument. The habit of arguing thus, however, I have, entirely left off for more than five years."

There are a number of things that are interesting about this statement, particularly in light of Lincoln's subsequent career. First of all, the Doctrine of Necessity he spoke of was hardly the typical ideology of the freethinking atheist—it derived from Puritan ideology, emphasizing the degree to which men and women could not know if they were saved. Saying that he no longer had the "habit" of making this argument might reflect a growing need for tact on his part politically or that he no longer believed in the doctrine. In any event, there was a notably ecumenical quality to Lincoln's invocation of religion for the next fifteen years, and even his meditations in 1862 were a strictly personal affair.

Yet as the war dragged on, his youthful convictions resurfaced, and he began making the argument again. By the final year of the war, Lincoln was no longer "almost" ready to concede God's will: he did so readily. "I attempt no compliment to my own sagacity," he wrote in a letter in April of 1864. "I claim not to have controlled events, but confess plainly that events have controlled me. Now, at the end of three years struggle the nation's condition is not what either party, or any man devised, or expected. God alone can claim it." Two weeks later, he went further, doing something he never did before: making his convictions public (albeit in a typically subtle way). "When the war began, three years ago, neither party, nor any man, expected it would last till now," he told a gathering in Baltimore. "Each looked for the end, in some way, long ere today. Neither did any anticipate that domestic slavery would be much affected by the war. But here we are; the war has not ended and slavery has been much affected—how much needs not now to be recounted. So true it is that man proposes, and God disposes." God, it appeared, cared more about slavery than Union: as Lincoln was speaking, the former was clearly dying and it was far from clear the latter would survive. (Nor was it clear Lincoln himself would be reelected, dealing as he was with a military stalemate and challenges from within his own party.)

Still, he told the crowd, there were reasons for optimism: "We can see the past, though we may not claim to have directed it; and seeing it, in this case, we feel more hopeful and confident in the future." In the classic formulation of the Dream of Upward Mobility, the past is irrelevant—except as a measuring stick for anticipated success. Now, however, the past is a source of hope in its own right. Moreover, Lincoln was no longer expressing the view, as he had for most his career, that one could will an outcome through hard work and a clean conscience. One simply had to trust in the ways of God—just as Augustine, a favorite of the Puritans, trusted that the fiery trials though which men would pass would lead them to the City of God.

The culmination of this line in Lincoln's thinking was his Second Inaugural Address, which he delivered on March 4, 1865. By this point in the war, slavery was abolished, the Union was virtually saved, and the end of the bloodshed was in sight. One might well imagine another man—especially another man with a deep investment in the American Dream—marking the occasion as a moment of triumph. It would not be altogether implausible, after all, to argue that the outcome really was a matter of right making might, of conviction carrying the day, and, above all, of a man from modest circumstances propelling himself to the pinnacle of national achievement, realizing a dream, and then leading his people to save that dream for others. Was this not, in fact, a crowning achievement, the culmination of all they fought for?

Amazingly, the answer was no. In this brief address—it could not have taken more than ten minutes—Lincoln repeated some of the ideas he had been mulling over for the past three years: that the course of the war had not been desired or expected, that its course had been unpredictable, and that both sides had invoked God's aid against the other. But, he said, God had his own idea about what this war was really about, and it seemed to be punishment for the sins of *both* sides:

If we shall suppose that American Slavery is one of those offences which, in the providence of God, must needs come, but which, having continued through his appointed time, He now wills to remove, and that He gives to both North and South, this terrible war, as the woe due to those by whom the offence came, shall we discern therein any departure from those divine attributes which the believers in a Living God always ascribe to Him? Fondly do we hope—fervently do we pray—that this mighty scourge of war may speedily pass away. Yet, if God wills that it continue, until all the wealth piled by the bond-man's two hundred and fifty years of unrequited toil be sunk, and until every drop of blood drawn with the lash, shall be paid by another drawn with the sword, as was said three thousand years ago, so still it must be said "the judgments of the Lord are true and righteous altogether."

Spiritually speaking, we are back in the world of the Puritans. The diction and themes of this passage call to mind the Gospel of Matthew, in which Christ's betrayal is both inevitable and blameworthy—and which influenced John Calvin's theories of predestination that proved so influential for the Puritans. One senses the death of Lincoln's Dream of Upward Mobility here, even as an older American Dream was reborn.

"Everyone likes a compliment," Lincoln wrote in thanks to the New York editor and political fixer Thurlow Weed, who he mistakenly believed had praised the Second Inaugural. Lincoln said he expected the address to wear "as well as—perhaps better than—anything I have produced." Perhaps he was especially gratified by Weed's putative praise because, as he explained, he did not believe it was very popular: "Men are not flattered by being shown that there has been a difference of purpose between the Almighty and them." Nevertheless, he wrote, "it is a truth which I thought needed to be told; and as whatever of humiliation there is in it, falls most directly on myself, I thought others might afford for me to tell it." A month later Lincoln was assassinated, an almost biblical casualty of the war he prosecuted with a firmness of purpose and humility that only grew more remarkable with the passage of time.

The Dream of Upward Mobility, however, lived on. If Franklin, Emerson, Clay, and others were its Old Testament prophets, then Lincoln was its Jesus Christ. In the decades that followed, countless admirers proclaimed themselves disciples of the Dream, spreading the Good News to anyone who would listen: that in America, it was possible to make your own destiny. Virtually none of these figures adopted the skepticism that shaded Lincoln's own understanding of the Dream as he aged, and all too many indulged a sense of complacency about the likelihood of success—and their own role in achieving it. Conversely, the Dream also served as a powerful vehicle for blaming those who did not succeed and for distracting those who might otherwise have sought structural changes by seducing them into thinking they weren't really necessary.

If there was one redemptive element in all of this, it lay in something that Lincoln cared very deeply about: that the purview of the Dream be expanded as widely as possible. By the end of the twentieth century, it wasn't just Hans, Baptiste, and Patrick who were pursuing—and occasionally achieving—upward mobility, but Elizabeth, Elena, and Kaneesha, too. The Russian-Jewish immigrant Mary Antin, who rose from illiteracy to become a successful writer (albeit one whose later career was marked by mental illness, financial insecurity, and disillusionment), felt with special intensity the very things Lincoln spoke about. "As I read how the patriots planned the Revolution, and the women gave their sons to die in battle, and the heroes led to victory, and the rejoicing people set up the Republic, it dawned on me gradually what was meant by *my country*," she explained in her own 1912 memoir *The Promised Land*. "The people all desiring noble things, and striving for them together, defying their oppressors, giving their lives for each other—all this made it my country." One is reminded here of something Lincoln said about immigrants and the Declaration of Independence in a speech in Chicago in 1858: "They have a right to claim it as though they were blood of the blood, and flesh of the flesh of the men who wrote that Declaration." And while you may consider it a matter of wishful thinking on my part, I find it hard to believe that Lincoln would have been all that upset to learn that one of the most vivid exponents of the American Dream a century and a half later is Oprah Winfrey, who built a media empire largely on pluck and the force of her own mythology as a self-made woman.

In the end, of course, the Dream of Upward Mobility will prove every bit as mortal as Lincoln himself. And despite all the passion he brought to it, I think he always knew, even before he became president, that it would. I say so because of the way he ended a speech in Milwaukee, Wisconsin, in September of 1859. The purpose of Lincoln's speech was to honor the rapid pace of Progress in the nineteenth century and to call for measures, like an increased public commitment to education, to foster it. Perhaps a part of him meant for the speech to close on a triumphant note, and I suppose it does. But here, at least, "Honest Abe" is not a particularly effective liar:

> It is said an Eastern monarch once charged his wise men to invent him a sentence, to be ever in view, and which should be true and appropriate at all times. They presented him the words: *"And this, too, shall pass away."* How much it expresses! How chastening in the hour of pride!—how consoling in the depths of affliction! "And this, too, shall pass away." And yet let us hope it is not *quite* true. Let us hope, rather, that by the best cultivation of the physical world, beneath and around us; and the intellectual and moral world within us, we shall secure an individual, social, and political prosperity and happiness, whose course shall be onward and upward, and which, while the earth endures, shall not pass away.

As Ernest Hemingway might have said, it would be pretty to think so.

CHAPTER 4

KING OF AMERICA:
THE DREAM OF EQUALITY

HOMER PLESSY was not a slave. Born in New Orleans on March 17, 1862—six months to the day before Abraham Lincoln issued the Emancipation Proclamation—he was the son of Creole parents. Although Plessy and his entire family were light-skinned and "passed" as white, his great-grandmother was of African descent. This meant, according to Louisiana law, that he was legally black. Unlike many African Americans—or "negroes," as they were called in polite circles at the time—Plessy, who grew up to become a shoemaker, had been a free man his entire life. Nobody owned him; nobody could buy or sell him. He could say what he pleased, go where he wanted. He enjoyed a series of constitutionally protected rights as a United States citizen.

Of course, as a negro, there were certain, shall we say, considerations. Nobody owned him, but if he was ever unfortunate enough to go to jail (something statistically more likely for him than for a white man), he might end up on a chain gang performing forced labor. He could say what he pleased, but as surely he understood, some things (particularly those critical of the state of race relations) could only be said at his own risk. He could go where he wanted, assuming he had the means (and obeyed the prevailing rules, like sticking among his own kind). He enjoyed a series of constitutional rights as a U.S. citizen—IF he could find officials willing (and able) to enforce them.

Fortunately, such considerations were relatively minor for Homer Plessy. No one could really tell his "true" identity, and as long as he was willing to lie now and then, everything would be fine. He was a free man—more free than most negroes.

On June 7, 1892, Plessy took a train ride from New Orleans to Covington, a town on the other side of Lake Pontchartrain. According to a new 1890 law in Louisiana, Plessy was obligated to ride in a separate car designated specifically for negroes, and thus to be segregated from white riders. Plessy ignored the law, ignored it as countless other light-skinned Americans surely evaded similar "Jim Crow" laws that were proliferating throughout the "redeemed" South of the late nineteenth century. Many of these laws were modeled on similar ones enacted by northern states in the decades before the war.

This time, however, Plessy did not get away with passing for white. Actually, he made sure he didn't: he and a group of collaborators *planned* for his arrest. Those collaborators included a citizens' committee of Creoles and the lawyer they hired, a northern white "carpetbagger" writer and lawyer named Albion Tourgée who moved to North Carolina briefly after the Civil War and was appalled by southern white racism. (The group also received quiet encouragement from the railroad company, which considered racial segregation economically onerous.) So it was no accident when a cooperating conductor approached Plessy and demanded he move to a white car; a private detective hired for the purpose arrested Plessy when he refused. He was charged by a Louisiana court and pleaded innocent, and a trial was set for the following month.

The trial was presided over by Justice John Howard Ferguson. A Massachusetts native, Ferguson, like Plessy's attorney Albion Tourgée, came south after the Civil War; unlike Tourgée, he stayed there and married the daughter of a prominent New Orleans attorney. In the weeks between Plessy's arrest and trial, Ferguson ruled in a similar case, also carefully orchestrated, involving a man riding an interstate train. In that case, Ferguson ruled that the Louisiana law, which called for "equal but separate accommodations for the white and colored races," was unconstitutional. This was because travel between states fell under the federal government's power to regulate interstate commerce, and a series of post–Civil War constitutional amendments and federal laws had strengthened the legal rights of African Americans. Of particular importance here was the Fourteenth Amendment, which asserted: "No State shall make or enforce any law which shall abridge the privileges or immunities of citizens of the United States; nor shall any State deprive any person of life, liberty, or property, without due process of law; nor deny any to any person within its jurisdiction the equal protection of the laws."

The Plessy case, however, did not involve interstate travel. Because of this, Ferguson ruled, federal law did not apply, because states had the right to regulate companies operating solely within their borders. When it came to some things—most things—states could do what they pleased without interference from meddling officials from Washington, and keeping the races separate was one of them. Plessy was found guilty.

This outcome had been anticipated. Indeed, Tourgée in particular hoped Plessy would be convicted; from the very beginning his plan was to appeal the case before the United States Supreme Court, which would be forced to strike down such "separate but equal" laws whatever their location or intent because they were so patently unfair. The Plessy team prepared carefully, delaying their case in the hope that the nation's racial climate (and the ideological makeup of the Supreme Court) would improve. When it became clear dramatic improvements were not forthcoming, they finally made their move, and the case went before the high court in April of 1896.

Plessy v. Ferguson, like many landmark Supreme Court cases, was a complex matter marked by abstruse theory and what many nonlawyers would regard as counterintuitive logic. In the most basic terms, the case was about the nature and meaning of equality, but a large body of legal doctrine had carefully distinguished between different *kinds* of equality: political equality (the rights of citizens in relation to the government), civil equality (the rights of citizens in the public sphere), and social equality (the rights of citizens in their personal dealings with each other). Such distinctions were crucial in the formulation of the Supreme Court's deliberations and featured prominently in the majority (7–1) decision written by another Massachusetts native, Justice Henry Billings Brown.

One paragraph in particular of Brown's ruling has long attracted particular attention:

> The object of the [Fourteenth] amendment was undoubtedly to enforce the absolute equality of the two races before the law, but in the nature of

things it could not have been intended to abolish distinctions based upon color, or to enforce social, as distinguished from political equality, or a commingling of the two races upon terms unsatisfactory to either. Laws permitting, and even requiring, their separation in places where they are liable to be brought into contact do not necessarily imply the inferiority of either race to the other, and have been generally, if not universally, recognized as within the competency of the state legislatures in the exercise of their police power. The most common instance of this is connected with the establishment of separate schools for white and colored children, which has been held to be a valid exercise of the legislative power even by courts of States where the political rights of the colored race have been longest and most earnestly enforced.*

The Court concluded that Plessy's case finally foundered in the idea that segregation itself was the problem. "We consider the underlying fallacy of the plaintiff's argument to consist in the assumption that the enforced separation of the two races stamps the colored race with a badge of inferiority. If this be so, it is not by reason of anything found in the act, but solely because the colored race chooses to put that construction upon it." If negroes feel inferior, Brown argues, they have only themselves to blame. The government is doing all it can, should—or will. After the case the free Homer Plessy drifted into anonymity, becoming a life insurance collector before his death in 1925.

Plessy v. Ferguson has long been considered among the worst decisions the Supreme Court ever made, one ranking with its *Dred Scott v. Sandford* decision of 1857, which ruled that African Americans "had no rights which the white man was bound to respect." *Plessy*'s reputation is partly a matter of hindsight—subsequent events would show it legally legitimated a racist state in which African Americans were systematically deprived of political, civil, *and* social equality for decades to come—but observers at the time (the few that were paying attention, that is) recognized it would have a disastrous impact. "In my opinion, the judgment this day rendered will, in time, prove to be quite as pernicious as the

---

* Brown is referring to *Roberts v. the City of Boston* (1850), a precedent that established the legitimacy of school segregation. Southern lawmakers were fond of basing their own segregation statutes on antebellum northern ones. Besides the obvious legal utility in cases like this one, it was also politically helpful when northerners began moralizing about "southern" racial problems.

decision made by this tribunal in the *Dred Scott* case," Supreme Court Justice John Marshall Harlan, himself a former slaveholder, wrote in a lone dissent. "The present decision, it may well be apprehended, will not only stimulate aggressions, more or less brutal and irritating, upon the admitted rights of colored citizens, but will encourage the belief that it is possible, by means of state enactments, to defeat the beneficent purposes which the people of the United States had in view when they adopted the recent amendments of the Constitution" (i.e., the Thirteenth, ending slavery, the Fourteenth, guaranteeing African Americans citizenship, and the Fifteenth, granting them the right to vote).

Abraham Lincoln may have made the slaves *free*, but not even he, as he pointed out repeatedly in the Lincoln-Douglas debates, was prepared to make them *equal*. The *Plessy* decision was part of a broader political effort to make two concepts that had been widely considered virtually interchangeable into two that were wholly separate, even antithetical.

Race relations wasn't the only area of American life where such a redefinition was taking place. The acceleration of industrial capitalism in the late nineteenth century, combined with the growing application of the Darwinian theory of "the survival of the fittest" to human affairs, popularized a notion of freedom as the right of the individual entrepreneur, like John D. Rockefeller, to make as much money as he could without interference that would drag down the progress of the human race as a whole. In this view, freedom meant freedom to dominate and freedom from regulation. Equality, by contrast, was a base "leveling" instinct that restricted freedom by insisting that everyone, even those who were evidently superior, had to play by the same rules, respect the same limits. Any assertion that people should be *more* equal than they theoretically already were smacked of socialism—and socialism, like other "foreign" ideas, was thoroughly beyond the pale. Such logic became the cornerstone of Republican ideology in the closing decades of the nineteenth century—and, for that matter, the closing decades of the twentieth as well.

But nowhere were the language, assumptions, and passion for inequality more entrenched than in race relations, and nowhere was the fear that attended the prospect of a truly egalitarian society more apparent. That might not have been a problem; many societies in world history have durably embraced inequality as the foundation for their social organization. Moreover, there have always been Americans in the South and elsewhere quite willing to deny the validity of equality entirely, and others who would pay it lip service lest meddlesome Yankees impose their will with lawsuits—and, once every century or so, with armed troops. But most of us have believed that equality must play a role in everyday American life, even if that role is almost wholly theoretical.

That's because the American Dream depends on it. At some visceral level, virtually all of us need to believe that equality is one of the core values of everyday American life, that its promises extend to everyone. If they don't, then not everybody is eligible for the American Dream—and one of the principal attractions of the American Dream, and its major moral underpinning, is that everyone is eligible: this has been the benchmark, commonsense notion of what equality has meant for quite some time. That the circumstances of everyday life routinely belie this belief is hardly a problem as long as the *principle* of equality is affirmed.

The way we typically square the difference between principle and reality is to cite the concept of equality of *opportunity*. The notion that everyone has the hypothetical possibility of being equal in public life is a standard we consider practical, as opposed to equality of *condition*, which we typically do not. We can accept, even savor, all kinds of inequalities as long as we can imagine different outcomes—that you *can* earn a million dollars (if you're lucky); that there's no obvious external barrier forcibly *preventing* a Latina child from attending an Ivy League university (if her test scores are good enough); that you too can hire jury consultants in your murder trial (if you're rich and/or famous); and so on. This allows us to believe we live in a reasonably fair country that bears some relationship to its founding ideals—in this case, that "all men are created equal," as usefully ambiguous as the phrase is—and gives us the hope that our own dreams are not impossibly out of reach.

In an insidious way, this commitment to a fuzzily defined equality of opportunity can actually prevent equality from ever being realized, in much the same way a cigarette smoker believes it's *possible* to kick the habit and thus remains free to maintain it a while longer. One is here reminded of 1972 presidential candidate George McGovern, who was surprised and dismayed by the negative reaction to his suggestion that large inheritances be heavily taxed. "They must think they're going to win a lottery," he mused. Rarely has it been so clear why a candidate lost.

Still, for all the laziness and hypocrisy our attitude toward equality has engendered, even the highly diluted equality of opportunity has never been wholly without transformative potential to regenerate the American Dream. Indeed, the great irony of *Plessy v. Ferguson* is that the legal basis of the ruling sowed the seeds of its own destruction. The Louisiana lawmakers who crafted the original state railway law knew the federal government would never let them get away with "separate" unless they at least made a *pretense* toward "equal." This is why most Jim Crow laws meant to deny blacks their constitutional rights never actually *said* African Americans could not vote but instead created standards (like literacy tests, poll taxes, and the like) that were supposedly racially neutral but effectively prevented only African Americans from exercising their rights. Beyond that, most Jim Crow laws didn't even bother with pretense: there was no point to them unless separate could mean *un*equal. Nevertheless, the standard, however flouted, provided the wedge that the National Association for the Advancement of Colored People—founded in the wake of *Plessy*—used to argue that the separate facilities typically provided for blacks were not in fact equal. This effort resulted in a string of legal victories in the 1930s and 1940s, culminating in *Sweatt v. Painter* (1950), in which the NAACP showed that the separate law school facilities provided by an institution in Texas failed to meet the *Plessy* standard. The NAACP advanced simultaneously on another front to show that even where theoretical equality existed, separation itself was inherently unequal. This was the basis of the celebrated *Brown v. Board of Education* decision of 1954, which overturned a practice—school segregation—that even Plessy's own lawyers took for granted in making their own case.

The fact that it took almost sixty years to overturn *Plessy*, however, is not exactly a resounding affirmation of the American legal system. Actually, Supreme Court justices themselves would be the first to say that law is an awkward instrument of social policy. (It's only fair to note that it took states like Louisiana decades after the Civil War to get those Jim Crow statutes on the books in the first place.) The most powerful, and meaningful, battles to infuse the spirit of equality have taken place not in the courts but on the streets. In 1892 Homer Plessy rode a train. In 1955, Rosa Parks—who, like Plessy (and, for that matter, Dred Scott) worked with a series of collaborators on a carefully planned scenario—opened a new phase of the struggle by riding a bus.

This historical movement embodied by figures like Parks has come to be known as "the civil rights movement." That name is accurate in that many of the issues that were fought over in the next fifteen years involved the ability of African Americans to avail themselves of political rights the law said they already had and to enjoy protection from discrimination that was not necessarily imposed by governments.

The civil rights movement is also sometimes known as "the black freedom movement." This, too, makes sense, in that what was at stake was often the freedom to exercise rights, like voting, or freedom from physical intimidation. Moreover, there have been few terms in the last thirty years that have had more allure in American life than "freedom," particularly among retail marketers and political conservatives.

In an important sense, however, names like "the civil rights Movement" and "the black freedom movement" obscure more than they reveal. In an important sense, this event of "the sixties" (another imprecise term) would perhaps most accurately be called the black *equality* movement. Such a designation would serve as a vivid reminder of what was really at stake in those years—and what has been so depressingly absent in the decades since.

The most famous figure in this struggle for equality was Dr. Martin Luther King Jr. Then and since, observers have noted that he was one figure among many and that the acts of daring that marked his life were matched by many others in the movement. This is, of course, correct. Yet a belief in King's preeminence in the movement, however inaccurate or even unjust, is not without a logical foundation. For it was he more than anyone else who articulated the moral and cultural basis for equality in American life—not only for African Americans, but for all Americans. The struggle for black equality is one of the great dramas of our national history, and its course and outcome remain an object lesson for those waging parallel struggles for equality in other, almost inevitably entwined, arenas in our national life.

He had a dream, you see. A dream that scares us, a dream that we often try to ignore. But it's one we can't forget, either, and don't entirely want to. That's because in our better moments, it's our dream, too.

Was the vision of a nation of equals flawed at the source by contempt for both the poor and the black? Is America still colonial Virginia writ large? More than a century after Appomattox, the questions linger.

—Edmund Morgan, *American Slavery, American Freedom: The Ordeal of Colonial Virginia,* **1975**

In the beginning, there was a kind of rough equality: an equality of death. Native or immigrant, male or female, rich or poor: the odds you would perish in early seventeenth-century North America were frighteningly high. "This month, thirteen of our number die," William Bradford reported of the Pilgrim settlement in March of 1621, the fourth month after arrival in Plymouth. "There sometimes die two or three a day. Of one hundred persons scarce fifty remain: The living scarce able to bury the dead; the well not sufficient to tend the sick." After the initial hardships for early settlers, though, New England proved to offer a relatively good climate for immigrants. The cold winters limited the possibilities for infectious disease; the Indians, who had been decimated by disease before the Puritan migration, were not in a good position to resist the invasion.

The Chesapeake colonies of Virginia and Maryland were another story. The bay harbored all kinds of deadly maladies, and the dank summer weather often proved to be too much for Anglo-Saxons from cooler climes. Nor were Indians quite as cooperative there. Virginia's first permanent settlement was established at Jamestown in 1607; nine years later the first tobacco crop, which would prove so central to the colony's economy, was planted. During the ensuing boom of the next few years, about 3,500 people, virtually all of them men, poured into Virginia. And yet, while its population should have been about 4,200, there were only about 1,240 alive in 1622.

The surest way to prosper in Virginia in those days was simply to survive. Most of those who had gone were poor young men from the streets of London with few prospects. They went over as indentured servants; if they made it to the end of their term of service, they literally received a stake in the land to make their own fortunes. Women in Virginia enjoyed a relatively powerful position, since they were relatively scarce and in some cases inherited the property of serial husbands who died before they did, making them very attractive indeed to suitors. Even the minute number of slaves, who began arriving in 1619, could own land, go to court, and have servants of their own. Here was a fluid frontier society of upward mobility, one marked by inequality from the beginning and yet full of possibility and danger for all.

Over the course of the century, however, Virginia and the other southern colonies stabilized, and as they did so the relative egalitarianism of these early years gave way to a growing sense of hierarchy. The governorship of Sir William Berkeley (1642–77) was pivotal in this regard; under Berkeley's watch the colony became an almost feudal society run in many cases by second sons of noblemen back home who seized opportunities to become lords of manors. The insurrection of Nathaniel Bacon in 1676 was in many ways a protest by relatively lowly "freemen" against the growing inequality of the colony—it was also a race war on the part of those who wanted to subjugate the Indians more decisively than Berkeley felt he needed to—but Bacon's sudden death allowed Berkeley to crush the rebellion. In its wake, wealthy Virginians became more inclined than ever to dispense with potentially trouble-some indentured white servants and make the investment in more durable, and reproducible, slaves, whose legal and social privileges were steadily circumscribed. Given Virginia's influence in the South and the colonies as a whole in the century that followed, the die was cast for a colonial culture whose stability rested on a foundation of racial inequal-ity. So did its understanding of freedom: the ambivalence and bad faith of Thomas Jefferson notwithstanding, it is clear the War of Indepen-dence was one of *white* independence, and the price of Southern ratifi-cation of the Constitution was the perpetration of a system of inequality based on slavery that spread across the South and beyond.

The great—inevitable?—paradox of this inequality is that for its white male citizens, the young United States was also the most egalitar-ian society the Western world had ever seen. "Among the novel objects that attracted my attention during my stay in the United States, noth-ing struck me more forcibly than the general equality of condition among the people," Alexis de Tocqueville wrote in an opening sentence of *Democracy in America* that set the tone for the entire work. Note that Tocqueville speaks of equality of *condition*; the phenomenon he observed was no mere principle or abstraction but an evident reality he experienced as he toured the continent.

That said, we can't necessarily accept Tocqueville at face value. For one thing, he was a member of the French aristocracy (albeit from a family out of favor), and there are few more entertaining passages in all of American historical literature than those where he describes, with evident irritation, the presumptuousness of some of the Americans he dealt with.* Indeed, Tocqueville regarded American equality as posing

---

* "I have often noticed that in the United States it is not easy to make a man understand that his presence may be dispensed with," Tocqueville observes in the second volume of *Democracy in America*. "Hints will not always suffice to shake him off. I contradict an Amer-

real problems, among them a tendency toward conformity in a culture where the acceptance of one's peers mattered far more than the patronage of one's betters.

It's also a little hard to see how Tocqueville could be so insistent on American equality in a slave society. In part, this may reflect the fact that most of his travels were in the North and Midwest. But Tocqueville was by no means ignorant of slavery and wrote about it with his usual psychological acuity. He recognized the powerful contradiction that equality fosters in the typical American—"he engenders to show that, for his part, he is an exception to the general state of things"—and described how this dynamic played itself out below the Mason-Dixon line: "The Americans of the Southern states have two powerful passions which will always keep them aloof: the first is fear of being assimilated to the Negroes, their former slaves; and the second, the dread of sinking below the whites, their neighbors." Tocqueville also saw the boundaries in the culture of egalitarianism. "If America undergoes great revolutions," he wrote in 1840, "they will be brought about by the presence of the black race on the soil of the United States; that is to say, they will owe their origin not to equality, but to the inequality of condition."

He was, of course, correct. He was correct in another sense as well: "If I were called upon to predict the future, I should say that the abolition of slavery in the South will, in the common course of things, increase the white repugnance for blacks." This was a matter of observation, not theory: "Inhabitants of the North avoid the Negroes with increasing care in proportion as the legal barriers of separation are removed by the legislature; why should not the same result take place in the South?" Tocqueville would have readily understood how it was that so many Jim Crow laws of the post–Civil War era drew their inspiration, even language, from northern laws.

Indeed, even before the Civil War, some African Americans began to realize that freedom and equality were by no means interchangeable and that the former was only a precondition for the latter. Frederick

ican at every word he says, to show him that his conversation bores me; he instantly labors with fresh pertinacity to convince me; I observe a dogged silence, and he thinks I am meditating deeply on the truths that he is uttering; at last I rush from his company, and he supposes that some urgent business hurries me elsewhere. . . . Democratic institutions generally give men a lofty notion of their country and themselves."

Douglass, as true a believer in democracy as black America ever created, seemed to regard the very northern air he breathed as somehow sweeter when he escaped from slavery to freedom in 1838. Douglass had been a caulker working in a Baltimore shipyard (where he was beaten by apprentices) prior to his escape. Upon achieving his freedom, he sought work in New Bedford, Massachusetts, and was "for once made glad by a view of extreme wealth, without being saddened by seeing extreme poverty." Douglass nevertheless encountered blanket discrimination against blacks in the shipyards there. He also found himself subjected to segregated seating on northern railroads, a practice he resisted even when it meant forcible eviction from the cars.

Such experiences fostered disillusionment but did not lead Douglass to give up. Indeed, if anything, they heightened his desire to achieve full citizenship and his anger at the betrayal of the core premises of national identity and the American Dream. Nowhere is this more obvious than in his famous 1852 speech "What to the Slave Is the Fourth of July?" in which Douglass dismisses self-serving "shouts of liberty and equality" as "hollow mockery." "For revolting barbarity and shameless hypocrisy, America reigns without rival," he concluded. And yet, despite this barbarity and hypocrisy, Douglass never gave up the pursuit of what he called in an 1883 address "making the nation's life consistent with the nation's creed." At the core of that creed was equality.

Frederick Douglass was in many ways an exceptional figure, but his hopes for his country were by no means unique, particularly among the nearly two hundred thousand black combatants, among others, who served on the northern side during the Civil War. Many of them did so with a clear sense of what was at stake. "We are fighting as hard as the white man is to restore the Union," one such soldier wrote in a letter to the editor of a black newspaper in December of 1864. "Why then should we not have equal rights with a foreigner, who comes to this country to fight for the preservation of the Government?" He then conjured his own Dream of Equality. "If we live to have families, we can sit down by the side of our wives, with our children around us, and relate to them what we have endured and witnessed upon the battlefields, to help us restore this now-broken Union." Another soldier, writing to the same newspaper a month later, evoked a similar vision of the day when he and his fellow soldiers would "surround our cheerful firesides, and relate to our wives and children, parents and friends, what we have witnessed during this struggle for freedom, liberty, and equal rights." This interracial vision of family and friends savoring the fruits of equality would prove to be a durable dream in black America, one that would be evoked a century later by Martin Luther King in his image of black and white sitting at the table of brotherhood in his most famous address.

Unfortunately, the Dream of Equality receded into the distance in the decades following the Civil War, largely because many white Americans were determined to see it do so. Edward A. Pollard, editor of the *Richmond Examiner* during the war and author of the 1867 manifesto *The Lost Cause*, spoke for many when he observed that the war may have decided "the restoration of the Union and the excision of slavery, but did not decide Negro equality." Indeed, in some quarters that had been decided before the war, and nothing had happened to change it. Democratic congressman Andrew Rogers of New Jersey, who opposed the Fourteenth Amendment, spoke for many whites, North and South, when he asserted that the American government "was made for white men and women" and that not even the Civil War could overturn God's "edict" against "social equality between the black race and white race." By the 1870s the views of people like Pollard and Rogers were in the ascendant again as increasing emphasis was placed on sectional reconciliation and decreasing emphasis was placed on black equality. The election of 1912 brought Woodrow Wilson, the first southern president since the Civil War, into office; in 1913, the federal government passed regulations following the southern practice of creating segregated facilities in government offices.

So: freedom? Yes. Fifty years after the Civil War, it remained a fait accompli, and even many avowed racists claimed, as former Confederate vice president Alexander Stephens did after the war, that "some of the strongest Anti-Slavery men who ever lived were on the side of those who opposed the Centralizing principles which led to the war." For such people, the war was never about slavery. (For some people, it still isn't; it's about "heritage," leading one to wonder what the people who make such an assertion think the South has a distinct heritage *of*.) In any event, slavery was no more, though to many former slaves the tenant farming system that replaced it was just as bad, even worse, forcing African Americans into unequal relationships with landlords who dictated terms with little or no economic, political, or legal recourse. The freedpeople were at liberty to sign onerous contracts if they chose to and free to starve if they did not.

But equality? No way, said the diehards. Not without another Civil War. Even then.

Yes, my friends. I want equality. Nothing less. I want all that my God-given powers will enable me to get, then why not equality. Now, catch your breath, for I am going to use an adjective: I am going to say I demand social equality. In this republic we shall be less than freemen, if we have a whit less than that which thrift, education, and honor afford other freemen. If equality, political, economic, and social is the boon of other men in this great country of ours, then equality, political, social, and economic is what we demand.

—John Hope, responding to the arguments of
Booker T. Washington in address before the Colored
Debating Society of Nashville, February 1896

The half century following the *Plessy* decision was a desert in the history of American race relations. To a great degree, this was because equality was simply not part of the national agenda—not in race relations or anywhere else. This was the age of the Robber Barons, men who relished inequality of condition because they believed in equality of opportunity. Any poor boy could theoretically become as rich as they were (and any poor girl could marry one of them).

To be sure, there were those, white and black, who swam against the tide. But such people knew that they were in a decided minority. The conventional wisdom of the era was expressed by Booker T. Washington in a much-celebrated 1895 speech in which he asserted, "In all things that are purely social we can be as separate as the fingers, yet one as the hand in all things essential to human progress." Even before *Plessy*, separate but equal was common sense.

Washington's racial philosophy has sometimes been perceived as naive at best, but he was no patsy. He ran a virtual empire out of his beloved Tuskegee Institute in rural Alabama, and his opinions won him and his followers positions of national power and influence. His emphasis on good work habits and vocational training made vivid sense to generations of African Americans, particularly working-class African Americans, in a way the work of other intellectuals we tend to regard highly today, notably W.E.B. DuBois, did not. He promoted a dream of upward mobility very much like that of Abraham Lincoln, and in principle, there was no reason why separate but equal couldn't work as long as African Americans were free to enjoy the fruits of their labor.

Indeed, in principle, even now there's no reason why separate but equal couldn't work—except that history shows that in the realm of race relations, it never has. And that's because, as a practical matter, separate but equal was simply a legal fiction whose entire reason for existence was a reality of separate but unequal. Proving this in court was very difficult; some exceptionally smart, dedicated people devoted their entire careers to upholding Jim Crow. But by the 1930s and into the 1940s, painstaking legal work was establishing an irrefutable gap between what we as a people said we believed and what we were actually doing.

This gap was proving increasingly difficult to ignore. The onset of the Great Depression showed that the price of national inequality was very great, even frightening, even for those most committed to the status quo: hopeless people have fewer compunctions about destroying fine things they don't believe they can ever have. The Scottsboro case of the 1930s, in which a group of black boys were wrongly convicted of raping a white woman, galvanized black-white solidarity in the North and drew attention to the gross inequities of the legal system. Above all, World War II raised troubling questions about the difference between a Nazi Germany that persecuted Jews and a United States that persecuted blacks. African Americans fought in that war, as they had in every other, and came back ready to fight still another. "I spent four years in the Army to free a bunch of Dutchmen and Frenchmen, and I'm hanged if I'm going to let the Alabama version of the Germans kick me around when I get home," said one black soldier in 1945. "No sirreee-bob! I went into the Army a nigger; I'm comin' out a *man*."

But it took another observer—this one, like Tocqueville a century before, a foreigner—to crystallize the untenable size of the gap between ideals and reality. Swedish sociologist Gunnar Myrdal doesn't use the term "American Dream" in his massive two-volume 1944 study *An American Dilemma*, but it looms large over Myrdal's work. What he does talk about is what he calls the national "Creed," which, as he defines it in his introduction, encompasses "liberty, equality, justice, and fair opportunity for everybody." (Note that "equality" and "fair opportunity" are *not* considered one and the same any more than "liberty" and "justice" are.) The dilemma Myrdal referred to was the conflict between this Creed and the way Americans were actually living their lives.

For Myrdal, inequality lay at the very heart of the American Dilemma:

> Liberty, in a sense, was the easiest to reach. It is a vague ideal: everything turns around *whose* liberty is preserved, to *what extent* and *in what direction*. In society liberty for one may mean the suppression of liberty for others. The result of competition may be who got a head start and who is handicapped. In America as everywhere else—and sometimes, perhaps, on the average, a little more ruthlessly—liberty often provided an opportunity for the stronger to rob the weaker. Against this, the egalitarianism of the Creed has been persistently revolting. The struggle is far from ended.

Indeed, as Myrdal himself presciently recognized, a new phase of the struggle was about to begin.

The question was where and how to wage it. In 1950 a young NAACP attorney named Thurgood Marshall convinced his colleagues to strike at the very heart of separate but equal: racially segregated public schools. This was a bold step. The legality of school segregation had been enshrined since 1850 in *Roberts v. the City of Boston*, a precedent that not even Homer Plessy dared challenge. (His lawyers pointed out that integrated train travel posed far less of a problem than the virtually unthinkable integration of schools.) In what became a group of cases collectively titled *Brown v. Board of Education*, the NAACP represented parents and children who were willing to risk ostracism—or worse—in the name of their aspirations. With admirable concision, historian James Patterson has explained what was at stake:

> What these and other parents yearned for above all was part of the American Dream: equal opportunities for their children. That is why schools, which later events indicated were among the toughest of all institutions to desegregate, became some of the fiercest battlegrounds in conflicts between the races in postwar America. Like many white people, the parents and students who engaged in these struggles believed in a central creed of Americans: schools offered the ticket to advancement in life. It was a creed that forced schools to the center of racial turmoil for the remainder of the century.

> Until 1950 these parents and their allies most often demanded educational quality, not desegregation: a separate-but-equal system of schools was tolerable if it was truly equal. It was only when they became con-

vinced that whites would never grant equality that they began to call for the dismantling of Jim Crow in schools.

In 1954 a unanimous Supreme Court decided in these parents' favor. "In the field of public education the doctrine of 'separate-but-equal' has no place," Chief Justice Earl Warren wrote in his opinion. "Separate educational facilities are inherently unequal."

Brown v. Board of Education is a landmark in American history, chiefly because it redressed a fundamental lapse in the American Creed represented by the *Plessy* decision. But there's a difference between revising the Creed and actually living it out, and the decision raised two unanswered questions. The first was whether the nation would really abide by the ruling; a half century later, the answer remains largely no.

The other question was whether separate but equal would continue in other areas of American life. But this argument, unlike *Plessy* or *Brown*, was no polite courtroom drama. Nor was it conducted in the language of legal briefs. This one played out against the rhythms of a lyrical American Dream.

Tell 'em about the dream, Martin.

**—Gospel singer Mahalia Jackson to Martin Luther King
at the Lincoln Memorial, August 28, 1963**

The American Dream is in many ways a story of omissions, and few omissions have been more glaring than that of the place of women in society. Abigail Adams's instructions to John notwithstanding, the Founding Fathers did not remember the ladies—or women who were not ladies. Frederick Douglass, a stalwart supporter of female suffrage, nevertheless sometimes seemed to regard the word "manhood," with its implication of a human condition that was universally shared, as a virtual synonym for "equality." Inequalities of opportunity *and* condition have been central features of the American experience for women, and while this has changed to some degree in modern times, the American Dream remains problematic. It has largely been a male dream, though one hopes that it does not have to be—will not always be—so.

But history is not entirely barren in this regard. Despite their neglect and exclusion, at least some women have always pursued the American

Dream, and black women in particular, who have historically been more disadvantaged than most, have played a crucial role in legitimating the Dream by extending its purview across gender as well as racial lines. One thinks here of figures such as Phillis Wheatley, the prodigiously gifted eighteenth-century slave poet who dreamed obliquely of freedom, and Madam C. J. Walker, the nineteenth-century entrepreneur of hair care products whose astounding success embodied the faith in the Dream of Upward Mobility with notable appeal for black Americans. But nowhere was the decisive role of women in the making of the American Dream more obvious than in the birth of the modern civil rights movement.

In March of 1954, two months before the *Brown* decision, the Women's Political Council of Montgomery, Alabama, met with the City Commission. The WPC, which had been founded by African Americans after its members were refused membership in the city's League of Women Voters, remonstrated with the commission about the city's treatment of African Americans on municipal buses. When nothing happened, the group began making plans for an organized protest movement.

A year later, in March of 1955, a high school student named Claudette Colvin was arrested for refusing to give up her seat to a white man on a crowded Montgomery bus. Knowing that civil rights activists wanted to make a federal case of it, the judge in the case dismissed the segregation and disorderly conduct charges and instead (implausibly) convicted her of assault. The WPC and other Civil Rights leaders decided not to pursue the case because, as an unwed teenage mother, Colvin made for less than a perfectly "respectable" defendant.

Nine months later, Rosa Parks—a figure civil rights historian Taylor Branch has described as "one of those blips of human nature, offsetting a dozen sociopaths"—was herself riding the bus home from her job as a seamstress at the Montgomery Fair department store. Parks was the executive secretary of the local chapter of the NAACP and had recently written a letter appointing the new minister in town, Martin Luther King Jr., to its executive committee. Parks had no intention of causing a scene, but when the bus filled up and the driver ordered her to give up her seat, something in her rose up. "Go on," she said so softly the driver could barely hear her despite the stunned silence that fell over the bus, "and have me arrested." She was, and the civil rights movement was under way in earnest.

Leadership was provided by the Women's Political Council, which quickly organized a boycott. Meanwhile, Parks's attorney, E. D. Nixon, organized a mass meeting and asked young Reverend King for the use of the basement of his conveniently located church. King agreed but hedged on Nixon's request that King endorse the plan to join the fight in the Parks case and begin a boycott.

Accounts differ as to what actually transpired before and during that meeting in the basement, but when it was over King, who arrived late, had been named president of the new Montgomery Improvement Association. Over the course of the next year, a King-led movement emphasizing community organization and a nonviolent philosophy became front-page news around the country, and King himself a household name. "We do not wish to triumph over the white community," he concluded in an article he wrote early in the boycott. "That would only result in transferring those now on the bottom to the top. But if we can live up to nonviolence in thought and deed, there will emerge an interracial society based on freedom for all." This notion of freedom, King is implicitly suggesting early in his career, is tightly woven with a notion of equality: it is a freedom defined in terms of inclusion ("for all"), not one where some benefit at the expense of others. It is also a notion of freedom that imposes responsibilities. "If the method we use in dealing with equality in the buses can eliminate injustice within ourselves, we shall at the same time be attacking the basis of injustice—man's hostility to man. This can only be done when we challenge the white community to reexamine its assumptions as we are now prepared to reexamine ours."

In many ways, Martin Luther King was an unlikely hero—and an even more unlikely prophet—of the dream of equality. He was born Michael Luther King Jr. on January 15, 1929, the second of three children. By that point, his father had already lived out a distinctively black version of the Dream of Upward Mobility. The son of an abusive Georgia sharecropper, the elder King left home with the help of his mother and educated himself well enough to be admitted to Morehouse College, an all-black institution in Atlanta, and win the hand of Alberta Williams, the daughter of the pastor at a leading black Baptist church in that city. He eventually took over the pastorate of that church and after a trip to Europe in 1934, changed his name, and that of his son, to Martin Luther King. Born into a milieu of privilege and expectation, the boy's destiny seemed chosen.

His gifts were not only material. By the time he was five, young King could sing hymns and recite biblical passages from memory, and he quickly skipped grades, entering Morehouse College when he was fifteen. To some extent, he was spared the petty humiliations of black life, though it was not possible to entirely forget his "place." When he was about fourteen, after delivering an address entitled "The Negro and the Constitution" to a black Elks Club, without notes, a bus driver insisted he give up his seat for two whites. "It was the angriest I have ever been in my life," he later said.

One could argue that even such anger was a luxury for black folks in those years, a callow reaction by someone who simply did not understand how relatively trivial such injustice was (or how dangerous challenging it could be). In any event, King enjoyed an adolescence of

UPLIFTING FIGURE *Martin Luther King Jr. at a press conference, November 1964.*
In shrewdly couching his vision for his country in terms of collective ideals, he redeemed the
American Dream by renewing its moral power. (Photo by Dick Marsico from the World-
Telegram & Sun Collection of the Library of Congress)

notable prerogative, even indulgence, and showed a soft spot for drinking, pool halls—and, especially, romance. He went to Morehouse hoping to become a doctor or lawyer, resistant to paternal pressure to
become a minister. Indeed, for all the lightheartedness of his youth,
there were also shadows and skepticism toward conventional notions of
propriety and success. King was particularly distraught at the death of
his grandmother when he was twelve; on at least one occasion he was
so overtaken with grief that he jumped out a second-story window. He
suffered no physical injury, but scars apparently remained: as he
explained in a reminiscence on her death, he shocked his Sunday-
school teacher by denying the bodily resurrection of Jesus. He did serve
as the assistant pastor at his father's church. But it was only after he was
arrested while working at his summer job in Connecticut—he had been
voted one of the two laziest tobacco harvesters the year before—that he
evaded his father's wrath by announcing his decision to go into the
ministry after finishing his bachelor's degree in sociology at Morehouse.

Which is not to say that he would do it on his father's terms. King
Senior reluctantly allowed his son to attend Crozer Theological Semi-
nary in Chester, Pennsylvania, where he earned another BA, this one in
divinity. It was at Crozer that King fell under the spell of the Social
Gospel, a liberal theological movement, and studied the work of figures
ranging from Karl Marx to Mohandas Gandhi. He was also influenced
by the work of theologian Reinhold Niebuhr, who in works like *Moral
Man and Immoral Society* (1932) emphasized the presence, and inevitabil-
ity, of evil. Upon the completion of his Crozer degree, King
announced his intention to pursue a doctorate in systematic theology at
Boston University. Although his father—still planning for his son to take
over his pulpit—was even more unhappy with this decision than the one
to go to Crozer, he agreed to foot the bill (again) and gave his son a new
Chevrolet for finishing at the top of his class.

King originally enrolled in BU's philosophy department to work
with the renowned theologian Edgar Brightman, best known for his
work on "personalism," which emphasized the human qualities of
God. When Brightman died, he transferred to the university's School
of Theology. He was perceived as a good student, though we now
know he routinely plagiarized his papers as well as his doctoral dissertation and even his subsequent books. He continued to have a busy social
life, ardently pursuing and finally marrying Coretta Scott, a student at

the New England Conservatory of Music, in 1953. He would be a habitual adulterer for much of his marriage.

There is little indication that he contemplated a life as an activist. "King left virtually no references to race or politics among his student papers at Boston University," Taylor Branch reports in his massive multivolume biography. "He took some courses from professors who were known crusaders for racial justice," Branch notes, but did most of his work with "sympathetic non-activists." When he finally began his ministerial career, he evaded his father's grasp once again, deciding, after some hesitation, to accept the pulpit at Dexter Avenue Church in Montgomery, Alabama, in 1954. He was twenty-five years old, and wholly unsuspecting of the events that would thrust him into international prominence the following year.

The point of this small biographical sketch is to suggest that while Martin Luther King Jr. was a boy raised with great expectations, he did not always meet those expectations and exhibited character flaws that could be attributed to the sense of privilege, even vanity, of his upbringing. He was a boy prince—albeit a prince with a common touch. "He told me, fairly early, that he was not a scholar, and that he wasn't really interested in the academic world," a Boston friend later recalled. "He said, 'I like people too much. I want to work with people.'"

This helps explain what brought King to Montgomery. What it doesn't explain—what no biographer has or probably ever will be able to explain—is how it was that King was transformed into the great leader he became. King himself seemed bemused by the transformation that the Montgomery bus boycott wrought. As he reflected in December of 1956: "If anybody had asked me a year ago to head this movement, I tell you very honestly that I would have run a mile to get away from it. I had no intention of being involved in this way." Once he did, though, something happened. "As I became involved, I realized that choice leaves your own hands. The people expect you to give them leadership. You see them growing as they move into action, and then you no longer have a choice, you can't decide *whether* to stay in or get out of it, you *must* stay in it."

In some sense, King was inaccurate or even misleading to say "you no longer have a choice." Of course "you" *always* have a choice: there were no slaves in the civil rights movement. Millions of Americans managed to calibrate their involvement in countless ways (something that Coretta Scott King must surely, and understandably, have told her husband throughout a stormy fifteen-year marriage that included four inevitably neglected children). What King really seems to mean here is that he was driven by a kind of inner compulsion, a moral imperative that for him and others overrode strictly personal considerations. He was a free man, but he was exercising his freedom in the most profound way a human being can: choosing to give it up by committing to something, or someone, else.

And for what did King exercise his freedom? To a great extent, the answer is an American Dream of Equality. Toward the end of his 1958 book *Stride Toward Freedom: The Montgomery Story*, he made this point, as he often would in the coming years, by invoking the charter of the Dream and noting the gap between what we say and what we do:

> Ever since the signing of the Declaration of Independence, America has manifested a schizophrenic personality on the question of race. She has been torn between selves—a self in which she has proudly professed democracy and a self in which she has sadly practiced the antithesis of democracy. The reality of segregation, like slavery, has always had to confront the ideals of democracy and Christianity. Indeed, segregation and discrimination are strange paradoxes in a nation founded on the principle that all men are created equal.

Slavery, which was now dead, was conquered by freedom. Segregation, which remained alive, could only be conquered by equality.

Over the course of the next five years, King was one figure in an extraordinarily diverse movement that fought a series of (nonviolent) battles for equality across a broad front. In places like Little Rock in 1957 and Birmingham in 1963, civil rights leaders won smashing victories by dramatizing the American dilemma, revealing to white America the jeering, ugly, repressive racism whites themselves found repulsive. In others, such as Albany, Georgia, in 1962, the movement was stymied by wily racists who denied leaders the opportunity to make their case quite as vividly. In still others, like the heroic voting rights campaigns of Bob Moses, the movement waged an excruciatingly slow and violent war of attrition that only bore fruit a decade or more later. Ella Baker taught young people leadership skills and helped launch the pivotal Student Non-Violent Coordinating Committee, which launched Freedom Rides; Septima Clark, the daughter of a former slave, taught literacy at her "citizenship schools" designed to create informed voters.

King, who raised money, led protests, and founded the Southern Christian Leadership Council to aid such enterprises, was above all the voice of the movement.

One of the key themes in his repertoire was the American Dream, which he invoked again and again in a series of contexts, all of them relating to equality. "I should like to discuss with you some aspects of the American dream," he told the graduates of Lincoln University, a historically black institution in Chester County, Pennsylvania, in June of 1961. "For in a sense, America is essentially a dream, a dream as yet unfulfilled. It is a dream of a land where men of all races, of all nationalities and creeds can live together as brothers." The following month, in a speech to the National Press Club, he sounded a similar, but more pointed, note. "We are simply seeking to bring into full realization the American Dream—a dream yet unfulfilled. A dream of equality of opportunity, *of privilege and property widely distributed*; a dream of a land where men no longer argue that the color of a man's skin determines the content of his character" (emphasis added). That fall, he saluted student protesters against segregation: "In sitting down at lunch counters, they are in reality standing up for the best of the American Dream." King would repeat versions of this line throughout the coming decade, most notably on the last night of his life. And in December, in an address to an AFL-CIO convention, King spoke of "a dream of a land where men will not take necessities from the many to give luxuries to the few."

The most famous of these invocations was King's celebrated "I Have a Dream" speech, which he delivered at the Lincoln Memorial as part of the March on Washington in August of 1963. "I still have a dream," he said toward the end of the speech, departing from his prepared remarks and improvising freely. "It is a dream deeply rooted in the American dream that one day this nation will rise up and live out the true meaning of its creed—we hold these truths to be self-evident, that all men are created equal." The speech culminated in a rhapsody demanding that freedom ring—a freedom defined by, not against, equality.

In some sense, "I Have a Dream" was the high-water mark for King and his American Dream. The coming years would bring victories—notably the passage of the Civil Rights Act and the Voting Rights Act, two of the most important laws in the history of American egalitarianism—but more defeats. King would encounter more subtle but intractable resistance when he tried to take the movement to northern cities like Chicago, and the movement itself was increasingly splintered. King himself was a target of criticism. Younger blacks derided him for his imperious manner and imperial style, secretly mocking him as "Da Lawd." Some colleagues, like Ella Baker, chafed at his thoughtless sexism, his difficulty in taking women seriously as peers. Others were dismayed by his gluttonous appetites, sexual and otherwise.

King was increasingly unpopular in white America as well, but for different reasons. The FBI under J. Edgar Hoover hounded him mercilessly, tapping his phone lines and spreading as much innuendo as it could without drawing attention to the bureau's role in spreading it. President Lyndon Johnson, who worked with King far more sympathetically and successfully than John F. Kennedy had, was furious at King for his growing opposition to the Vietnam War, metaphorically comparing that opposition to King raping his daughter. But the disenchantment was more widespread than that. In 1967 King failed to make the Gallup Poll list of the ten most admired Americans for the first time in a decade, a telling indication of moral fatigue.

King himself was increasingly disenchanted. His biographers agree he was a depressed man in the final years of his life, which may explain some of his personal excesses. He was particularly dismayed by the ebbing commitment to nonviolence in the movement, a development he understood even as he lamented it. He was even more dismayed at the depth of resistance to change in white America, which belied their—and his—faith in the Creed. Perhaps as a result, King seemed to speak less of the American Dream after 1963.

What he *didn't* stop speaking about—indeed, what he spoke *more* about, and what may explain his sagging popularity—was equality. It is a kind of poetic justice that he was killed in Memphis while working on behalf of striking sanitation workers, engaged in what was often viewed as the lowliest of professions. At the end of his life, King decided he could no longer be silent about things he had held his tongue about, among them the disproportionate impact of the Vietnam War on African Americans—and the immorality of the war in general. His last major organizing effort, the so-called Poor People's Campaign, explicitly widened its scope to cross racial lines, and not only white-black ones. And he became less inspirational, more explicitly challenging, to his national audience. The opening chapter of his final book, *Where Do We Go From Here: Chaos or Community* (1967), is revealing in this regard:

Negroes have proceeded from a premise that equality means what it says, and they have taken white Americans at their word when they talked of it as an objective. But most whites in America in 1967, including many persons of good-will, proceed from a premise that equality is a loose expression of improvement. White America is not even psychologically organized to close the gap—essentially it seeks only to make it less painful and obvious but in most respects to retain it. . . . A good many observers have remarked that if equality could come at once the Negro would not be ready for it. I submit that the white American is even more unprepared.

His irritation at white hypocrisy is apparent in "Remaining Awake Through a Great Revolution," his final Sunday morning sermon. In it, King suggested disgust with the false pieties of the American Dream of Upward Mobility:

In 1863 the Negro was told he was free as a result of the Emancipation Proclamation being signed by Abraham Lincoln. . . . It simply said "You're free," and left him there penniless, illiterate, not knowing what to do. And the irony of it all is that at the same time the nation failed to do anything for the black man—through an act of Congress it was giving away millions of acres of land in the West and Midwest*—which meant that it was willing to undergird its white peasants with an economic floor.

But not only did it give the land, it build land-grant colleges to teach them how to farm. Not only that, it provided county agents to further their expertise in farming: not only that, as the years unfolded it provided low interest rates so that they could mechanize their farms. And to this day thousands of these very persons are receiving millions of dollars in federal subsidies not to farm. And these are so often the very people who tell Negroes that they must lift themselves up by their bootstraps. It's all right to tell a man a man to lift himself up by his bootstraps, but it is a cruel jest to tell a bootless man that he ought to lift himself up by his own bootstraps.

Freedom is not enough. Nor is an equality of opportunity that is nothing more than an empty abstraction. For the Dream to live, it has to be more than that.

* King is referring to the Homestead Act.

How much more? Is the solution equality of condition? Not even King went this far, and even if he had, it is abundantly clear the country would never have gone along with him. If anything, such a possibility is even less likely now. There is something in our collective imagination that refuses to accept it. As libertarians are fond of reminding us, equality can restrain freedom, depriving people of the possibilities of achieving their potential, of achieving their dreams (thus the frequent arguments in favor of "gifted and talented" programs in public schools). But even if we cannot, or should not, demand equality of condition, it is clear that the very imprecision, even vagueness, of equality of opportunity demands a vigilance that we tend to resist out of laziness or fear. Equality without freedom may be a totalitarian nightmare. But freedom without equality has been an oppressive reality for much of American history—and that's the "better" half. To survive in a new century, the American Dream must be more than an excuse to ignore or forget.

The Negroes of this country may never be able to rise to power, but they are very well placed indeed to precipitate chaos and ring down the curtain on the American Dream.

This has everything to do, of course, with the nature of that dream and the fact that we Americans, of whatever color, do not dare examine it and are far from having made it a reality. There are too many things we do not wish to know about ourselves. People are not, for example, terribly anxious to be equal (equal, after all, to what and to whom?) but they love the idea of being superior.

—James Baldwin, *The Fire Next Time*, 1963

"I didn't like him much," Jack tells me.

I've been describing my latest book project and my recent reading about Martin Luther King at a dinner party in Providence, Rhode Island, with a small group of septuagenarians hosted by my graduate school mentor, Jack Thomas. But then one of the guests, the kindly widow of another one of my teachers, Bill McGloughlin (himself a much-beloved political activist), mentions that she had actually met King some thirty-five years before when he gave a talk at Brown University. She found him a man of great bearing and dignity, even intimidating. "But I liked him very much," she says.

Jack had also met King. He had been at Brown at the time of King's visit but described shaking his hand during a different encounter, when he and his wife saw him emerging from the Copley Plaza Hotel in Boston. Whether it was King's manner in that exchange or some preconceived notions of the civil rights leader, he was not impressed. King seemed formal to the point of arrogance, a man far too enamored of the exalted role of the African American preacher to be a convincing leader of the masses.* It's a reaction he regrets in retrospect, one he is now far more inclined to think says more about him than King. More than ever, he's inclined to trust the instincts of women like his now-dead wife (whose idea it had been to shake King's hand) or of Virginia McGloughlin, who is sitting beside him, rather than his own.

Listening to these people talk unself-consciously about a legend, I feel a little like a kid a century earlier eavesdropping on the reminiscences of Civil War veterans describing momentary interactions with Abraham Lincoln. The encounters themselves are trivial, and yet all the more striking, even meaningful, because this triviality somehow conveys an authenticity that you can't get out of a book.

It also makes me wonder: how would I have reacted to meeting Martin Luther King? I can't say for sure. At some visceral level, I suspect my reaction would be something like Jack's. But I'm not sure I'd be wrong to feel the way he did any more than I think he was. In part, this is because King himself would hardly treat a white stranger the same way he would have a member of his congregation (or, for that matter, a black stranger). But this is also a matter of the "two selves" King once alluded to in one of his sermons, selves that loosely correspond to public and private, formal and informal—good and evil.

As any Puritan would have said, the struggle between good and evil is to a great extent one between pride and humility. So did King. In the last sermon he delivered from his pulpit—his father's pulpit, which he finally consented to take over in 1960—King spoke of "the drum-major

---

* This was not an isolated reaction. Journalist Marshall Frady, who covered King for *Newsweek* in the 1960s, describes him in a recent biography as having "a manner of unremitting and ponderous gravity in his deacon-sober suits. His round face, black as asphalt, wore a bland gaze of almost Oriental impassiveness, an improbable bourgeois placidness—yet with, I still remember, almost meltingly sweet eyes. But on the whole, he could have been a comfortably prosperous funeral home director, or merely what among other things he indeed was, the Baptist preacher of a big-city church."

instinct," a thirst for individual distinction that competes with a truer desire for equality and justice. As is true of any good sermon, the power of King's words derived from their honesty, their willingness to confront his own weakness as part of a process that asked his listeners to confront theirs. Speculating on his own death, which would occur exactly two months later, King implored the congregation not to remember him for accomplishments like the Nobel Peace Prize he received in 1964. Instead, he said,

> I'd like somebody to mention that day, that Martin Luther King, Jr., tried to give his life serving others. I'd like for somebody to say that day that Martin Luther King, Jr., tried to love somebody. . . . I want you to be able to say that day that I did try to feed the hungry. And I want you to be able to say that day, that I did try, in my life, to clothe those who were naked. I want you to say, on that day, that I did try, in my life, to visit those who were in prison. I want you to say that I tried to love and serve humanity.

He tried. It's clear that he came up short, both in meeting his own standards and in realizing the Dream of Equality. May we all dream, and fail, as well as he did.

CHAPTER 5

DETACHED HOUSES:
THE DREAM OF HOME OWNERSHIP

In 1969, MY PARENTS, sister, and I moved from our row-house apartment in the Jackson Heights section of Queens, New York, to a first-floor rental in a two-family house on Long Island. The reason was the racial desegregation of our neighborhood public schools. The civil rights movement, whose first stirrings had focused on southern school systems in the 1950s, had spread across the country and was increasingly coming closer to home. This was apparent in the racial violence that now engulfed cities like Newark no less than Birmingham. Perhaps even more frightening than spectacular eruptions like the riots that followed the assassination of Martin Luther King were more lasting structural changes in everyday life. The previous year, a political struggle over school integration erupted in the Brooklyn neighborhoods of Ocean Hill–Brownsville, and in the ensuing arguments, which resulted in a state takeover of the schools, even former allies—the teachers' union, black activists, Jewish residents—found themselves bitterly divided.

My father, a New York City firefighter who worked in the largely black Brooklyn neighborhood of Bedford-Stuyvesant, was not the kind of man to participate in protests or to carefully follow Supreme Court rulings. But he knew which way the political winds were blowing. He was unhappy about the fact that as a kindergartener, I knew much more about Martin Luther King Jr. than about George Washington, about whom I knew nothing. He was also opposed to my pending transfer, via busing, to a more remote school. But in the broadest terms, he had concerns about the safety and quality of a system that, to put it more euphemistically than he would, was undergoing a difficult transition. So when he learned about an available first-floor apartment in a house in the nearby suburban town of Port Washington, he and my mother, who tended to share his views on such matters, left the city in which they had spent their entire lives in search of better ones for their children.

Port Washington, only about ten miles east of the Queens border, was demographically much further away, and not only because of its racial composition. Though we lived in its least affluent neighborhood of Manorhaven, the town was decidedly upscale. The street I lived on was a dead end, and I would often cut through some woods and end up among the mansions of Sands Point—the thinly fictionalized "East Egg" of *The Great Gatsby*. My mother, who as early as I can remember inculcated both a sense of pride in our working-class origins and an expectation for upward mobility, strayed far outside her decidedly urban background to serve as a den mother for my Cub Scout troop, a stretch she made to further my socialization in this new world. I look back on this period of my childhood fondly.

But Port Washington was also problematic for my parents. For one thing, they were in a sense only pseudo-suburbanites, because they were tenants in someone else's home, not owners of their own. For another, my father was not entirely comfortable with the progressive educational style of Port Washington public schools, which emphasized newfangled ideas like open classrooms and a nontraditional curriculum. Finally, while I don't believe any member of our family was ever subject to condescension or ill-treatment, the gap in class status between us and many of the people we dealt with troubled him greatly. I've been told on a number of occasions that my father became determined to move again after learning that I had called home from a friend's parents' car phone, such things being much more exotic than they are now. My mother, who loved the town but who also worried about her children growing up with their noses pressed up against the glass of their classmates' windows, reluctantly agreed.

Unlike some of their contemporaries, who jumped at the chance to buy houses at the first available opportunity, my parents were ambivalent at best. They did not particularly welcome the burdens of debt, repairs, and taxes that home ownership entailed, and the real estate business held little charm for them. And yet for them, no less than for those with a penchant for carpentry or gardening, the decision to buy a house reflected a series of hopes and fears inextricably (if silently) bound in mortgage. One factor, as I've already suggested, was racism. But there were others, too, ranging from a thirst for privacy and autonomy (I remember vividly my parents' rage when our landlord in Port Washington raised the rent, and how my parents refused to make eye contact with him) to a Dream of Upward Mobility that perhaps paradoxically rested on family stability—and good schools.

After what my sister and I regarded as an agonizingly boring search, my parents finally found something they liked and could afford. They scraped together two thousand dollars of their own and borrowed two thousand dollars of my paternal grandmother's money, and, with the help of a Federal Housing Authority–backed mortgage, they were able to buy a quarter-acre split-level ranch for thirty-five thousand dollars in Northport, a small town about twenty-five miles east of Port Washington. My mother still lives there. The mortgage, along with a 1988 home equity loan that financed a finished basement apartment, was paid off in 1999.

And so it was that I finished my childhood at the tail end of the Baby Boom in a virtually all-white suburban town with friends who were generally (but not outrageously) wealthier than I was. The three-bedroom house in which I played, ate, and slept is, by almost any standard, an unprepossessing one, if for no other reason than there are about fifty more just like it in the postwar circular housing development in which it is situated. But, you see, it was *mine*: the bedroom, which could barely fit my bed, a desk, and a bulletin board that I filled with movie ticket stubs, newspaper cartoons, and photographs; the yard, bounded by a six-foot stockade fence, in which I reenacted entire sporting events single-handedly to imagined audiences of millions; the kitchen, with its gleaming Formica counters and enameled appliances. Each autumn, there were leaves to rake, and each spring, a lawn to mow.

It wasn't until later that I began to reckon with the historical forces that brought me to that house. To some extent, this is because my parents didn't want me to know. (Alcoholism, mental illness, poverty, and fraud figure in the fragments I've picked up from both sides of the family.) I don't doubt that the move to Long Island was principally a matter of devotion to my sister and me, but I suspect it also represented an opportunity for them to clean the slate, to start over. Indeed, every trip we made back to the city to visit my relatives' apartments somehow seemed like a trip back in time, our car a sealed capsule protecting us from a harsh frontier environment that would swallow us up if we ever broke down or even stopped. I was always a little afraid, and always a little excited, by the visits.

Looking back now, however, I see their flight from Queens—and our forays back there—in a less heroic light. Although racial and class segregation have more or less become a given in U.S. history, I feel shame about my essentially segregationist beginnings—as well as a sense of shame about my shame over my parents' actions. I have tried to take refuge in any number of justifications: that they were far from unusual; that the concerns they had about educational safety and quality were legitimate in their own right; that my father could say not only that some of his best friends were black but that he in fact had pulled black and Latino children out of burning buildings; and so on. At the very least, the facts surrounding my childhood complicate my nostalgia.

But if I cannot in good conscience straightforwardly celebrate this myth, I don't regard it as an outright lie, either. Frequent statements to the contrary, the United States was never a "free," "open," or "virgin" land. It has, nevertheless, afforded opportunities for a great many people (including some black and Latino people, among others) to do something that was previously difficult, if not impossible: acquire a place they could call their own.

"The American Dream of owning a home," we call it. No American Dream has broader appeal, and no American Dream has been quite so widely realized. Roughly two-thirds of Americans owned their homes at the start of this century, and it seems reasonable to believe that many of the remaining third will go on to do so. And if, like other American Dreams, this one is imperfect, even fatally flawed, it is also extraordinarily resilient and versatile. My story was only a fragment in a late chapter of what had already been a very long story.

*For the Lord thy God bringeth thee into a good land. A land of wheat, and
barley and vines, and fig trees and pomegranates; a land of oil olive and
honey; A land wherein thou shalt eat bread without scarceness, thou shalt not
lack any thing in it; a land whose stones are iron, and out of whose hills thou
mayest dig brass.*

—Deuteronomy 8:7–9, King James Bible, 1611

In the beginning, there was land. The United States of today may be a
"welfare" state, but as Dorothee Kocks reminds us in her evocative
book *Dream a Little,* it began as a frontier state. If the basic currency of
the welfare state was cash, the coin of the realm in the frontier state
was land. For much of American history, in fact, land was a more practical and accessible financial instrument than cash, which was rare,
unstable, and, given the lack of a national currency, difficult to use.
While other goods could function as a medium of exchange (the
wampum of Indians and tobacco of farmers, for example), land was of
particular importance very early in American history.

Land, however, was not always viewed as a desirable or even obvious commodity. At least initially, many indigenous American peoples
thought land could no more be bought or sold than the air they
breathed or the water they drank. Spanish and French colonists typically measured wealth in terms of the gold, fish, furs, or other forms of
wealth they—or in many cases, their slaves—extracted from North
America and shipped home for mercantile purposes. Controlling land
was of course important for such enterprises, but more as an instru-
mental means to an end than something to be prized in its own
right—particularly because so much of their dominions consisted of
deserts, bayous, forests, mountain ranges, or other environments that
seemed unprofitable at best and dangerous at worst.

Still, even many of these people knew that land, particularly arable
land, could produce great wealth as well as confer less direct benefits
for strategically minded generals, evangelically minded missionaries, or
thrill-seeking adventurers. Moreover, land was a cheap way for imperial
governments to court or reward important subjects. From the beginning, then, in America not only was an abstraction such as money
important, but so too was the development of a particular place where
a variety of people could transform, acquire, or lose lives.

A notion of America as a particular place was especially important for British colonists. In many cases, their motives were the same as their European rivals, but as relatively late arrivals in the colonial free-for-all, they began by claiming a stretch of territory—the Atlantic seaboard— that was far less remunerative than, say, the sugar plantations of the Caribbean or the gold mines of Peru. Of course, the British did acquire Caribbean colonies in short order, and the tobacco plantations of Virginia soon began generating revenue for the Crown. And like their counterparts, English monarchs also used land as a commodity; Pennsylvania, for example, was acquired as a whole and sold off in pieces by William Penn, who gained the right to do so as payment of a debt to his father.

But far more than the Spanish, French, or Dutch, the British saw the American landscape itself as an asset in its own right. Moreover, it could be more than a mere marketable commodity: it could serve as a *home*. Indeed, it quickly became apparent to everyone, especially the Indians, that the English came to stay. For many settlers, America was a refuge from hostile outsiders as well as a livelihood that could confer upward mobility: a land of dreams. This belief, whatever its factual validity (which, needless to say, varied widely), established the framework for the frontier society that would sweep across the continent.

Insofar as the British government looked at the possibilities of this frontier, it was as likely to see problems as possibilities. The mercantile orientation of English politics and economics made the Atlantic Ocean, not the American interior, the focus of imperial policy. Given the threat of French and Indian military power and the costs of containing it, the West was to serve as a perimeter that demarcated limits, not a seedbed for development—and certainly not a homeland that had to be protected. Many American colonists, among them George Washington, chafed at this policy. Indeed, tension over the disposition of western territory was a major factor in the political imperatives that led southerners in particular to support the Revolution.

With the achievement of independence the United States truly became a frontier state, in that land became an avowed instrument of government policy. Individual colonies like New York and North Carolina had claimed ownership of territory extending directly west to the Mississippi River but surrendered such claims in return for the national government assuming their debts. Led by Thomas Jefferson, Congress in 1785 drafted a plan for survey and sale of this land. Seeking to avoid the tangled claims that had characterized the settlement of Kentucky, they divided western territories into townships composed of thirty-six sections of one square mile (640 acres) each. These grids—one in each town to be designated for the support of public schools—would have a decisive impact on the future landscape of the nation, ranging from the street-and-avenue patterns of many midwestern cities to the quilt-like landscape seen from an aircraft. In 1787 Jefferson played a pivotal role in congressional passage of the Northwest Ordinance, which codified federal supervision of these territories and the criteria for statehood for the states of Ohio, Indiana, Illinois, Michigan, and Wisconsin. Subsequent acquisitions like the Louisiana Purchase from France, Florida from Spain, and Texas from Mexico were integrated into the nation on the tracks laid down in the Ordinances of 1785 and 1787.

To be sure, the circumstances surrounding these developments were not always orderly: treaties were made with Indians and Mexicans under duress, and thousands of settlers squatted illegally. Moreover, Congress rejected Jefferson's proposals to give the land away for free, to allow community self-government rather than the rule of appointed judges and governors, and to ban slavery in the Southwest (though it was banned in the Northwest Territory). But for all the limits and omissions of such policies, they nevertheless held out promise for a society in which an unprecedented proportion of a national polity could, and did, literally have a stake in their country. Though this vision is often rightly attributed to Jefferson, it was Washington who expressed it with unusual clarity and optimism. "I wish to see the sons and daughters of the world in Peace and busily employed in the . . . agreeable amusement of fulfilling the first and great commandment—*Increase and Multiply*: as an encouragement to which we have opened the fertile plains of the Ohio to the poor, the needy, and the oppressed of the Earth," he wrote in a letter to the marquis de Lafayette, at the end of the Revolution. "Anyone therefore who is heavy laden or who wants land to cultivate, may repair thither & abound as in the Land of promise, with milk and honey."

Still, if the United States professed a far more egalitarian basis for distributing national wealth than had ever existed, the fact remained that ordinary farmers and their families were not the only, or even primary, beneficiaries of the frontier state. Speculators of widely varying scrupulousness were always a very large part of the equation, and the prospect of road, canal, and, especially, railroad construction promised to make very small groups of people very rich. Politicians promoted the frontier state for reasons that did not completely overlap: as a vehicle for extending trade to the Far East; as a means for rapid industrialization; as a "safety valve" for teeming cities facing the prospect of urban unrest. (Newspaper editor Horace Greeley issued his famous call "Go West, young man, go forth into the country" in 1837 as a means for dealing with financial panic that engulfed the nation that year.)

Amid this panoply of motives, however, there remained those who championed the value of the independent farmer cultivating a home as an end unto itself: Jefferson's republican dream of the independent yeoman still loomed large. Illinois politician Stephen Douglas, who wanted a transcontinental railroad as much as anyone, nevertheless emphasized the need to "subdu[e] the wilderness, and people it with a hardy and industrious population," an objective at least as important as increased trade with India and China.

This desire to extend what was widely called an "Empire of Liberty" made land not only the defining criterion of what it meant to be truly free in the United States but also a check on the growth of slavery. This was not immediately apparent. In the early nineteenth century, slavery entered new territory easily. Alabama and Mississippi, for example, were settled by southerners and quickly integrated into the plantation system. But by mid-century, it was apparent that much of the territory acquired from the Louisiana Purchase (and later Mexico) would become nonslave states, less for moral reasons than because of the relative economic impracticality of the slave system—a system that to a great degree depended upon people working land they did *not* own. While many southerners remained enthusiastic about territorial expansion in the decades before the Civil War, others were increasingly skeptical that a nation of freeholders was really in their interest.

As a number of historians have noted, the key to the eventual success of the Republican Party in 1860 lay in the way it could unite a number of disparate and even conflicting constituencies: abolitionists and racists; easterners and westerners; entrepreneurs and factory workers. The fulcrum of their ability to do this was land—specifically their proposal for a Homestead Act that would finally enact Jefferson's vision for giving away western territory to individuals. Interestingly enough, much of the early energy for this proposal originated in the East, not only among boosters like Greeley but also among more radical figures like activist-actress Frances ("Fanny") Wright and George Henry Evans, leader of the Workingmen's Party that became a powerful presence in New York politics during the 1830s and 1840s. More prominent national eastern leaders were indifferent to giving away land to home-steaders—U.S. Senator William Seward of New York complained in 1854 the idea would give "the interested cupidity of the pioneer" undue influence in national policy—until western politicians made clear that such a proposal, which enjoyed widespread support, would provide a crucial incentive to bring the region into an emerging political coalition that fused free soil, free labor, and free men.

As proposed in the Republican platform of 1860 and signed by President Abraham Lincoln in 1862, the Homestead Act was fairly simple. Any family head or adult male who was a citizen (or, in the case of immigrants, a male who simply declared an intention to become a citizen) could claim 160 acres of land in the public domain. In return, the recipient need only pay a small registration fee and promise to remain there for five years, at which point the title would be transferred to the settler. At the time of its passage, eighty-three million acres were available for settlement; fifteen million more from California, Colorado, Washington, and Wisconsin were added later.

The Homestead Act enjoyed its greatest success in the central and upper Midwest, where soil and climate conditions could support family farming. By 1880 a little over half of the 242,000 new farms in Kansas, Nebraska, the Dakota territories, and Minnesota were acquired this way. (The Act accounted for about two-thirds of Minnesota's new farms.) In 1866 a faction of Republicans in Congress sought to extend the homesteading to former slaves, but when Senator Thaddeus Stevens sought to add the forfeited estates of Confederates to the pool of available land, the measure was decisively defeated. Two days later, Congress did pass the Southern Homestead Act introduced by Indiana representative George Julian, an energetic supporter of the original act, which was a more modest measure that gave black and loyal white Americans the opportunity to acquire land that would not interfere with existing property rights. Here, in effect, was a law that could largely realize the celebrated promise of "forty acres and a mule"—a temporary ad-hoc war measure implemented by General William T. Sherman in Georgia and South Carolina in 1865, but one African Americans never forgot.

Unfortunately, the original Homestead Act and its successors never lived up to their original promise. Blacks and whites alike had trouble acquiring the knowledge, materials, and capital necessary to farm even land that was given away free, and speculators gobbled up much of it. Moreover, much of the American West, particularly as one crossed into the arid, grassy Great Plains—known for much of the nineteenth century as "the Great American Desert"— was not really suited to farming, and not even measures like the Enlarged Homestead Act of 1909, which offered larger tracts to settlers willing to irrigate it, made it attractive. Ironically, the cavernous spaces of virtually uninhabitable land led many westerners to congregate in cities and towns; as early as 1880 the West was the most urbanized region of the country. It still is.

But if the *reality* of the independent freeholder left a lot to be desired, the *dream* of the independent freeholder demonstrated great resilience, one that went to the very heart of American identity. Frederick Jackson Turner, whose 1893 essay "The Significance of the Frontier in American History" gave this vision its most systematic expression, laid out the premises of the frontier state with unusual directness as an 1896 school dedication in his hometown of Portage, Wisconsin:

> Americans had a safety valve for social danger, a bank account on which they might continually draw to meet losses. This was the vast unoccupied domain that stretched from the borders of the settled area to the Pacific Ocean. . . . No grave social problem could exist while the wilderness at the edge of civilizations [*sic*] opened wide its portals to all who were oppressed, to all who with strong arms and stout heart desired to hew a home and a career for themselves. Here was an opportunity for social development continually to begin over again, wherever society gave signs of breaking into classes. Here was a magic fountain of youth in which America continually bathed and was rejuvenated.

The "social development" and "rejuvenation" Turner spoke of was a seamless process whereby the Indian gave way to the explorer and hunter, who in turn gave way to the trader, who then gave way to the rancher, who in turn gave way to the (beloved) farmer who tended land on which he built his home. Eventually, family farms gave way to towns and cities, but by then the process was presumably beginning over again somewhere out West. To his critics—in decades to come, there would be many—this was pure fantasy. Moreover, even those who embraced it most fully were plagued by an unsettling feeling. Note the elegiac tone of Turner's speech: he spoke in the past tense. Indeed, Turner's purpose in writing his celebrated "Significance of the Frontier in American History" (which he delivered at the 1893 Chicago Columbian Exposition honoring the four hundredth anniversary of the European discovery of America) was to declare the frontier, which he defined as an area with less than two people per square mile, was closed. "And now," he concluded, "four centuries from the discovery of America, at the end of a hundred years of life under the Constitution, the frontier has gone, and with its going has closed the first period in American history."

This notion of a closed frontier would haunt many Americans for the next century. In 1920, Turner himself, finishing a career that in some ways was a disappointment (he failed to write a book-length masterwork), wrote that "it is to the realm of the spirit, to the domain of ideals and legislation, that we must look for Western influence on democracy in our own days." A political Progressive, he hoped public institutions ranging from the federal government to state universities could provide a viable alternative. For the rest of the twentieth century, his imagined heirs proclaimed a series of disembodied "new" frontiers—from space exploration to the Internet—that would somehow extend the original one. The hunter, trapper, cowboy, and farmer would be replaced by the researcher, engineer, bureaucrat, and consumer. A livelihood would be made not in fields but in factories and office buildings. And the homes they returned to would not be "open" tracts but rather planned "developments" specifically zoned to house such workers.

Amid all these technological, political, and symbolic displacements, however, land never disappeared. Indeed, in the twenty-first century it remains as important as ever. To be sure, the local supermarket has taken the place of the family farm, which was virtually supplanted by agribusiness. But if anything, the desire for—and yes, even the reality of—a family homestead was as widespread as ever. Amber waves of grain may have receded into the distance. But a new frontier vista offered a clear view of an indigenous weed in much of North America: crabgrass.

Americans have long tended to see city and country as separate places, more isolated from each other than connected. We carefully partition our landscape into urban places, rural places, and wilderness. Although we often cross the symbolic boundaries between them—seeking escape or excitement, recreation or renewal—we rarely reflect on how tightly bound together they really are.

—**William Cronon,** *Nature's Metropolis: Chicago and the Great West,* 1991

In 1920, as Frederick Jackson Turner's career was ending, the official U.S. census showed that for the first time, more Americans lived in cities than on farms. This was a much-discussed statistic then and for decades afterward, and one that marked the arrival of a new social order. And yet that order was relatively short-lived. While cities remained important in American life—notwithstanding a tendency to fear and deride them as a source of many evils—the nation was not decisively urban for very long. The census of 1990 confirmed something that many had taken for granted much earlier: that most Americans lived in neither city nor countryside but in that demographic hybrid known as a suburb.

Conceptually, the American suburb can trace its origins to an unlikely union of Thomas Jefferson and Alexander Hamilton. From the Jeffersonian strain in American history, it drew on widely shared assumptions about the beneficent influence of nature, small communities, and home ownership. At the same time, the suburb reflected Hamiltonian realities about the centrality of cities as the source of Americans' livelihoods, and of commerce, not self-sufficient farming, as the true engine of national development. The resulting hybrid was pastoral—a managed geography that combined human effort and repose.

Strictly speaking, the suburb is of English origin and, in the larger scheme of human history, somewhat unusual. On most of the earth for most of the time, the outskirts of cities were considered unattractive terrain and relegated to the poorest people; the very prefix of the word "suburb" suggests precisely this inferiority. In the twentieth century, for example, the slums of cities from Paris to Rio de Janeiro were located on their outskirts, while their central districts remained the most sought-after residential turf. Beginning in the eighteenth century, however, Londoners began to construct what one historian has called "bourgeois utopias": strategically located garden communities outside

HOUSES REPRESENTATIVE *Aerial view of Levittown, New York, 1954. The product of an unlikely marriage between the Jeffersonian love of the country and the Hamiltonian emphasis on the centrality of the city, suburbia has long been the site of the most widely realized American Dream: home ownership. (Photo from the World-Telegram & Sun Newspaper Photograph Collection of the Library of Congress)*

of, but within commuting distance of, large cities. Such communities were the repositories of an emerging domestic ideology that emphasized close family connections, Protestant religion, and a belief in pastoral settings as the best havens for nurturing a responsible citizenry. Among the first was the town of Clapham Common, a village about five miles from London Bridge when the first families began moving there in the 1730s. By the end of the century, it had become recognizably suburban in a modern sense: a low-density community dependent on the city economically but dominated by single-family houses in park-like settings.

In the United States, the first traces of a suburban style surfaced at the turn of the nineteenth century in places like Beacon Hill, a vacant lot at the edge of Boston. This was, however, still part of the city, a neighborhood within walking distance of downtown. A more direct forerunner of suburbia was the early nineteenth-century town of Brooklyn, New York, located across the East River from Manhattan. It began growing rapidly when ferry services began moving commuters for a standard fare of two cents each way. Indeed, Brooklyn grew so fast that it soon became a major city in its own right before it became part of greater New York City in 1898. Meanwhile, in a manner reminiscent of Turner's frontier, other western Long Island towns—Williamsburg, Bedford-Stuyvesant, Bushwick—evolved from rural hamlet to city neighborhood, pushing the urban frontier still farther back.

Ferries notwithstanding, suburban development for anyone not rich enough to own a horse and carriage could not really begin to develop until new forms of transportation—notably the railroad—made it possible to transport people beyond city limits relatively quickly and cheaply. Once that began to happen, increasing numbers of the well-to-do began to leave the central cities, with their bustling workshops, jostling social classes, and increasing urban problems, for homes on the perimeter. The towns along Philadelphia's fabled Main Line—Ardmore, Haverford, Bryn Mawr—became bywords for suburban affluence after the Civil War. So, too, did Chicago suburbs like Evanston, Lake Forest, and Highland Park.

The steam-engine railroad, however, was only one form of the urban transportation revolution of the late nineteenth century. Other varieties, which involved intracity travel, were at least as important. The horsecar, which combined the efficiency of a vehicle on tracks with the economy and flexibility of a horse, was first employed in New

York in the 1830s and remained in use across the country until the end of the century. Cable car service was popular in Chicago and especially San Francisco, where it was particularly well adapted to steep inclines like Nob Hill. The most important variation on locomotion, though, was the streetcar (and its close relation, the subway), particularly those that ran on electricity rather than steam or coal. First used in Cleveland in 1884, the streetcar spread widely and by the turn of the century had become the dominant form of transportation in the United States, accounting for over half of the nation's twelve thousand miles of electrified tracks. It is interesting to note how quickly the streetcar spread when one considers how long it took the automobile, which was invented at about the same time, to achieve its dominance.

In the short run, these developments helped cities, which grew not only in population but also in geographic size. The most striking example was Philadelphia, whose geographic boundaries grew from 2 to 130 square miles in 1854, briefly making it the largest city in the world. (Paris replaced it five years later.) Many towns annexed to Philadelphia were suburbs, which, like many such communities across the country, agreed to the change in status to cut their costs, raise their prestige, or satisfy (often corrupt) politicians and businessmen. Chicago expanded in a similar fashion in 1889, adding 133 miles to city limits. More common, however, were cities that grew in piecemeal fashion, such as Detroit, which annexed a series of townships, from Greenfield to Grosse Point, between 1880 and 1918.

By the late nineteenth century, however, there were already signs that urban growth would have limits. Beginning in 1868 the city of Boston doubled its area by annexing the cities and towns of Roxbury, West Roxbury, Dorchester, Charlestown, and Brighton. But in 1874 Brookline, a community that called itself "the richest town in the world," voted decisively against annexation. From that point on, affluent suburban areas, like Chicago's Oak Park or Oakland's Alameda County, rejected incorporation with cities. When Greater New York was created in 1898, the eastern part of Queens broke off to form the new county of Nassau. And while the southern part of what had once been Westchester County became the borough of the Bronx, border communities like Bronxville incorporated themselves to prevent precisely this possibility. Only in western cities did annexation remain common. In 1870, Los Angeles consisted of 29 square miles; by 1980 it was 465, with its greatest growth occurring between 1910 and 1930.

Cities like Houston (25 to 556), Indianapolis (11 to 279), and San Antonio (36 to 267) are comparable.

The reluctance of many communities to integrate with cities reflects the growing class and racial segregation of the nation's metropolitan areas, a segregation apparent everywhere from the types of work being done to the types of music being listened to. At the same time, however, what may be most striking about the course of urbanization and surburbanization in the United States is the degree to which it cut across American society as a whole. Horace Greeley of "Go west, young man" fame had it backwards: as industrialization proceeded, the country was not the safety valve for the city, but rather the *city* served as a refuge from the *country*. And, increasingly, the suburb served as a refuge from both.

Wherever they happened to live, Americans seemed united by an exceptional penchant for home ownership. It is notable, but perhaps not coincidental, that the greatest fervor appeared to come from immigrants. One study of Detroit, for example, showed that in 1900, 55 percent of Germans, 46 percent of the Irish, and 44 percent of Poles owned their own homes—figures that would have been virtually inconceivable in Europe at the time, particularly in Ireland and (what was once) Poland, whose residents were often virtual prisoners of foreign powers. In the immigrant-laden Massachusetts city of Newburyport in the 1930s, Irish and Italians tended to make home ownership an even greater priority than their children's educations; the percentage of those with property holdings who lived in the city for twenty years ranged from 63 to 78 percent. Still another study, this one of cities with more than a hundred thousand residents at the turn of the century, found that the proportion of immigrants who owned their own homes ranged from 11 percent in New York City to 58 percent in Toledo. Among the native-born, by contrast, 15 percent owned homes in New York City; the figure reached 40 percent in Los Angeles. As one noted historian, Kenneth Jackson, has observed, "Obviously variation by city and by ethnic group was enormous, but from an international perspective what is most important about these statistics is that it was not a native-American, or middle-class, or urban phenomenon, but an American phenomenon." Moreover, Jackson noted, while African Americans tended to encounter discrimination that blunted their own aspirations for home owning, and Jews' religious practices tended

toward group cohesion, all other ethnic groups were migrating to suburbia in the early decades of the twentieth century.

A number of interrelated factors contributed to the widespread
opportunities for home ownership. Some, like the plenitude of wood on
a continent whose forests had not been denuded, were intrinsic to the
land itself. Others were more technological. The advent of the balloon
frame house in the 1830s in Chicago revolutionized American architecture by making housing far cheaper and simpler to construct. (The
characteristic wooden beams that define a building long before it is finished continue to be widespread in American contracting into the
twenty-first century.) Still other factors were economic: though one
often hears assertions about cheap labor being crucial for national economic health, the United States was to a great degree a country built
on high wages, which not only stimulated labor-saving technological
innovation but also gave workers sufficient wages to buy houses, which
furthered economic development still more. Finally, the elaboration of
a transportation infrastructure effectively brought more (and cheaper)
land within the purview of a metropolitan area, creating an ever-
widening radius of housing within commuting distance of cities.

All these elements were firmly in place by 1900. At that point,
though, a new element appeared on the scene that would have a transformative effect: the automobile. Its impact on American society in
general and on suburbs in particular has been so great that it is hard to
believe that suburbs were really suburbs without it.

At the most fundamental level, the car transformed the physical
geography of the metropolis. Before, the organizing principle had been
the rail line extending outward. Now, however, the suburbs were defined
not so much by a radius from the center as by a circumference circling it
(like the Beltway that loops around Washington, D.C.). Cars also transformed the built environment, whether in the growing prominence of
the garage or in the oversized signs, parking lots, shopping centers, or
other kinds of architecture that were specifically designed to attract
motorists. They also hastened the decline of cities by decentralizing
many of their social functions and by draining financial resources away
from their infrastructure. (The proverbial story of the huge Los Angeles
rail system, eviscerated by funding for highways, comes to mind.)

Like the house, the car became widely celebrated as an emblem of
democracy even for those who had not yet acquired one, and for many

of the same reasons. As with housing, cars were the focus of endless technological refinement. They also became relatively less expensive over time, allowing virtually all families (and even individuals) to acquire them. Like houses, too, cars were typically bought on borrowed money, which was lent in large measure because relatively high wages permitted it and in turn provided an ever-expanding market for those who sold them and related products. And Americans took to cars as passionately—and perhaps as irrationally—as they did to houses. "We'd rather do without clothes than give up the car," one working-class housewife told researchers Robert and Helen Lynd in their classic 1937 study of Muncie, Indiana. "I'll go without food before I'll see us give up a car," asserted another. Such sentiments were impressive when one considers them in light of the relatively severe economic conditions that preceded and followed that era, but car ownership, like home ownership, points to one more distinctively American trait: relative wealth. When Soviet authorities tried to discredit American capitalism by showing the 1940 film *The Grapes of Wrath*—a movie whose emotional power derives from a story line about the homelessness of displaced tenant farmers—it was yanked out of theaters after six weeks when it became clear that viewers were more impressed by the fact that the impoverished Joad family nevertheless owned a family car. Literally and figuratively, the automobile embodied personal mobility, and as such was the perfect complement for the anchorage provided by a privately owned homestead.

The most important contribution of the automobile to suburbia, however, may have had less to do with its use than with its means of construction. Henry Ford revolutionized American manufacturing by exploiting the principles of assembly line manufacture for what was at the time an extremely complex consumer appliance. But could the same techniques of mass manufacturing—control over large quantities of raw materials, a fixed sequence of assembly using fewer workers, economies of scale to lower per-unit price, and sufficient capital to provide financing for a wider array of buyers—be used to construct residential housing?

Abraham Levitt knew the answer. Levitt and his sons William and Alfred had been relatively small-scale contractors before the Second World War, when they received a government contract to build more than two thousand homes for war workers in Norfolk, Virginia. The experience, which proved difficult, nevertheless allowed them to develop a system for laying dozens of foundations every day and pre-assembling walls and roofs. Just as important, the coming economic forecast—which included a huge demand for housing in the wake of the Great Depression and the end of the Second World War, as well as the prospect of government aid to veterans and others—made the construction of large housing developments appear to be a worthwhile gamble. Returning to Long Island after the war, they built some high-priced residential housing but also acquired a four-thousand-acre tract of potato fields in the township of Hempstead. Their development, which was known at the time as Island Trees, was soon renamed Levittown.

The formula was simple. Trucks dropped off building materials at sixty-foot intervals. All the houses had concrete foundations (no cellars), asphalt floors, and rock-board walls. Freight cars delivered Levitt-owned timber to lumberyards, where one man could cut parts for ten houses in a day. The houses were constructed in twenty-seven steps by workers who specialized in particular jobs, aided by new electrically powered tools. Preassembled parts and appliances were provided by wholly owned subsidiaries, and the company used nonunion labor, making up for rainy days on weekends. At the height of production, thirty houses went up a day.

When complete, Levittown consisted of over seventeen thousand houses and eighty-two thousand residents, making it the largest housing development ever built in the United States. The Cape Cod–style homes, which were built in a few standard variations, typically offered about 750 square feet of space and were sold for as low as $6,990, including a washing machine. As little as 10 percent was all that was necessary for a down payment, and because the mortgage, interest, principal, and taxes were often less than rent, virtually all were owner-occupied—particularly since government aid in the form of VA and FHA guarantees allowed the Levitts both the capital to build the houses and freedom from risk in lending it. In the coming years, they would build similar developments in Pennsylvania and New Jersey—and, more important, these would be followed by a wave of similar developments across the country.

Jefferson would have been disappointed: the United States never became a nation of yeoman farmers. And yet, in important ways, the surburbanization of the United States realized a Jeffersonian vision of small stakeholders. It realized some of the less attractive dimensions of that vision as well: a wish that black Americans and other minorities would simply disappear. The explicit government policy of redlining certain towns, cities, and neighborhoods with high minority populations—declaring them too risky to insure—made them virtually worthless to banks and buyers. Nor could minority families escape such places, for reasons that included individual irresponsibility, government neglect, and the self-fulfilling prophecies of mass abandonment. Levitt himself refused to sell to African Americans for fear that it would hurt his business. In this regard, of course, both he and the government simply reflected the attitudes of the voters and customers they served. "We can solve a housing problem, or we can try to solve a racial problem," Levitt explained in the isn't-it-obvious, commonsense logic of the early postwar years. "But we cannot combine the two." In 1960 not a single resident of Levittown was black.

That would change, very gradually, as many of those with African and other minority backgrounds made their fitful entrance into realms of American life from which they had formerly been excluded. To begin to understand why they may have done so—and to begin to understand the cost they and others paid for doing so—one must shift the tenor of the discussion away from the more external, structural elements in the American Dream of Home Ownership into a more psychological and symbolic realm. Only then can one begin to understand what kind of people this modern-day Dream of Home Ownership produced.

> *Eden is that old-fashioned house*
> *We dwell in every day*
> *Without suspecting our abode*
> *Until we drive away.*

—undated poem by Emily Dickinson (1830–86)

That attempt to understand began early. Among the first people to explore the cultural ramifications of the emerging suburban order was David Riesman, a sociologist whose widely read 1950 book *The Lonely Crowd* traced what he considered a historic shift from the goal-oriented, work-minded, "inner-directed" individual to a more self-conscious, consumer-minded, "outer-directed" one. Riesman did not focus on postwar surburbanization, which was barely getting under way, and he carefully noted the implicit problems with inner-direction as well as outer-direction (the typical neurosis for the former is shame and guilt, while the latter is subject to a more free-floating sense of anxiety). But many of the elements Riesman and his colleagues noted in *The Lonely Crowd* would resurface in later studies as highly characteristic of the suburban personality.

Perhaps the best known of such works was William Whyte's 1956 study *The Organization Man*. Whyte, who specifically linked the arche-typal figure of the title to Riesman's other-directed person, noted the high degree of social conformity that characterized postwar suburban life—in the offices of men who commuted to the city as well as in the communities they returned to each night. (He used the affluent Chicago suburb of Forest Park as his case study.) For Whyte, as for Riesman, this emphasis on "togetherness" imperiled the sense of inde-pendence and autonomy that had characterized much of earlier Amer-ican culture, replacing it with a sense of conformity that was at best bland and at worst deeply hostile to pluralist traditions of democracy. As Whyte recognized, this critique was similar to the one Tocqueville had made a century before. But now, he felt, those most invested in the sense of individualism that once made the United States distinctive had lost the lineaments of the Protestant ethic that once animated the soci-ety. Even as these people heartily insisted "that there are some people left—e.g. businessmen—to defend the American Dream," they were suc-cumbing to the blandishments of an organization man who lacked the spine to keep the American Dream alive.

The work of people like Riesman and Whyte received a fair amount of attention in the 1950s, in large measure because one did not have to look very hard to find evidence of what they were talking about. As one suburbanite explained, "If you have any brains, you keep them in your back pocket around here." Added another, "In the city I knew a lot of intellectual, progressive-type people. I'll admit they are more stimulat-ing, full of ideas, always wanting to talk about India or something. But I like the stodgy kind now. It's more comfortable." Stodginess, however, coexisted with yearnings for alternatives that ranged from pathetic to pathological. Such yearnings could be glimpsed in sources like Alfred Kinsey's celebrated 1948 study *Sexual Behavior in the Human Male* (his report on females followed five years later) but more commonly in fic-tion with titles like *The Man in the Gray Flannel Suit* and "The Secret Life of Walter Mitty." In varied ways, all these works questioned—if not explictly condemned—the enervating compromises implicit in the suburban ethos. Not that any of this mattered. Like much of their audience, the fictional Ricardo family (and their friends the Mertzes) would themselves be making the move to Connecticut in the hugely popular television series *I Love Lucy*. In both its content and the way it was watched, television soon became the quintessential mass medium of suburbia.

In the sixties, a previously latent unease with suburbia would become more explicit and intense, and it would appear from what had been largely quiet quarters. Betty Friedan's 1963 book *The Feminine Mystique* may have been elliptical in describing an emerging female consciousness as a response to "the problem that has no name," but there can be little doubt as to suburbia's role as one of the principal sites of that problem. The economic crisis of the Great Depression had eroded the centrality of a man's role as the family breadwinner; the military crisis of the 1940s had given women a new sense of participation in the public workplace. After the war, many women—willingly as well as unwillingly—returned to their homes to become the seemingly ubiquitous suburban housewives of the 1950s. In fact, many began to drift back to offices and factories, if indeed they had ever left, but that tended to be played down in the reigning domestic ideology of the era. Such suburban women, who were educated or longed to be, chafed at the deadening routines and mindless suppositions about family life that passed as common sense. Friedan's particular form of feminism was subsequently criticized for presuming all women were like middle-class whites, but, if nothing else, her work—as well as its enthusiastic reception—shows the degree to which a widespread sense of anomie in the post–Second World War culture of suburbia affected those living at the center of it.

It fell to the children of such women, however, to mount the most furious attack on the culture that created them. Indeed, it seems that the youth movement of the 1960s, one whose memory lingers as a byword for American narcissism, was nothing so much as a sustained rejection of the "Little Boxes"—to quote the title of a song by folksinger Malvina Reynolds—and everything they stood for. For better and worse, the pastoral mythology of Woodstock *and* the urbanity of Haight-Ashbury (that is, the country *and* the city), free love *and* antiwar militancy, civil rights communalism *and* hippie self-indulgence, drew their power from the degree to which they effectively negated suburban values of moderation, conformity, and the pursuit of happiness via a plot of land.

In retrospect, though, what seems most remarkable is not the power of such challenges, as compelling as they were, but suburbia's ability to (blandly) repel them. Despite a vast and varied critique of suburbia that was at my parents' disposal by 1969, they either rejected or were oblivious to it. They bought a house not because they wished to make a political statement or, unlike some of their peers, because they had an overriding emotional predilection for home owning. They did it because it made sense for them economically and because they felt it was the best means to their end of upward mobility for their children. If it was pointed out to them that even unconscious choices had political implications and consequences, they would shrug and say they wouldn't have done anything differently. And if, in sympathy for their position, it was pointed out to them that the fiery black leader Malcolm X also bought a house on Long Island for the safety and long-term security of his wife and four children, they would shrug and say that's very interesting and still maintain they wouldn't have done anything differently—unless, of course, he bought a house in their neighborhood. In this regard, I think, my parents were little different than millions of previous generations of Americans, whether they huddled on farms in the Midwest or managed to acquire a multiple-family dwelling in an urban neighborhood.

This is not to say that the character of suburban life was wholly static. From the perspective of a half century later, the most remarkable thing about *The Organization Man* is how dated it seems in its anxiety about conformity. This is less because conformity has altogether ceased to be a problem than because individualism seems to have run amok, typified by the so-called gated communities in which wealthy homeowners virtually barricade themselves from the outside world (except perhaps to admit servants; complaints about the difficulty in finding good help now seem as common as they were among the affluent a century ago). What Betty Friedan called "the problem that has no name" in the 1960s was replaced by a different one in the next generation: mothers who worked outside the home and struggled to find the resources—time, money, quality day care—for their families and themselves. The gradual creation of a large black middle class and the reform of the most flagrant government abuses have allowed African

Americans and other minorities to make their own migration to the suburbs, where class segregation is now in some places almost as obvious as racial segregation. The revitalization of some city neighborhoods, along with the general spread of city amenities—and city problems—has led to a blurring of just what constitutes a suburb.

Indeed, perhaps the biggest and most obvious change in suburbia is structural. Some suburbs are, or have become, cities in their own right. Yonkers, New York, for example, is both a commuting haven for Manhattan and the fourth-largest city in the state. Instead of leaving home to go work in the city each day, more and more Americans live in one suburb and work in another. So-called edge cities such as Towson, Maryland, or La Jolla, California, owe their existence to large metropolises (Washington, D.C., and San Diego, respectively) yet serve as surrogates or carve out economic niches independent of them for residents and those living in adjacent communities. Meanwhile, surburbia continues to sprawl, reaching into hinterlands and converting them into exurbia. The process seems almost Turnerian: exurbs suburbanize, suburbs urbanize, and restless settlers flee to frontiers—from Vermont to Idaho—in search of a "simple" life.

But for all the changes, suburbia remains a recognizable phenomenon. It also seems like a relatively stable one; my own suburban upbringing in the 1970s was not fundamentally different from that of young people in the 1950s or the 2000s. Like my predecessors and successors, I too knew a world of McDonald's restaurants, shopping-center parking lots, and four-bedroom colonials surrounded by chemically treated lawns. Like them, I watched parades go down Main Street, went swimming in backyard pools, and shoveled snow to create easier pedestrian access for homes and automobiles. The routines, trivial in themselves, had a cumulative effect that felt like security.

This is why, shortly after our first child was born and my wife and I both got reasonably solid jobs, we bought a four-bedroom colonial in lower Westchester County, New York. (I use the term "we" loosely; the truth is that my wife's parents gave us the down payment.) And when it came time for that child to begin his education, we sent him to private school. Ironically, a major factor in this decision involved a desire to avoid the rather severe racial segregation of our community and allow him to learn and socialize with African-American and Latino children. Not that I'm proud of, or can even finally defend, the decision. My wife and I both wished our local public schools weren't so mediocre, or that we could afford to buy a house in a community where the commitment to public schooling was greater (though in our view the kind of cultural homogeneity that characterized those communities in some sense constituted another kind of mediocrity). We viewed our choices as the best we could make of an inherently flawed situation, recognizing our complicity, our hypocrisy. Still, we may yet pay in other ways (and suffer with bad plumbing for the foreseeable future). Built as a bulwark against the ravages of time, nature, and the less pleasant realities of American life, home owning—from its rural beginnings to its exurban end—cannot finally be a refuge from any of them. But I'm grateful it still seems that way.

CHAPTER 6

DREAM OF THE GOOD LIFE (III): THE COAST

THE AMERICAN DREAM was never meant to be a zero-sum solution: the goal has always been to end up with more than you started with. Even the Puritans, whose dream in its purest formulation was about as selfless as any in American history, and who were as skeptical of human will as any people in the Western world of the last five hundred years, nevertheless acted from this premise. There's really no other way to understand their migration except as motivated by a belief that it could procure *some* gain, if not for themselves in providing a reassuring sense of purpose, then at least for the good of their children and community, who might yet be saved even if they themselves were not. Other believers then and since were not nearly as circumspect about their errands in the wilderness, acting with confidence that they could secure their futures in the next world through good works in this one. In all these cases, however, this was the Dream of the Good Life as a spiritual affair.

As we've seen, another Dream of the Good Life was also a spiritual affair, though it tended to be focused (at least in the short term) on this world at least as much as the next one, offering a kind of psychic satisfaction that sustained one through the journey of life—and, ideally, conferring benefits beyond. The foundation of this dream, upward mobility, was a belief that one could realize the fruits of one's aspirations through applied intelligence and effort. This was the dream of Abraham Lincoln and his heirs. A similar emphasis on applied intelligence and effort also animated the Dream of Home Ownership, which typically required investments of many kinds—money, time, labor, among others—in order to yield a domestic dividend.

There is one other Dream of the Good Life, however, that is decidedly different from these other two. For the most part, it is insistently secular (though there are times when the fervent desire for mortal goals such as wealth, fame, looks, or health becomes so ardent as to assume a kind of religiosity). This dream does not celebrate the idea of hard work, instead enshrining effortless attainment as the essence of its appeal. Which is not necessarily to say that applied intelligence and effort don't play a role. Very often they do, sometimes far more than these dreamers would like to acknowledge to themselves, let alone anyone else. But it's the rewards that are least strenuously earned that are the most savored, and even those that *are* strenuously earned tend to be discussed in ways that suggest they aren't.

One might say that the difference between this dream and that of upward mobility is more quantitative than qualitative. After all, there are few Americans who object to the idea of getting rich, and the rising value of a home is one of the things that contributes to the sense of security that inheres in it. But at some point—it's hard to say exactly where—a line gets crossed. A lot of people work hard for their money, but in what sense does one ever really *earn*, say, a million dollars a year, never mind ten million or a hundred million? In any event, very little of the wealth of rich people comes from their salaries; instead, it comes from investments whose value lies precisely in the way they produce income *without* labor on the part of the shareholder. Yet to focus too rigidly on accumulating wealth finally misses the point of this particular American Dream. It's less about accumulating riches than about living off their fruits, and its symbolic location is not the bank but the beach.

The American Dream is very much a national, even global, phenomenon, but some dreams have a strong geographic orientation. The Puritan dream, of course, was grounded in New England, though Puritan values ultimately stretched across the continent. Similarly, the Dream of Equality appeals broadly but owes its deepest resonances to the South, where inequality was most obvious and resistance to it most heroic. The Dream of Upward Mobility has a strong midwestern accent, as suggested, for example, by the strength of the region's state university systems, which have served as vessels of the American Dream. Abraham Lincoln may have been a national figure, but the Land of Lincoln, as the license plates remind us, is Illinois. And like the Dream of Home Ownership, the dream I'm talking about here has a strong western orientation. It is a dream with roots in the South (specifically colonial Virginia) and one that traverses the mines, wheatfields, and deserts of the West. But its apotheosis is California. This American Dream is finally the dream of the Coast.

. . . the serene confidence which a Christian feels in four aces.

—Mark Twain, letter to *The Golden Era* **(San Francisco),**
May 22, 1864

It's not easy to get something for nothing. Even the most highly leveraged speculator usually has to come up with some collateral, and in those cases where there isn't a lot of money at stake, there may be other things that count at least as much: time, energy, reputation, a sense of hope. Gains demand gambles.

America itself—in the broadest sense of that term—is a world built on gambling. Christopher Columbus, Hernan Cortés, Sir Francis Drake: these men were nothing if not gamblers. Ponce de Leon must have known that the Fountain of Youth was a long shot; Henry Hudson had far more confidence than his men did that he'd find the Northwest Passage; a normally cautious Montcalm went for broke and personally led the attack on the Plains of Abraham in the struggle for Quebec. All these men and countless others—among them the Indians who tried to stop this New World from emerging—took their chances. Naturally, because the odds were against them, most lost. But they felt there was no way they'd ever get (or keep) anything worth having here unless they made their wagers.

There's no need to be metaphorical about this. Those who fret about government-sponsored gambling may be surprised to learn that lotteries were among the most important financial instruments in building colonial North America—not only in raising funds for initial settlement but also for homes, schools, and other community institutions. Queen Elizabeth I authorized the first official raffle in 1566 to finance

English harbor improvements, though the practice remained uncommon until the early seventeenth century, when James I authorized the Virginia Company to use lotteries to help prop up its sagging investments overseas. (Those who bought the lottery tickets were known as "adventurers.") Later colonial governments used them as a popular alternative to taxation. The city of Philadelphia actually began speculating in lottery tickets itself in the mid-eighteenth century, and the omnipresent Benjamin Franklin organized a successful contest to raise money for the city's defense during the War of the Austrian Succession in the 1740s.

Such public gambling, much of it conducted by wealthy elites, was accompanied by far more widespread private gaming throughout colonial society. Cards, dice, horseracing, and cockfighting were very early arrivals in America. The publication of books like Charles Cotton's *Compleat Gamester* (1674) and Edmond Hoyle's *Short Treatise on the Game of Whist* (1742) outlined rules and showed readers how to recognize cheating. *The Compleat Gamester* was also something of a philosophical defense of gambling, emphasizing the need for recreation and the likelihood it would take a number of forms, not all of them universally popular—or approved.

Indeed, denunciations of gambling have been a fixture of American life as long as gambling itself has. The Puritans in particular objected to it on the grounds that it abetted idleness and especially because gambling so often took place on the Sabbath, a day when people typically did not work and so had time to play games. But perhaps even more than the contests themselves, it was gambling's corollary effects that led lawmakers to write and enforce antigambling ordinances to prevent "much waste of wine and beer," "the corrup[t]ing of youth and other sad consequences," and "hazard" to the "Limbs and lives" of those who conducted horseraces.

Underlying such presumably practical concerns was a more fundamental issue. The behavior fostered by gambling grew out of a different, competing notion of the American Dream. For those who felt that the universe was a fair and orderly place—and, especially, for those who enjoyed a lofty place in their communities—the underlying assumptions of the gambling mentality were profoundly disturbing. At bottom, the gambler does not instinctively regard the universe as a fair or orderly place, tending instead to believe that the world's arrangements are, if not arbitrary, then not finally knowable in any rational way. A Puritan could well agree that life is inscrutable. But a Puritan could not take the next step a gambler typically does: that rules, even morality, are irrelevant at best and a thinly veiled attempt to take control at worst. This is one reason why gambling tended to promote "undesirable" behaviors like sex and drinking. While the Puritan was inclined to reflect, perhaps even to try and overcome, inscrutability, the gambler tried to gain as much as he could, not feeling compelled to explain success *or* failure. In the end, the appeal of gambling proved too strong even for the Puritans as well as the Quakers, who found it difficult to control the practice as their colonies became increasingly diverse and settlement at their frontiers extended beyond the reach of civil authorities. By the time of the Revolution there was far less difference in attitudes between North and South about gambling than there had been 150 years earlier.

As the western frontier—a mere hundred miles from the eastern seaboard at the time of the Revolution—receded in the nineteenth century, the patterns and arguments about gambling were continuously reenacted. "From the seventeenth century through the twentieth, both gambling and westering thrived on high expectations, opportunism, and movement, and both activities helped to shape a distinctive culture," historian John Findlay explains in his history of American gambling. "Like bettors, pioneers have repeatedly grasped at the chance to get something for nothing—to claim free land, to pick up nuggets of gold, to speculate on western real estate." This dream fostered its own culture, a culture that fostered not only raucous games like cockfights and duels but also a raucous southwestern popular idiom that would furnish the raw material for later writers like Mark Twain and Herman Melville, who set his 1857 novel *The Confidence Man*, a metaphysical meditation on gambling, deception, and faith, on a Mississippi riverboat. Yet even here there was resistance. The professionalization of gambling and presence of sophisticated conmen helped contribute to a feeling that the West was a disreputable, even dangerous, place. One perhaps ironic result of this fear of disorder was vigilantism: in 1835 a group of settlers in Vicksburg, Mississippi, lynched five gamblers and declared martial law. Similar incidents (notably in San Francisco in 1856) demonstrated that not all the hostility toward gambling came from traditional guardians of morality such as elite women and church leaders.

Such opposition reflected the threat that unrestricted gambling posed for another American Dream: home ownership. Gambling culture has always been fundamentally antidomestic in orientation.

Wagering—of money, land, even human beings—was an intrinsically destabilizing cultural practice and part of what made frontier life so worrisome to those who really desired to *settle* the West. As countless observers from James Fenimore Cooper to Frederick Jackson Turner on down have noted, settlers in a given locale typically succeeded in stamping out gambling culture, only to have the frontier that sustained it move on. The culture of gambling, in short, was a moving target.

Nor did it move in a straight line. As a number of historians have made clear, the American frontier was an irregular and shifting affair as likely to go east as it did west. For much of the nineteenth century, the general area between the Great Plains and the Pacific coast was commonly known as "the Great American Desert"—terrain to move *through*, not settle *on*. Only after (northern) California was firmly integrated into the Union were Americans tempted—often by the lure of highly deceptive advertising circulated by railroad companies—to settle places like eastern Montana. All too often, this was a wager that proved to be a losing proposition.

Nowhere was this interplay of domesticity and gambling, movement and settlement, played out more vividly than Las Vegas, Nevada. Everything about early Nevada—from the Spanish trails blazed through it to connect Santa Fe and southern California to its hasty, improvised admission to the Union in 1864 to help cushion Abraham Lincoln's electoral majority—testifies to the transience of its beginnings. Significantly, it was the Mormons, who had a Puritan-tinged dream of a holy community rooted in home ownership, who made the first sustained effort to make the area now known as Las Vegas a permanent settlement, part of Brigham Young's plan to extend Mormon influence to southern California and provide travelers with a safe haven along the way. To that end, construction of a fort and missionary activity with the Paiute Indians got under way in 1855. But the effort was abandoned three years later.

That evangelical Christians would first try to colonize a place that would become synonymous with vice is only one of many ironies surrounding the rise of Las Vegas. Another is that, the American celebration of the entrepreneurial loner notwithstanding, it was the federal government, not enterprising individuals, who ultimately put the city on the map. Land grants to railroads—a classic example of corporate handouts that proved far less risky and far more profitable than any casino table—ultimately allowed the construction of rail lines that led to Las Vegas's first identity as a way station between Salt Lake City and Los Angeles in 1905. Construction of the Hoover Dam in nearby Boulder City in the 1930s brought salaried workers into Las Vegas's orbit. (Not until 1945 did gambling replace the Dam as the principal source of tourist traffic.) And military bases, contracts, and testing—the most notable tests being nuclear bomb explosions—brought large sums of money to an area that would otherwise have been impoverished. Nevada's historic stinginess with local and state spending on schools, health care, and other social services belies the federal government support that continues to sustain it (and much of the rest of the West).

Ultimately, however, it would not be government-sponsored industry that made Las Vegas famous. That activities like drinking, prostitution, and gambling did points to yet another irony. At the turn of the century, city officials limited such activities by ordinance to two blocks of clubs near the railroad station that catered to passengers on layovers. The idea, of course, was to limit (and profit) from what could not otherwise be prevented. It increasingly became obvious, however, that vice was the tail that wagged the civic dog. Recognizing the economic potential in such activities—particularly in a state that was otherwise uncongenial to economic development—Nevada legalized prostitution and gambling by 1931 and determinedly looked the other way during Prohibition. It also avowedly made itself the easiest state in the Union in which to obtain a divorce. The promise of secular fulfillment, in all its forms, became the basis of its existence.

Las Vegas also became a proving ground for the elasticity of the American Dream, showcasing its penchant for absorbing ethnic influences and in turn being shaped by them. Beginning in the 1940s, organized crime figures from back east began showing an interest in the city for achieving their own American Dream of Upward Mobility—and doing so in an alluring new climate that presented a more attractive life of ease than any they had previously known. These urban frontiersmen were in effect gambling on gamblers; the risk was not so much in making money on gaming (this was something they had been doing successfully for a long time) but rather risking exposure and arrest by bringing their underground economy into the desert and laundering their gains with glittering new enterprises. The most famous of these figures was Benjamin Siegel (or "Bugsy," as he was known to non-friends). Siegel, who had been sent to Los Angeles in the thirties to reorganize crime there, first came to Las Vegas in 1941 with his associate Moe Sedway as part of an effort by Meyer Lansky and other gangsters to find a legally sanctioned base for their business empires. Siegel's role in the construction of the Flamingo, one of the first major Las Vegas* resorts when it opened in 1946, has become legendary. Plagued by cost-overruns and poor returns that cost Siegel his life, the Flamingo nevertheless became a gold mine that served as a pioneer for a number of other major casino-hotels, among them the Desert Inn and the Stardust. Like Moses—or perhaps more to the point, Daniel Boone—Siegel had glimpsed the promised land. By the early 1950s Las Vegas had become the Great American Playground, a frontier town for the age of jet airplanes.

Film director Martin Scorsese, among others, has vividly depicted the almost biblical fable that followed, as a small group of men gained and lost paradise through their own excesses, greed chief among them. By the late 1970s the implacable hand of corporate capitalism supplanted mobsters and the union pension funds that had sustained them. Las Vegas became an increasingly well organized and financed business.

To a great degree, Las Vegas was also domesticated. This can be largely attributed to the logic of capitalism, a logic that is also predicated on gambling but that tries to square the circle wherever possible in the name of maximizing profit as efficiently as possible. In this case, that means providing safe, reliable, "family" entertainment to go along with gambling, which itself has been carefully circumscribed by an elaborate series of rules and regulations to ensure order. (In the United States, as it turned out, the Puritan and the gambler are never that far apart.)

But the sanding of the city's hard edges also reflects a broader cultural shift—or, at any rate, a variation on this particular Dream of the Good Life. The American Dream embraced most fully by earlier incarnations of Las Vegas, which remains present even now, focuses on get-

---

* Technically, neither the Flamingo nor any of the subsequent wave of resorts built on the so-called Strip was actually in Las Vegas city limits—in fact, their location was specifically chosen so as to be beyond that city's municipal regulations. Such establishments were situated in the coyly named, regulation-friendly city of Paradise, which has since been absorbed into Las Vegas.

ting something for nothing. Yet an air of exertion, even anxiety, suffuses this dream, as suggested by the recent remarks of this casino shift manager who sympathizes with the players:

> I have felt that same rush gambling, and you want to know the really weird part of it all? When I'm gambling, I am having the best time of my life and I am having the absolute worst time too. I'm talking about those nanoseconds when you are waiting for that white ball to drop into the red or black or the dice to stop rolling. It can be absolutely terrifying and absolutely beautiful. You are standing there wishing like hell that you hadn't put down your complete paycheck. You are thinking "Am I nuts? What am I going to do if I lose?" You are terrified and you are totally alive. . . . People will tell you that they gamble to win, but I don't believe them. It's those brief seconds before you know the outcome that really turn you on. Those are the moments when you learn if you are a player or a real gambler, a winner or a loser. Those are the moments that really count because you are up there flying without a net.

There's a curious tension here, something akin to a work ethic: gambling doesn't really count unless there's really something at stake. It's the gambling, not the winning or losing, that finally matters.

There can be little doubt that this person is describing a common psychological profile in the world at large. But the validity of these observations notwithstanding, it must also be true that many people have always gambled to win—have been happy to do so *without* spine-tingling risk or suspense (many no doubt work in the accounting department of this very casino). From the plantation owner happy to survey his fields from the comfort of his porch to the Wall Street executive contentedly savoring the fruits of paper profits at a Caribbean resort, the purest expression of the Dream of the Coast rests on a quest for placidity, not the thrill of risk.

Ground zero for this particular variant is not Las Vegas but rather California. Indeed, for much of its history, Las Vegas looked west, not east, for cultural direction. The gambling houses of San Francisco, with their sense of often garish splendor and (relative) permanence, furnished the model for early Las Vegas casinos. But it was geographically closer Southern California that most decisively shaped the modern American Dream. The rise of the interstate not only brought Los Angeles within the orbit of Las Vegas, but also influenced the pattern of settlement in ways ranging from roadside architecture to patterns of racial and social segregation. Perhaps the most notable example of this segregation was the shift in the locus of gaming culture from downtown gambling houses—the so-called "Glitter Gulch," whose very name harkened back to the Old West—to the more exotic and often futuristic resorts of the automotive-friendly Strip.

But to really understand the Dream of the Coast, you have to go back to the beginning, when to many California itself was at least as much a dream as it was a place.

. . . these States tend inland and toward the Western sea, and I will also.

Walt Whitman, "A Promise to California," 1867

In March of 1816, two American sailors jumped off a ship on the California coast and found their way to land. One was a Bostonian named Thomas Doak; the other, a black man known simply as Bob. The two took out Spanish citizenship, married local women, and converted to Catholicism; Doak was baptized as Felipe Santiago and Bob as Juan Cristóbal. The former became a well-respected, well-paid carpenter; the latter found at least some of a racial stigma not quite as sharp as it was back home.

It seems fitting that these two became the first recorded permanent American residents of California: their lives suggest the Dream of the Coast. In coming from the East, discarding their identities, and leading a less onerous existence, they resembled many of those who followed—or, at least, the fondest *hopes* of many who followed.

Indeed, for hundreds of years, California was above all else a matter of potential. Despite the staggering beauty of its mountains, valleys, and deserts, the region was notably light in population for much of its history. (The south, for example, was too arid to support the large native populations common elsewhere in North America.) In 1535 the legendary Spanish conqueror Hernan Cortés landed in what is now Baja peninsula and named the place "California" after the island mountain kingdom in a popular Spanish romance of the time, *Las Sergas de Esplandían* (in which the protagonist, Esplandían, converts the Amazons of California to Christianity). In 1542 the Spanish explorer

Juan Rodriguez Cabrillo sailed into what is now San Diego Bay and continued north along the Pacific coast, making frequent trips ashore to claim the land for Spain. Despite the relative lack of resistance from the notable variety of native peoples, the Spanish showed little interest in the region. In 1579 the English explorer Sir Francis Drake reached northern California, which he named Nova Albion and claimed for England. But it would be almost two hundred years before Europeans settled in the region, and when they did, it was the Russians and French who established naval posts and contemplated the establishment of imperial outposts in the Pacific. It was to prevent this that the Spanish governor of lower California established a presidio, or military post, in San Diego in 1769. He also sent Junípero Serra, a Franciscan missionary, to San Diego to establish the first of many missions that formed a chain between San Diego and San Francisco. The purpose of the missions was to convert Native Americans, who were forced to live and work in what were essentially authoritarian religious communes. The collapse of Spanish authority in the 1820s brought California under nominal Mexican rule, but a steady influx of outsiders and internecine factionalism raised questions as to who would finally claim it as their own. The growing presence of maritime Americans from New England and trappers traveling overland from the South and border states gave the United States the upper hand in this imperial contest—though not without cost. The almost mythic tale of the Donner Party, trapped in the mountains during an overland journey into California and forced to eat human flesh, became a potent symbol of the nightmares that could result from the pursuit of this dream.

The process whereby the United States realized what its boosters called its manifest destiny began with the outbreak of the Mexican War in 1846, which provided the pretext for a detachment of U.S. soldiers under the command of General John Frémont to support an insurrection and the creation of the so-called Bear Flag Republic, named for the grizzly bear that adorned the flag of the revolutionaries. A series of American-led invasions, some unsuccessful, followed, but in 1848 California was ceded to the United States as part of the treaty of Guadalupe Hidalgo. The United States promised to honor the rights of Mexican landholders, but the demand that they document their claims in Washington, D.C., typically led to expensive litigation that effectively stripped Mexicans of ranches that were in some cases themselves the spoils of the Franciscan missions. Two years later, California became a (free) state as part of the Compromise of 1850, though its native, Mexican, and Chinese populations would work in ways all too similar to those of southern slaves and tenant farmers.

The treaty of Guadalupe Hidalgo had not even been signed when an unexpected event transformed California—and the American Dream. In 1839, the Mexican government, seeking to check American expansion, made a huge land grant to a Swiss immigrant, John Sutter, who established a large ranch near Sacramento. Sutter needed lumber and turned to his American partner, James Marshall, to build him a sawmill on the South Fork of the American River. On January 24, 1848, Marshall was inspecting the construction site when he picked up a yellow nugget: gold. Marshall and Sutter tried to keep the discovery quiet, but it was no use. The gold rush was on. In 1848 there were twelve thousand émigrés in California; six years later there were three hundred thousand. In the century between 1860 and 1960, the state's population would double every twenty years.

The California gold rush is the purest expression of the Dream of the Coast in American history. The notion that transformative riches were literally at your feet, there for the taking, cast a deep and lasting spell on the American imagination. Paradoxically, the prospect of seemingly effortless riches led Americans to move mountains in pursuit of this dream. It goes without saying that most failed. Sutter, for his part, died bankrupt; Marshall drank himself to death. Yet even when the promise of the gold rush proved illusory—except for the mining companies, which quickly gobbled up the land and created a large-scale industry—it continued to have enormous metaphorical power for generations of Americans, for whom California (a.k.a. "the Golden State") offered the potential for riches of many kinds.

One of these was railroads. As in so many other ways, California's experience was much like the rest of the country's, only more so. Shrewd speculators were given vast tracts of land by the federal government, which they then used to finance the railroads by selling off pieces of it at an exorbitant profit. The first railroad within the state, a twenty-two-mile line between Sacramento and Folsom, was completed in 1855. Two railroad companies built the first transcontinental railroad: the Union Pacific Railway laid tracks west from Omaha, and the Central Pacific Railroad, under the leadership of Sacramento businessmen Leland Stanford, Charles Crocker, Collis P. Huntington, and Mark Hopkins, laid track east from Sacramento. The two lines were joined at Promontory, near Ogden, Utah, on May 10, 1869. In 1876 the Central Pacific was extended southward, reaching Los Angeles. Railroads became major players in the California economy, dictating the commercial and political development of the state and who would prosper in it. Men like Stanford and Huntington became rich—obscenely rich, in the eyes of some—while others paid the price for lacking their luck, timing, or social connections.

But it wasn't only modern industries like mining and railroads that dangled the prospect of the Good Life before a lucky few. Farming, perhaps all the more alluring because it was familiar to most Americans, also played a role. In the 1860s and 1870s California became the nation's breadbasket, as farmers depleted the soil at an extremely rapid rate, sometimes planting two or three crops a season. This was not the work of small homesteaders tilling dreams of upward mobility; it was agribusinessmen like Dr. Hugh Glenn, who owned sixty thousand acres and employed six hundred workers (one of whom murdered Glenn after he was fired for drinking, suggesting the frustration and violence that often accompanied the quest for the American Dream). The advent of refrigerated rail cars in the 1880s made it possible to ship perishables like fruit over long distances, transforming California's agricultural economy. In 1904 the advertising agency for the California Fruit Growers Exchange created a new trademark, Sunkist, to market individually wrapped oranges. Millions of Americans became devotees of a fruit most had never seen a few years earlier.

In a sense, they became even more devoted to the *image* that Sunkist promoted. Crates containing the oranges were illustrated with vivid, idyllic lithographs of Southern California landscapes. One, "Sea Side," from 1919, showed a family at the beach; another, "Suburban," from 1915, depicted a bungalow in an orange grove. The name of yet another illustration, this one of two peacocks in a grove near a castle, made explicit what was really being presented in these images. It was called "California Dream."

Indeed, to focus too much on the broad economic transformation of California runs the risk of losing sight of its deeply personal appeal in ways that were as much psychological as material. Eastern journalist Charles Nordhoff's best-selling book *California for Health, Wealth, and*

Residence (1872) was only one well-known example of a large literature promoting the good life to be found there. "I think nothing can be more delightful than the life of a farmer of sheep or cattle in Southern California," Nordhoff reported. "The weather is almost always fine; neither heat nor cold ever goes to extremes; you ride everywhere across country, for there are no fences; game is abundant in the seasons; and to one who has been accustomed to the busy life of a great city like New York, the work of a sheep or cattle *rancho* seems to be mere play." More than the prospect of great riches per se, it was the idea of easy living that captured the national imagination. You would happily let the industrial barons divide the world among themselves if you could just simply enjoy yourself back at the (economically self-sufficient) ranch.

By the turn of the twentieth century, California, north and south, had established itself as a kind of American Mediterranean—a haven of sorts from the hard-driving tenor of much of the rest of national life. San Francisco in particular enjoyed a reputation as a cosmopolitan entrepôt, notable for quality restaurants, its arts community, and ethnic diversity, while Los Angeles grew rapidly as railroads, the oil industry, and the completion of its new harbor in 1910 allowed its population to triple over the course of the decade. Not even earthquakes, frontier violence, or racism stopped newcomers, who often found themselves facing daunting odds. For few were the odds more daunting than for the Japanese, whose triumph over such obstacles in accumulating land so infuriated Anglo-Californians that state legislators made it illegal for them to do so. Yet none of this displaced the sunny visage California presented to the outside world.

That sunny visage in what was still a remote location could also prove quite practical for some enterprises. The first decade of the twentieth century was pivotal in the new industry of motion pictures, which had rapidly developed from an arcade attraction to be viewed through a peephole-like device called the kinetoscope to a mass medium projected onto screens in nickelodeons. Much, though not all, of the early movie industry was concentrated in metropolitan New York, the stomping grounds of inventor—and speculator—Thomas Edison, whose trust controlled key patents on projectors and demanded royalties from filmmakers. (The idea that you could make something once in a fixed period of time and earn income from it continuously thereafter without further effort is one of the most cherished scenarios in the Dream of the Coast.) Edison believed that the key to mastery of the movie industry lay in controlling the means of production. A group of Jewish immigrants with names like Fox and Warner, however, realized the money really lay in content, that is, in making movies that people truly wanted to see. (Edison regarded films themselves as a virtual afterthought, something he'd let someone else do—as long as he was paid.) Over the long run, the future would belong to these people, who proved much better at making sure *they* were paid.

In the winter of 1907, a director named Francis Boggs and his cameraman, Thomas Persons, had finished shooting the interior scenes for their film *The Count of Monte Cristo* in Chicago. They needed good weather to shoot the exterior scenes, but it was overcast in the Windy City, so they went to Los Angeles. A steady stream of filmmakers followed, lured not only by the weather and the lack of strong unions but also because Southern California was generally beyond the reach of Edison's lawyers, who served subpoenas to those they suspected of evading his trust (which was declared an illegal restraint of trade in 1915). In the event of legal problems, it was useful for filmmakers to simply pick up and move their operations across the border to Mexico, which some occasionally did.

In 1910 the hugely ambitious actor/writer/director David Wark Griffith began making regular trips to Southern California to make films that would culminate in the epic *The Birth of a Nation* (1915), widely regarded as the first major feature film. He brought with him a troupe of actors, among them a seventeen-year-old girl named Mary Pickford, whom he deployed in a series of movies, which he shot with the consummate skill of a genius inventing an entirely new artistic grammar. Griffith based his operation in Hollywood, a small city created in 1888 by Horace and Daeida Wilcot, a wealthy midwestern couple bereaved by the loss of a child. A small, sober-minded community that did not allow alcohol—or movie theaters—Hollywood was in some ways an unlikely site for an international capital of popular culture. But its absorption by Los Angeles in 1910 made this possible, and D. W. Griffith (himself soon to be left behind) became a founding father of a shimmering new American Dream.

At its most compelling, California could be a moral premise, a prescription of what America could and should be. At its most trivial, it was a cluster of shallow dreams, venial hankerings which mistook laziness for leisure, selfishness for individualism, laxity for liberation, evasion and cheap escape for redemption and a solid second chance.

—**Kevin Starr,** *Americans and the California Dream,* **1973**

It was, if you were to believe the newspapers, magazines, radio, and newsreels, the most fabulous house in America. The two-story colonial had an **L**-shape, its varied rooms a mélange of Frederic Remington paintings, Oriental carpets, and hand-carved Italian chairs. Outside, one could find kennels, stables, a tennis court, a miniature golf course, a swimming pool, and a bathhouse fitted with swimsuits of all sizes. The estate's fifteen servants had their own dormitory (the majordomo,

COASTING *Douglas Fairbanks and Mary Pickford at Pickfair in the mid-1920s. The couple's marital merger was one of the first, and most alluring, examples of modern celebrity culture. (Photo Collection / Los Angeles Public Library)*

Albert, had his own cottage). Located in the hamlet of Beverly Hills—which, like nearby Hollywood, had recently become part of Los Angeles—the house became a mecca for a new breed of people who were settling the frontier of American entertainment.

The house was called "Pickfair" in honor of its residents—Mary Pickford and Douglas Fairbanks. Pickford, the premier movie star of the 1910s and 1920s, was known as "America's Sweetheart" (which, in typical fashion, her handlers would revise to "the World's Sweetheart"). While seductresses like Theda Bara and Greta Garbo played the role of vamp, Pickford was cast as the eternal child in films like *Poor Little Rich Girl* (1917), *Daddy-Long-Legs* (1919), and *Pollyanna* (1920). Fairbanks, who went to Harvard not as a student but to socialize with people who were actually enrolled, was renowned for his grace and sex appeal in films like *The Mark of Zorro* (1920), *The Three Musketeers* (1921), and *Robin Hood* (1922). In 1919 Fairbanks and Pickford teamed up with D. W. Griffith and Charlie Chaplin to form United Artists, their own movie studio. Chaplin, a frequent guest at Pickfair, had his own room there, even though he owned a house a block away.

Pickford and Fairbanks's marital merger was a little more difficult to execute than their business partnership. Both had been married prior to their 1920 wedding. The two, along with Chaplin, had generated much good will in their Liberty Bond fundraising drive in support of World War I, but divorce carried a strong social stigma, particularly for women. When the Catholic Pickford stretched Nevada's already lax divorce laws by leaving the state almost immediately upon procuring a settlement, marrying Fairbanks the same month after openly insisting she had no plans to do so, and having a Baptist minister perform the ceremony, she provoked the wrath of the Church, the Nevada Attorney General, her former husband, and a good deal of the public. But lawyers, money, and a European honeymoon largely defused the furor. The leading fan magazine of the period, *Photoplay,* reflected the new consensus when it published a telegram that ended COME HOME ALL IS FORGIVEN. The couple returned to the house Fairbanks owned before the marriage, renaming it "Pickfair."

By 1922, according to one biographer, Pickfair had become a kind of collective dream house, a place fans felt they instinctively knew even if they had never actually been there. "No one much cared about how Mrs. Harding or Mrs. Coolidge ran 1600 Pennsylvania Avenue, but Mary's boudoir, her servant problems, the table she set, her scheme of interior decoration—these were fascinating topics for the American public, and the papers kept readers informed of each new development at Pickfair," explained one biographer. Albert Einstein, Babe Ruth, and Lord and Lady Mountbatten were typically atypical guests; the dinner table was automatically set for fifteen and was usually full each evening.

Yet great care was taken at Pickfair not to suggest anything resembling decadence. This was a real concern in the Hollywood of Fairbanks and Pickford, which had seen its share of squalor. In 1920 Pickford's sister-in-law Olive Thomas, a former showgirl and rising actress celebrated for her beauty, poisoned herself in a Paris hotel room. (Her husband, Pickford's brother Jack, also an actor, was reputed to have a heroin habit.) A year after Thomas's death, another actress, Virginia Rappe, also died in a hotel room, this one north of San Francisco, after a party hosted by the famed comic actor Roscoe "Fatty" Arbuckle. Arbuckle, arrested on charges of first degree murder, was ultimately acquitted, but his career was nevertheless in shreds. Incidents like these—and there were many—led the new movie moguls to hire a powerful Washington lawyer, William Harrison Hays, who gave up his position as postmaster general of the Harding administration to orchestrate the public relations of the film industry through an internal censorship operation known as the "Hays Office." His help wasn't needed at Pickfair, however. No liquor was served there (at least officially—these were the days of Prohibition), and the movie screenings that followed dinner always ended by ten P.M. so that Fairbanks and Pickford would arrive fresh on the set by six the next morning. In short, Doug and Mary were nice young people.

They were also *forever* young people. Writing in 1973, movie critic Richard Schickel marveled at the durable power of Fairbanks's image: "No one has quite recaptured the freshness, the sense of perpetually innocent, perpetually adolescent narcissism that Douglas Fairbanks brought to the screen." Pickford, for her part, was cherished as an eternal child; well into her thirties she was playing characters in golden curls and frilly dresses in what were popularly known as "Mary pictures."

One might say that Fairbanks and Pickford lived out a dazzling American Dream, but to leave it at that would obscure the way their lives reflected new currents in the Dream that have shaped it ever since. Some versions of the American Dream stressed the value of hard work for its own sake; others recognized it as a necessary evil, but one that afforded the promise of a leisurely life of many happy returns on profitable investments. In an important sense, however, the appeal of Doug and Mary rested less on what they did or what they acquired than on playing themselves. Simply being Doug and Mary was in *itself* perceived to be desirable (and profitable). To be sure, these were people with real talent, but exercising that talent was something that presumably came naturally, something that simply happened in the course of a normal day. To put it another way: the American Dreams of Benjamin Franklin, Abraham Lincoln, and Andrew Carnegie rested on a sense of *character*; those of Douglas Fairbanks and Mary Pickford rested on *personality*. They were celebrities, people whose fame rested not on talent, however defined, but on simply being famous. One of the strangest paradoxes of subsequent American history would be the histories of other Americans, among them Frank Sinatra and Elvis Presley, who emerged from highly particular cultural communities possessing enormous talent and yet who trivialized, even discarded, their gifts in a desperate desire to live the Dream of the Coast.

The contrast between an older American Dream rooted in character and its replacement, a Dream rooted in personality, is vividly apparent in the 1916 film *His Picture in the Papers*. Fairbanks plays a young man who works for his father, a cereal manufacturer. He is a quiet rebel against parental strictures, dutifully bringing a bag lunch to work only to pull out a martini mixer to drink on the job. (He also defies his family's vegetarianism by eating steaks at restaurants.) In his free time, he goes slumming among immigrants, distinguishing himself in Irish boxing matches. But if such activities bring him censure at home, they pay clear dividends elsewhere: he is a magnet for the attention of women and has the necessary manliness to rescue a fellow businessman when thugs attack him. When reporters ask him the secret of his strength, he answers with "Pringle Products," the food made by his father. Overnight, Pringle's cereal becomes a hotter commodity than it had ever been, advertised as a means to build strong bodies and sex appeal rather than as a sensible vegetarian staple. A charismatic personality makes and breaks his own rules, succeeding in business without really trying.

The key to his success is *lifestyle*, a term that, like "the American Dream," entered common parlance surprisingly recently.* The world

---

* According to *The Facts on File Dictionary of Cliché* (2001), the term "life style" was coined by psychologist Alfred Adler in 1929 to describe the psychological profile of an individual as defined in childhood. But according to *Brewer's Dictionary of Twentieth-Century Phrase and Fable* (Boston: Houghton Mifflin, 1992), use of the term to denote attitudes, values, and styles of consumption did not become commonplace until the 1980s.

of Pickfair was not about wealth or achievement but physical beauty, grace, fun. For the Beautiful People, a work ethic does not mean deferred gratification, but rather gratification through novel and exciting work—work that can be talked about on talk shows or in magazine stories, or work not tethered to a clock the way most American jobs are. To be sure, Benjamin Franklin and Andrew Carnegie were famous in their own right (as indeed they wished to be), and they lived in a style that could be considered analogous to that of Pickfair. But neither celebrated—in fact, they explicitly condemned—the values celebrated in *His Picture in the Papers*.

Even from the heights of hypocrisy, they did so for good reason: the values embodied in Pickfair are a fraud, and we all know it. Fairbanks and Pickford did not live happily ever after in a storybook romance; in fact they divorced in 1935, years after their marriage had become a sham. The economic and personal freedom they won was paid for, especially by Pickford, with a cult of youth and beauty that was not only oppressive but would inevitably leave them behind. Their accomplishments, real as they may have been, were not only fleeting but outstripped by ambitions that would be forever beyond them—movies unmade, roles unrealized, a studio that never quite attained the heft of its rivals. Franklin and Carnegie left behind libraries that remain with us; the principal legacy of Pickford and Fairbanks is made of deteriorating celluloid, fading pictures of a world that never was.

And yet that world continues to exert an enormous allure that has only grown more powerful. Doug and Mary were replaced by Clark and Carole, Liz and Dick, Tom and Nicole; the newsreel has been replaced by the website; the stars have their own production companies rather than serving at the convenience of studio chiefs who paid them fixed salaries. While Hollywood remains their home, their values seem to have taken root in other dream capitals, from Washington, D.C., to the Harvard Fairbanks could only pretend to attend.

I know I sound a little skeptical, even dismissive, when I write about people like Douglas Fairbanks. That's hardly surprising coming from someone who began this book by admitting his affection for the Puritans. But I, too, feel the undertow of the Coast. Most of us do. Indeed, a longing for a life of leisure has virtually universal appeal, and given the grind of exertion and duty that has characterized everyday existence for most of human history, it's not hard to understand why.

Nor can I entirely dismiss such longings, which Americans seem to have an uncanny ability to capture, package, and distribute, as superficial. Despite the enormous gap between what the creators of Pickfair portrayed and what their audience lived, their dream world has a paradoxical immediacy and accessibility that make it a democracy of desire. We have fun watching them have fun, and we almost believe they really do represent us. In a crude way, the box office is a kind of voting booth—one rife with corruption, certainly, and yet the repository of a collective hope that I can't help but feel has not only a kind of reality but also a kind of tattered validity. I know the beautiful figure I see on a screen has no life beyond it, and that character, if real, would have no truck with the likes of me (nor should I with her). I know the fable of abundance depicted on the page of a magazine is a marketing ploy, but the magic it appropriates has a life that cannot be wholly contained by a slogan, an image, a bill of goods. I know that the culture of consumption that is finally at the heart of the Dream of the Coast preys on my worst impulses—greed, lust, gluttony. But every once in a while there is good to be seized among the goods. The smell of the paper in a freshly printed book; the sound of an electric guitar that emanates from the radio; the grace of an actress, now dead, in a movie on television: so much senseless beauty. Amid all the striving, some worthwhile and some appalling, the American Dream is most fully realized in works of art.

I'LL BEGIN TO END this discussion of the Coast, and this book generally, by heading back east for one final tale of the American Dream. It's a fairly simple story. James Gatz (or "Jimmy," as his father calls him) is born sometime around 1890 in North Dakota. After attending St. Olaf's College in southern Minnesota for two weeks, the seventeen-year-old boy drifts to Lake Superior, where he works digging clams, fishing for salmon, and holding other odd jobs. While there, Gatz meets Dan Cody, a millionaire copper magnate who hires him to serve as a steward-mate-skipper for his yacht. For the next five years, Gatz sails the world with Cody, who adopts the boy as a protégé and trusts him to keep tabs on him when he drinks too much. When Cody dies in 1912, he leaves Gatz twenty-five thousand dollars, but Gatz never receives the money because of the machinations of Cody's mistress.

Gatz's whereabouts are unknown between 1912 and 1917, at which point he appears in Louisville, Kentucky, as a lieutenant in the U.S.

Army awaiting transport to France to fight in the First World War. Here, he falls in love with the beautiful young Daisy Fay, whose background is far more distinguished than his own. Visiting her house with other officers from the local army base, and then alone, brings his life into vivid clarity: she will be the love of his life. But Daisy, while returning his attentions, is out of reach. This is not only because he is about to go to war, but also because his lowly origins pose a serious financial and social obstacle. Nevertheless, he is determined to win her.

After being decorated for distinguished service in the war and a stint at Oxford, he returns to make his fortune via shadowy means. (Apparently he has something to do with the notorious Black Sox Scandal of 1919, in which the Chicago White Sox allegedly collude with bookmakers to intentionally lose the World Series.) Meanwhile, Daisy Fay comes out as a debutante and marries Tom Buchanan, a Yale graduate from a respectable family. Daisy bears a daughter, Pamela, and the young family moves from Santa Barbara to Chicago, finally completing its migration from west to east by settling on a waterfront estate on Long Island.

How do we know all of this? We learn most of it secondhand from Nick Carraway—who himself learns it secondhand. Nick, a fellow midwesterner, is Daisy's second cousin once removed and knew Tom at Yale. Nick comes to New York in the spring of 1922 to become a bond trader and rents a small house on a peninsula across a bay from Daisy and Tom. It soon emerges that Nick's rich next-door neighbor, who throws wild parties* at his baronial estate and who is the source of endless gossip (Is he a bootlegger? Did he kill a man?), is Daisy's old suitor. Those parties, as it turns out, have a determined purpose: to lure Daisy. Nick becomes the agent of their reunion—and the man who bears witness to the ensuing tragedy.

At some point in reading the last four paragraphs, you probably realized this is the plot of F. Scott Fitzgerald's *The Great Gatsby*. It was published in 1925, a time when the Dream of the Coast was both consolidating and spreading. The book has long been considered the quintessential Great American Novel—and, surely not coincidentally, the quintessential expression of the American Dream. The reason is less

---

* Those parties include glamorous figures from the new world of motion pictures, among them the head of a studio and a "gorgeous, scarcely human orchid of a woman" the host points out to other guests, who stare at her "with that peculiarly unreal feeling that accompanies the recognition of a hitherto ghostly celebrity of the movies."

the plot than a gift for language that here, for example explains the appeal of his protagonist:

> There was something gorgeous about him, some heightened sensitivity to the promises of life, as if he were related to one of those intricate machines that register earthquakes ten thousand miles away. This responsiveness had nothing to do with that flabby impressionability which is dignified under the name of "creative temperament"—it was an extraordinary gift for hope, a romantic readiness as I have never found in any other person and which it is unlikely I shall ever find again.

One need not be an especially acute reader to know from the outset that Gatsby's quest for Daisy is not promising. We meet her even before we meet him, and so we know how shallow she is, and most of us know from experience that such strong desire is an unstable compound. Any plausible hopes we might have for Gatsby's dream of Daisy evaporate when Nick advises him not to "ask too much of her" because "you can't repeat the past." To which Gatsby responds: "Can't repeat the past? Why of course you can!" Subsequent events in the novel reveal just how disastrous it can be to railroad through hard realities like time, space, and the fickleness of the human heart.

But the skepticism that *The Great Gatsby* engenders about its protagonist's American Dream is not only a matter of its fable-like plot of a man who pursues unseemly ends through unseemly means and pays for his dream with his life. Fitzgerald also gives the reader other cues, the most important of which is the famous image of the "valley of ashes," presided over by an optometrist's advertisement featuring the enormous eyes of Doctor T. J. Eckleburg. This haunting image, which opens the second chapter of the novel and is the setting for its climax, has sometimes been interpreted as a kind of modernist metaphor for the wasteland of humanity in a godless age. There's a mute quality to Eckleburg and the valley of ashes that makes them all the more unnerving, and at the same time a notion of divine judgment is not wholly absent.

There are also unmistakable allusions to Gatsby as a Christ-like figure as the novel approaches its climax: he's a man who dies for someone else's sins, at three in the afternoon, and has his true identity revealed three days later by his father. It is, of course, highly ironic that this pathetic fraud of a man, an unregenerate sinner, would be the redeeming figure in the novel. But that's also what makes it all the more appropriate and satisfying.

There's also a mystical strain that runs through the novel. It's apparent, for example, at the point when Gatsby feels his dream is just about within his grasp, a moment when Nick makes some deeply suggestive remarks:

> Through all he said, even through his appalling sentimentality, I was reminded of something—an elusive rhythm, a fragment of lost words, that I had heard somewhere a long time ago. For a moment a phrase tried to take shape in my mouth and my lips parted like a dumb man's, as though there was more struggling upon them than a wisp of startled air. But they made no sound and what I had almost remembered was uncommunicable forever.

The problem with the American Dream, this passage implicitly suggests, is not exactly that it's corrupt or vain. Indeed, the great paradox of *The Great Gatsby* is that even as Gatsby pursues his dream through instruments of fraud and adultery there is a deeply compelling purity about his ambition, especially given the smug pieties of those around him (hence Nick's sincere pronouncement that Gatsby is "worth the whole damn bunch of them put together"). Rather, the real problem is that any American Dream is finally too incomplete a vessel to contain longings that elude human expression or comprehension. We never reach the Coast we think we see.

Still we go on dreaming. Even those of us who have the means and desire to pursue their dreams finally have no power over what they happen to be: dreams usually come to us unbidden and are not typically practical or easy to achieve (otherwise they wouldn't be dreams). What makes the *American* Dream American is not that our dreams are any better, worse, or more interesting than anyone else's, but that we live in a country constituted of dreams, whose very justification continues to rest on it being a place where one can, for better and worse, pursue distant goals. This is something Fitzgerald understood very well. "Gatsby believed in the green light, the orgastic future that year by year recedes before us," he writes in the soaring conclusion of the novel, his vision pulling back out to encompass the whole of American history all the way back to Dutch sailors—themselves seeking a west coast—who encountered a new world "commensurate with [their] capacity to wonder."

LOOKING BACK *F. Scott Fitzgerald in 1937. "I look at it—and think it is the most beautiful history in the world," Fitzgerald wrote of the nation's past at the end of his life, when he
was living in Hollywood, burnishing the dreams of others. "It is the history of me and my
people. And if I came here yesterday . . . I should still think so. It is the history of all aspiration—not just the American dream but the human dream." (Photo from the Van Vechten Collection of the Library of Congress)*

At the core of many American Dreams, especially the Dream of the Coast, is an insistence that history doesn't matter, that the future matters far more than the past. But history is in the end the most tangible thing we have, the source and solace for all our dreams. In his 1991 book *The True and Only Heaven*, the late historian and social critic Christopher Lasch suggests its role in sustaining a sense of hope essential to the American Dream:

> Hope implies a deep-seated trust in life that appears absurd to those who lack it. It rests on confidence not so much in the future as in the past. It derives from early memories—no doubt distorted, overlaid with later memories, and thus not wholly reliable as a guide to any factual reconstruction of past events—in which the experience of order and contentment was so intense that subsequent disillusionments cannot dislodge it. Such experience leaves as its residue the unshakable conviction, not that the past was better than the present, but that trust is never completely displaced, even though it is never completely justified either and therefore destined inevitably to disappointments.

Gatsby, like other strivers for the Dream of the Coast, lacked such an understanding of the past, seeing it only as an explanation for limits he would inevitably overcome. His creator had a more sophisticated view, though the tragic course of his subsequent life suggests that the past may have been more of a nostalgic refuge than a source of courage with which to confront his demons (alcohol, among others). "I look at it—and think it is the most beautiful history in the world," Fitzgerald wrote of American history at the end of his life, when he was living in Hollywood, burnishing the dreams of others as a largely unsuccessful screenwriter. "It is the history of me and my people. And if I came here yesterday . . . I should still think so. It is the history of all aspiration—not just the American dream but the human dream and if I came at the end of it that too is a place in the line of pioneers." But it was not the end. That will come, but it hasn't yet.

In the meantime we beat on, boats with the current, forced forward ceaselessly into the future.

CONCLUSION: EXTENDING THE DREAM

IT IS A STORY as singular, and as old and familiar, as America itself:

Renu Pidurutagala* was born in Columbo, the largest city in the island nation of Sri Lanka, in 1950. Actually, her native land only *became* an island nation two years before: reputedly settled by Hindus from northeastern India circa 500 B.C., but largely Buddhist after 300 B.C., the island was successively colonized by a series of invaders, culminating in the Portuguese (who named it "Ceylon"), the Dutch, and finally the British, who ultimately granted the Singhalese their independence. Renu was the third of nine children and the eldest daughter. Her father, a technical engineer who trained himself via British correspondence courses, owned a business in the radio industry and was a great believer in education. That's why he paid to have his children educated in schools run by Catholic missionaries rather than in what were then considered inferior public schools. And that's why he allowed his daughter to earn a degree from a Montessori school in Columbo, where she was trained to practice early childhood education in the mid-1970s.

---

* I have changed some names and places to respect a desire for anonymity on the part of my subjects.

But daughters, of course, had to be married off. Sri Lankan society was changing, but it still had a caste system comparable to neighboring India's, and Renu's boyfriend of the time came from a lower stratum of society. This would not do, for arranged marriages were still the order of the day. Renu's brother was marrying into a local family, and her father hoped she could marry into the same one—a doubleheader, as it were. Renu would have none of it. She pleaded with her mother, who then turned to her father's aunt, who convinced him not to insist. Perhaps the girl was not ready.

She never would be. "I wanted to be an independent person," she said simply. So when she learned that a friend had gone to New York and would help her if she, too, made the trip, Renu applied for and received a visiting visa. Her friend introduced her to an African-American couple in nearby Mount Vernon, and she became a nanny to their son. When the child was old enough to go to school, her patrons suggested she use their basement to open a day care center. Renu had begun taking courses that would lead to a bachelor's degree in business administration (training that would be useful in running her business) and was well on her way to acquiring a "green card," giving her legal alien status. She received the necessary permits and began operating her day care center in 1984.

This is where Sheela Galle entered the picture. She, too, was a native of Columbo, two years younger than her good friend Renu, whom she met at the Montessori school. Sheela was an only child, but her experiences and aspirations were not unlike Renu's, though at the time she was working as a bookkeeper in Columbo. It was on a vacation in London in 1984 that she decided to visit the United States.

Renu met her at the airport. It was a dank October day, and Sheela was repelled by the chilly climate. But it didn't take long for Renu to convince her to stay. Sheela got a student visa (she ultimately earned an undergraduate degree in computer science and a master's degree in educational computing) and began working with Renu, who incorporated her day care center in Yorktown Heights with a name suggested by her old patron: Open Vistas.

Open Vistas grew. The 1980s were a time of rapid expansion in the day care industry—American women, who traditionally had primary responsibility for their families, were becoming a permanent presence in the paid workforce, too—and Renu and Sheela were deluged by more requests for placements than they could handle. In 1994 they bought a home in Yorktown Heights and converted the first floor into a new facility. Renu became an American citizen in 1992 and began following American politics as avidly as she did tennis. Sheela's path to citizenship has been slower, but she is on her way. There has been talk of opening a second facility, but the women are committed to keeping the business to a manageable size.

This is the kind of story we like to hear, a story where hard work pays off and aspirations are realized. And a story where the principals speak of their adopted land with accents of love and loyalty. "I'm so grateful to this country," Renu tells me over brunch at an Indian restaurant in the immigrant-rich city of Mamaroneck. "I got my dream to come true." What was that dream? I ask her. "To become an independent person," she replies. When I press her as to just what it means to be independent, she spells it out: "To own my own business and get an education. I live the way I want to live. I do my duty, but I have no boundaries." Besides paying taxes and following regulations, her "duty" includes tending to family affairs back in Sri Lanka, attending her temple in Queens, and making meals for the poor one weekend a month. Independence does not mean freedom from responsibility, but it does mean a degree of autonomy in meeting those responsibilities that was simply not possible where she came from.

Sheela expresses similar sentiments. Though one often hears horror stories about the notoriously overtaxed and inefficient Immigration and Naturalization Service, a circumspect Sheela refuses to rise to the bait. "The system is fair," she says flatly. Individual people, she notes, aren't always honest, but this is true everywhere.

Surely the women have some complaints. I query them about racism, and while they acknowledge its existence, they do not believe they have been personally subject to it, perhaps because they live in a fairly tight-knit community that includes nearby French immigrants as well as Latino natives. I continue to try to press them on what they believe to be the nation's shortcomings, on the ways they've been mistreated. But Renu, whose patience and placidity make her a marvel in interacting with children, finally tells me, with the earned serenity of a committed Buddhist, "Life is not easy, Jim. You've got to face those things."

There are, of course, other stories to be told. Stories of Salvadorean migrants driven out of their country amid a war on communism and prevented from entering this one amid a war on drugs. Stories of Pakistani fathers taken from their wives and children and held indefinitely without charges amid a war on terror. Stories of immigrants who do not speak or act toward the United States in terms of love or loyalty but rather in terms of hatred and destruction. The saga of what might be called the "Dream of the Immigrant"—a subset of the Dream of Upward Mobility—has long been marked by ambivalence and despair. For much of our history, we could never quite decide whether we finally regarded immigrants as a blessing or a burden. (Can we assimilate them? Will they drive down our wages? Will our children marry them?) Immigrants themselves have been unsure about whether to stay—and even how to navigate tensions between old-timers and newcomers.

So the saga of the Dream of the Immigrant is far from over. Indeed, it seems anything but static. Once the hopes and anxieties surrounded the Irish and Germans; then it was the Italians and Japanese. Now it's the Arabs and Mexicans. Once bias against Catholics was commonplace; then it was Jews. Now it's Muslims. But it isn't all a game of ethnic musical chairs; the overall trend has been toward greater acceptance and opportunity. For example, starting a business was always largely a male aspiration, for immigrants or anyone else. But as the case of Renu Pidurutagala shows, now women can do it, too, though it hardly seems a coincidence that professional opportunities open to women continue to cluster around caring for children, the sick, and the elderly. In these ways and others, the American Dream continues to be stretched, not always comfortably, by those from elsewhere—which, in the final analysis, is where every American, even those Native Americans who crossed the Bering Strait thousands of years ago, is from.

Not all of this stretching has come from without, however. Indeed, even without a huge surge in immigration, the closing decades of the twentieth century were a time of increased awareness of demographic differences in American society, in large measure because of the civil rights movement of the 1960s. One legacy of that movement has been a heightened awareness of the ways minority experiences have not corresponded to the presumptions or practices of "normal," "mainstream," or "traditional" Americans and of the ways in which a dominant American culture has overshadowed, even repressed, such alternative experiences. And one result of this heightened awareness has been an effort to recover and celebrate these alternatives, an ongoing collective effort that has revitalized American society as a whole in ways that range from more eclectic restaurant cuisine to better legal protections.

Nowhere has this collective effort been more obvious than in the American academy, where for the last twenty-five years a large body of scholarship has explored the ways various Americans have struggled with—and, in happier cases, overcome—legacies of racial, ethnic, sexual, and other forms of discrimination. Taken as a whole, this work has not only sharpened our national awareness in ways that even the most dedicated conservative cannot ignore, but has also broadened the prospects for new generations of Americans who may enjoy a greater sense of possibility—what Renu calls "independence"—than their predecessors.

But for a variety of reasons that relate to these developments, as well as resistance to them, many Americans of all varieties believe themselves to be living in a time of social fragmentation. One can't help but wonder whether the nation can be infinitely elastic and can incorporate people and traditions that are not necessarily democratic, or even pluralistic. In such a time, it may be useful—actually, it may be essential—that the skeptic of diversity as well as the true believer identify, and seek to strengthen, any sense of truly shared ground.

In writing this book, I hoped to show that the American Dream has functioned as shared ground for a very long time, binding together people who may have otherwise little in common and may even be hostile to one another. Which is not to say that the Dream should be uncritically upheld as a kind of miracle glue. Indeed, I have also hoped to show that all too often it serves as a form of lazy shorthand, particularly on the part of those who use it to ignore, or even consciously obscure, real divisions in American society.

Instead, what I would hope is that the American Dream could serve as a rigorous standard that we can use to ask a series of searching questions. What does it really mean, for example, to leave no child behind? How have we defined equality in our everyday lives, and are widely accepted terms like "equality of opportunity" more than empty abstractions? What is the price of any given American Dream, and who pays it? Are some dreams better than others? To ask, and begin to answer, such questions can transform the Dream from a passive token of national identity to a powerful instrument of national reform and revitalization.

"What happens to a dream deferred?" asked the great American poet Langston Hughes in his oft-cited 1951 poem "Harlem." The problem, he suggests, is that when dreams deferred are perceived as dreams denied, an explosion may erupt, one that will blow away living as well as dead aspirations. In an age when the American Dream still seems alive, even well, his troubling question remains as insistent as ever. The survival of our society depends on addressing it seriously, and addressing it seriously requires a willingness to work with the energy of a Puritan. This is a job for all of us. Not even the best child care can spare us the exertion.

NOTES ON SOURCES

Though, as I have tried to show, the American Dream retains enormous relevance and appeal in contemporary American life, I have written this book with the impression that many professional scholars regard it as a dowdy, if not downright disreputable, topic. Much of the reason for this is generational. Writers like Herbert Croly and James Truslow Adams addressed the American Dream directly or indirectly in their work in the first third of the twentieth century, but one might say that its golden age in academic (and, more specifically, historical) circles was the decades following the Second World War. In the aftermath of a struggle against fascism, and amid a struggle against communism, writers of a so-called consensus or exceptionalist sensibility, among them Daniel Boorstin and Richard Hofstadter, identified those aspects of American life that might help explain why the United States has not succumbed to—and should actively resist—the pull of totalitarianism. In his 1965 book *The Promise of America*, Yale historian John Morton Blum named those aspects and their larger significance:

> Social mobility, the prudential virtues, and universal education; land,
> free government, free thought, and human dignity; economic plenty
> and industrial power—all these sometimes overarching elements were
> reconciled within one overarching edifice, that of the American nation,
> the United States. The various parts merged to form the promise of
> American life. It was a promise that offered the chance of fulfillment to
> men of diverse ambitions and diverse ideals.

In other words, the American Dream.

In fact, of course, not all consensus historians uncritically celebrated the culture they observed. (Richard Hofstadter, for example, was dismayed by, even afraid of, the conformity he described.) But they thought they were describing a powerful reality that had to be dealt with as such.

Blum's book represented the high-water mark of this ideological outlook. In the years that followed, the Vietnam War, the rise of the black power movement, and a new wave of feminism raised pointed questions about whether the United States really *did* offer "the chance of fulfillment to men of diverse ambitions and diverse ideals." Historians such as Lawrence Levine, Ronald Takaki, and Patricia Limerick analyzed who was implicitly excluded in such a formulation. The intellectual spirit of the closing decades of the twentieth century could plausibly be termed an age of particularism, as scholars moved beyond inverting the conventional wisdom of exposing the promise of "Amerika" as a hypocritical lie to recovering lost visions and silent voices. The hope of many of these people—though I think this aspiration has gotten lost in the shuffle at times—is a reconstituted American Dream.

In some sense, I think of this book as part of a broader attempt to move beyond a now-stale debate over multiculturalism and identify shared common ground even as we recognize, even affirm, particularism (part of which involves acknowledging that the United States is in some respects unique in its development, but by no means insisting that our model represents the best or only way to go). I finish this project keenly aware of my intellectual shortcomings as well as my provincialism, but I hope at least to raise questions or furnish elements for others to use in preserving—which, in its purest form, is finally adapting—a vision of life that I can't help but feel, amid some grave doubts, has some redeeming value.

Because *The American Dream* was written more for students of American history (broadly construed) than professional scholars, I have not included endnotes, a bibliography, or other elements of the traditional academic apparatus. Instead, what follows is a brief description of some of the people and works that influenced me most. This bibliographic essay is by no means comprehensive of all the sources I consulted, nor should it be viewed as anything more than a basic primer on the topics in question. Yet to a degree I find remarkable, it does not simply describe sources that were significant in shaping this book but rather limns a body of historical literature from which my intellectual profile was cast. I am humbled by, and grateful for, the work of these people.

INTRODUCTION: A DREAM COUNTRY

Information on James Truslow Adams came from a number of sources, including Adams's entry in the *Dictionary of American Biography*, a classic reference work I accessed on CD-ROM (New York: Charles Scribner's Sons, 1997), and *James*

Truslow Adams: Historian of the American Dream, a memoir/collection of letters
written and edited by Allan Nevins (Urbana: University of Illinois Press, 1968).
As noted, *The Epic of America* was first published by Little, Brown in Boston in
1931. The copy I consulted was a reprint edition published by Blue Ribbon
Books in Garden City, New York, in 1941.

Alexis de Tocqueville used the phrase "the charm of anticipated
success"—which, incidentally, was once the title of this book—in the second volume of *Democracy in America,* the Henry Reeve translation annotated by Phillips
Bradley and first reprinted in 1945 (New York: Vintage Books, 1990). All subsequent references to either volume of *Democracy in America*—and there are
many—come from this edition.

Political scientist Jennifer Hochschild's *Facing Up to the American Dream: Race,
Class, and the Soul of the Nation* (Princeton, N.J.: Princeton University Press, 1996)
focuses mostly on the attitudes of African Americans, but its analytical rigor
makes it one of the more impressive explorations of the American Dream generally and one of the few works that tries to measure attitudes empirically.
Richard Sennett and Jonathan Cobb's *The Hidden Injuries of Class* (New York:
Knopf, 1972) has a more psychological and impressionistic approach, but its
observations about blue-collar workers parallel those found in Hochschild.

I'd like to express particular gratitude for the insights of Andrew Delbanco's
The Real American Dream: A Meditation on Hope (Cambridge: Harvard University
Press, 1999). The chapters in this remarkably evocative volume were first delivered as a series of lectures at Harvard in 1998 and greatly deepened my understanding of the Dream.

DREAM OF THE GOOD LIFE (I): THE PURITAN ENTERPRISE

My primary sources for Puritan literature were anthologies. The most important of these is the superbly edited and annotated *The Puritans in America: A Narrative Anthology,* edited by Alan Heimert and Andrew Delbanco (Cambridge:
Harvard University Press, 1985). Heimert was the premier Puritan scholar of
his generation; Delbanco is currently the commanding figure in his, and he has
augmented this volume with *Writing New England: An Anthology from the Puritans to
the Present* (Cambridge: Harvard University Press, 2001). Older but still useful
anthologies include *A New England Reader: William Bradford to Robert Lowell* (New
York: Antheneum, 1962), *The Puritans: A Sourcebook of Their Writings,* edited by
Perry Miller and Thomas H. Johnson (2 vols., New York: HarperTorchbooks,
1938), and *The Puritans: Their Prose and Poetry,* edited by Miller (New York:
Columbia University Press, 1956).

Perry Miller is to Puritan scholarship what Sigmund Freud is to psychology:
a giant whose conclusions have been questioned, even discarded, but whose
reputation is nevertheless secure. His magnum opus is *The New England Mind:*

The Seventeenth Century (Cambridge: Harvard University Press, 1939) and its sequel, *The New England Mind: From Colony to Province* (Cambridge: Harvard University Press, 1953). Other major secondary works that shaped my thinking include Edmund Morgan, *The Puritan Dilemma: The Story of John Winthrop* (Boston: Little, Brown, 1958), David Hall, *Worlds of Wonder, Days of Judgment: Popular Religious Belief in Early New England* (Cambridge: Harvard University Press, 1989), Andrew Delbanco, *The Puritan Ordeal* (Cambridge: Harvard University Press, 1989), and David Hackett Fischer's section on the Puritans in *Albion's Seed: Four British Folkways in America* (New York: Oxford University Press, 1989). In addition to Fischer, my understanding of everyday life in early New England was amplified by James Deetz, *In Small Things Forgotten: The Archeology of Early American Life* (New York: Anchor, 1977), Bruce Daniels, *Puritans at Play: Leisure and Recreation in Colonial New England* (New York: St. Martin's Press, 1995), and James Deetz and Patricia Scott Deetz, *The Time of Their Lives: Life, Love and Death in Plymouth Colony* (New York: W. H. Freeman, 2000). A more critical reading of Puritanism and New England culture generally can be found in Jill Lepore, *In the Name of War: King Philip's War and the Origins of American Identity* (New York: Knopf, 1998), a work that distills and extends a more skeptical historiographic tradition that includes scholars such as Francis Jennings and James Axtell. For an excellent one-volume overview, see Francis J. Bremer, *The Puritan Experiment: New England Society from Bradford to Edwards* (1971; Hanover, N.H.: University Press of New England, 1995).

DREAM CHARTER: THE DECLARATION OF INDEPENDENCE

Three pivotal twentieth-century works have shaped understandings of, and arguments about, the Declaration of Independence. The first is Carl Becker's *The Declaration of Independence: A Study in the History of Political Ideas,* first published in 1922 and revised in 1942 (my edition was published by Vintage in 1958). Becker emphasizes the influence of John Locke on Jefferson and the Founders. The second is Garry Wills's *Inventing America: Jefferson's Declaration of Independence* (1978; New York: Vintage, 1979). Wills makes much of the Scottish philosophy on Jefferson and the communitarian accents in his thinking. He also points out the very different way Jefferson and other Founders understood things like freedom, merit, and education, a topic also analyzed by Daniel J. Boorstin in *The Lost World of Thomas Jefferson* (1948; Chicago: University of Chicago Press, 1981). The third major twentieth-century work on the Declaration is Pauline Maier's *American Scripture: Making the Declaration of Independence* (New York: Knopf, 1997). Maier's work pointedly keeps Jefferson out of the title, emphasizing the degree to which earlier British political theory and local declarations of independence played a key role in the way Jefferson's draft was revised prior to final adoption. As the title also suggests, Maier explores the way in which the Declaration has been remembered, a point of departure for my own thinking on the subject.

Also important in this regard is the work of Michael Kammen, notably *A Season of Youth: The American Revolution and the Historical Imagination* (New York: Knopf, 1978) and his magisterial *Mystic Chords of Memory: The Transformation of Tradition in American Culture* (New York: Knopf, 1991).

My understanding of the cultural and intellectual backdrop for the American Revolution was shaped by a number of works by major American historians. The oldest of these is John Franklin Jameson's *The American Revolution Considered as a Social Movement* (1926; Princeton, N.J.: Princeton University Press, 1967). Like many students, I have been strongly influenced by the work of Bernard Bailyn, particularly his classic *Ideological Origins of the American Revolution* (Cambridge: Harvard University Press, 1967). Bailyn's student Gordon Wood has written two widely cited works: *The Creation of the American Republic, 1776–1787* (1969; New York: Vintage, 1972) and *The Radicalism of the American Revolution* (1991; New York: Vintage, 1993). Also important are a number of essays by Edmund Morgan, collected in *The Challenge of the American Revolution* (New York: Norton, 1976) and *The Meaning of Independence: John Adams, George Washington, and Thomas Jefferson* (1976; New York: Norton, 1978). Finally, Theodore Draper's *A Struggle for Power: The American Revolution* (1996; New York: Vintage, 1997) is a major work by a maverick historian who spent his scholarly career outside the academy. I found it bracing, provocative, and authoritative.

As far as general narrative accounts go, Robert Middlekauff's *The Glorious Cause: The American Revolution, 1763–1789* (New York: Oxford University Press, 1982) is the regnant scholarly text. Countless college students have been well served by Edmund Morgan's brief *The Birth of the Republic, 1763–1789*, which has undergone multiple editions since it was first published by Norton in 1956.

The literature of republicanism could easily make for an extended bibliographic essay in its own right, one that would include the work of Bailyn, Morgan, Wood, and Maier as well as scholars such as Sean Wilentz and Joyce Appleby. Those looking for an overview would be well served by *American Quarterly* 37:4 (Fall 1985), an issue of the journal devoted to the subject. See also Daniel Rodgers, "Republicanism: The Career of a Concept," *Journal of American History* 79:1 (June 1992), pp. 11–38. My understanding of the nuances of difference between Adams and Jefferson on natural aristocracy were clarified by Nicholas Lemann, *The Big Test: The Secret History of the American Meritocracy* (New York: Farrar, Straus, Giroux, 2000), a book that explores the legacy of natural aristocracy in contemporary American life.

DREAM OF THE GOOD LIFE (II): UPWARD MOBILITY

Information on upward mobility in colonial Virginia came from a variety of sources, the most important of which is Edmund Morgan's magnum opus, *American Slavery, American Freedom: The Ordeal of Colonial Virginia* (1975; New York: Norton, 1995). The other landmark account is Winthrop Jordan's *White over*

Black: Attitudes Toward the American Negro, 1550–1812 (Chapel Hill: University of North Carolina Press, 1968), condensed as *The White Man's Burden: Historical Origins of Racism in the United States* (New York: Oxford University Press, 1974).

All quotes from Benjamin Franklin, including his autobiography, letters, and Poor Richard maxims, can be found in the 1993 Oxford University Press edition edited by Ormond Seavey. Franklin is also the subject of two major recent biographies: Esmond Wright's *Franklin of Philadelphia* (Cambridge: Harvard University Press, 1986) and H. W. Brands's *The First American: The Life and Times of Benjamin Franklin* (New York: Doubleday, 2000). I'm happy to report that my thinking about Franklin was also influenced by the work of a former student, Aubrey Spath, whose superb 1997 Harvard College honors thesis, "Those Extraordinary Twins: Mark Twain and Benjamin Franklin," analyzed Twain's ambivalent (and often hilarious) opinions on the sage of Philadelphia.

My understanding of Andrew Jackson has developed over many years with the help of scholars like Robert Remini, Arthur Schlesinger Jr., Michael Rogin, and others. But one work worth singling out is *Andrew Jackson: Symbol for an Age*, a small gem by John William Ward (New York: Oxford University Press, 1955). Ward is a founding father of American Studies; his work has served as a model for my own ever since I encountered it in graduate school.

Unless otherwise indicated, all quotes from Abraham Lincoln are taken from the two-volume collection of speeches and writings edited by Don Fehrenbacher (New York: The Library of America, 1989). This 1,500-page set is less authoritative than the standard scholarly source, the nine-volume *Collected Works of Abraham Lincoln* (New Brunswick, N.J.: Rutgers University Press, 1953) edited by Roy P. Basler, but much more accessible. Indeed, this chapter came into existence precisely because I have lived with these two cherished books in my home ever since they were published, sifting, annotating, and distilling them. A one-volume edition with an introduction by Gore Vidal was published by the Library of America in 1992.

Lincoln's life and work has of course been the subject of a voluminous literature, some of which I survey in my chapter on the multivolume biography by Carl Sandburg in *The Civil War in Popular Culture: A Reusable Past* (Washington, D.C.: Smithsonian Institution Press, 1995). The most important recent biography is David Donald's *Lincoln* (New York: Simon & Schuster, 1995). My initial reaction to this book was one of irritation over Donald's emphasis on Lincoln's self-perceived lack of agency as president, but I have been increasingly convinced of its cogency and have incorporated it into my view of the American Dream.

The most important scholar to explore the relationship between Lincoln and the American Dream specifically is Gabor Boritt. As its title suggests, his *Lincoln and the Economics of the American Dream* (Memphis: Memphis State University Press, 1978) treats the issue from a materialist perspective. But over the course of his long career, Boritt has examined this and other aspects of Lincolniana in a large body of work that includes a number of edited anthologies, among them *The Lincoln Enigma: The Changing Faces of an American Icon* (New York: Oxford University Press, 2001). No work has been more important in shaping this chapter, however, than Richard Hofstadter's remarkably suggestive essay "Abraham Lincoln and the Self-Made Myth," from his classic *The American Political Tradition* (1948; New York: Vintage, 1959). Hofstadter's suggestion that the source of Lincoln's greatness lay in the way that he was "chastened and not intoxicated by power" was the seed from which all my thought has proceeded (by way of Stephen Oates, Garry Wills, James McPherson, et al.). One book published as I was finishing this one, William Lee Miller's *Lincoln's Virtues: An Ethical Biography* (New York: Knopf, 2002), was also very helpful.

KING OF AMERICA: THE DREAM OF EQUALITY

The background, text, and related documents for the *Plessy* decision can all be found in *Plessy v. Ferguson,* edited with an introduction by Brook Thomas (Boston: Bedford/St. Martin's, 1996). Another book in the same series offers comparable information for *Dred Scott v. Sandford,* edited by Paul Finkelman (1997). Two volumes from Longman Publishers' "Primary Sources in American History" series—*Women in the National Experience,* edited by Ellen Skinner (1996), and *Sources of the African American Past,* edited by Roy Finkenbine (1997)—were also helpful sources of documentary evidence for this chapter.

A number of works cited for earlier chapters—notably Edmund Morgan's *American Slavery, American Freedom* and David Hackett Fischer's *Albion's Seed*—illuminated the ideological foundations of inequality in the colonial South. David Blight's biographical *Frederick Douglass' Civil War: Keeping Faith in Jubilee* (Baton Rouge: Louisiana State University Press, 1989) helped shape my understanding of Douglass's thinking about slavery, freedom, and equality. Blight is the editor of an edition of *The Autobiography of Frederick Douglass* in the Bedford series cited above (1993) and is also the author of *Race and Reunion: The Civil War in American Memory* (Cambridge: Harvard University Press, 2001), a treasure trove of quotes and analysis. No account of the late nineteenth- and early twentieth-century South can be complete without C. Vann Woodward's *The Strange Career of Jim Crow* (1955; 3d rev. ed. New York: Oxford University Press, 1974), one of the most important works of American history ever published.

Of comparable, if not greater, stature is Gunnar Myrdal's landmark work of sociology, *An American Dilemma: The Negro Problem and Modern Democracy* (2 vols., New York: Harper & Brothers, 1944), regarded by many as the opening salvo of the civil rights movement. James T. Patterson traces the origins and outcome of another pivotal moment with his customary meticulousness and clarity in *Brown v. Board of Education: A Civil Rights Milestone and Its Troubled Legacy*

(New York: Oxford University Press, 2001). For those seeking a brief narrative history of the movement, I suggest Harvard Sitkoff, *The Struggle for Black Equality 1954–1992* (1981; New York: Noonday Press, 1993).

The best single-volume resource of primary source material on Martin Luther King is *A Testament of Hope: The Essential Writings of Martin Luther King Jr.* (San Francisco: HarperSanFrancisco, 1986). Two Pulitzer Prize–winning biographies are of crucial importance: David J. Garrow's *Bearing the Cross: Martin Luther King, Jr. and the Southern Christian Leadership Conference* (1986; New York: Vintage, 1988) and Taylor Branch's gigantic *Parting the Waters: America in the King Years, 1954–1963* (New York: Simon & Schuster, 1988). Garrow's book is a one-volume treatment of King's life and work; the second volume of Branch's biography, *Pillar of Fire: America in the King Years, 1963–1965*, was published by Simon & Schuster in 1998. (A third volume, *At Canaan's Edge*, is forthcoming.) I was also greatly aided in my understanding of King thanks to Michael Eric Dyson's *I May Not Get There with You: The True Martin Luther King* (2000; New York: Touchstone, 2001). See also Marshall Frady's evocative *Martin Luther King Jr.* in the "Penguin Lives" series of short biographies (New York: Penguin, 2002).

DETACHED HOUSES: THE DREAM OF HOME OWNERSHIP

The source of my assertion that roughly two-thirds of Americans at the turn of this century own their own homes is the *New York Times*. See "To the Surprise of Many Experts, Housing Boom Keeps Rolling," May 27, 1999, p. A1.

Some of the most important historical scholarship on the United States ever written concerns the American West. A case in point Henry Nash Smith's *Virgin Land: The American West as Symbol and Myth* (Cambridge: Harvard University Press, 1950), one of the founding works of American Studies. But the fountainhead of this literature is Frederick Jackson Turner's 1893 essay "The Significance of the Frontier in American History," which can be found along with other pioneering work in *Frontier and Section: Selected Essays of Frederick Jackson Turner* (Englewood Cliffs, N.J.: Prentice-Hall, 1961).

The Turner thesis has of course spawned a voluminous literature; a few important responses can be found in *The Turner Thesis Concerning the Role of the Frontier in American History* (Lexington, Mass.: D. C. Heath, 1972). For a particularly compelling intellectual portrait of Turner, see Richard Hofstadter, *The Progressive Historians: Turner, Beard, Parrington* (Chicago: University of Chicago Press, 1969). The preeminent contemporary critic of Turner is Patricia Nelson Limerick. See *The Legacy of Conquest: The Unbroken Past of the American West* (New York: Norton, 1987). Another major writer about the West in particular and American land generally is William Cronon; see particularly his towering *Nature's Metropolis: Chicago and the Great West* (New York: Norton, 1991). Other scholars on the subject who shaped my thinking include Jonathan Raban, *Bad Land: An American Romance* (1996; New York: Vintage, 1997), John L. Thomas, *A*

Country of the Mind: Wallace Stegner, Bernard DeVoto, and the American Land (New York: Routledge, 2000), and my graduate school classmate, Dorothee Kocks, from whom I borrow the term "Frontier State." See *Dream a Little: Land and Social Justice in Modern America* (Berkeley: University of California Press, 2000).

The literature of surburbanization has also attracted a distinguished body of writers, some of whom (David Riesman, William Whyte, Betty Friedan) are discussed in the chapter as primary sources. For me, the single most important work is Kenneth T. Jackson's *Crabgrass Frontier: The Surburbanization of the United States* (New York: Oxford University Press, 1985). Other important works include Robert Fishman, *Bourgeois Utopias: The Rise and Fall of Suburbia* (New York: Basic Books, 1987), Elaine Tyler May, *Homeward Bound: American Families in the Cold War Era* (New York: Basic Books, 1988), Joel Garreau, *Edge City: Life on the New Frontier* (New York: Anchor, 1991), Jane Holtz Kay, *Asphalt Nation: How the Automobile Took Over America, and How We Can Take it Back* (New York: Crown, 1997), and *Suburban Nation: The Rise of Sprawl and the Decline of the American Dream* (New York: North Point Press, 2000).

DREAM OF THE GOOD LIFE (III): THE COAST

A number of works indirectly contributed to my formulation of the term "the Coast" to describe a particular American Dream. Godfrey Hodgson's *America in Our Time: From World War II to Nixon, What Happened and Why* (1976; New York: Vintage, 1978) charts the almost utopian dreams spawned by postwar affluence and a collective yearning for effortless success. James T. Patterson makes a similar argument in *Grand Expectations: The United States, 1945–1975* (New York: Oxford University Press, 1996). See also Loren Baritz's *The Good Life: The Meaning of Success for the American Middle Class* (1982; New York: Harper & Row, 1990) and Robert J. Samuelson's *The Good Life and its Discontents: The American Dream in the Age of Entitlement, 1945–1995* (New York: Times Books, 1995). Of particular interest to me were those works that explored the more psychological dimensions of this dream in the realm of consumer culture. In particular, see William Leach, *Land of Desire: Merchants, Power, and the Rise of a New American Culture* (1993; New York: Vintage, 1994), and T. J. Jackson Lears, *Fables of Abundance: A Cultural History of Advertising in America* (New York: Basic Books, 1994). But probably the most important of all are the enormously suggestive essays of Warren Susman. See especially "Personality and the Making of Twentieth-Century Culture" and other pieces in *Culture as History: The Transformation of American Society in the Twentieth Century* (New York: Pantheon, 1984).

On the culture of gambling, my most important source was John Findlay, *People of Chance: Gambling in American Society from Jamestown to Las Vegas* (New York: Oxford University Press, 1986). My account of Las Vegas's origins came from a number of general accounts, the most rigorous and useful of which was Eugene Moehring's *Resort City in the Sunbelt: Las Vegas, 1930–1970* (Reno: University of

Nevada Press, 1989). Another useful source was Robert D. McCracken's *Las Vegas: The Great American Playground* (Reno: University of Nevada Press, 1997). See also Pete Earley, *Super Casino: Inside the "New" Las Vegas* (New York: Bantam, 2000).

The preeminent historian of California is Kevin Starr, author of multiple volumes in a series entitled "Americans and the California Dream," all published by Oxford University Press. The most important for my purposes were *Americans and the California Dream, 1850–1915* (1973) and *Inventing the Dream: California Through the Progressive Era* (1985). Another pivotal writer on Southern California in particular is Mike Davis; see in particular *City of Quartz: Excavating the Future in Los Angeles* (1990; New York: Vintage, 1992).

The literature of the early film industry in general and Hollywood in particular is enormous. (It is to some degree encapsulated in Jim Cullen, *The Art of Democracy: A Concise History of Popular Culture in the United States,* 2d ed. [New York: Monthly Review Press, 2002].) Of special significance here is Lary May, *Screening Out the Past: The Birth of Mass Culture and the Motion Picture Industry* (1980; Chicago: University of Chicago Press, 1983), which has an excellent chapter on Douglas Fairbanks, Mary Pickford, and Pickfair. See also Gary Carey, *Doug and Mary: A Biography of Douglas Fairbanks and Mary Pickford* (New York: Dutton, 1977), and Richard Schickel, *His Picture in the Papers: A Speculation on Celebrity in America Based on the Life of Douglas Fairbanks Sr.* (New York: Charterhouse, 1973). Schickel is also the author of a major biography of D. W. Griffith, *D. W. Griffith: An American Life* (New York: Simon & Schuster, 1984).

CONCLUSION: EXTENDING THE DREAM

The literature of immigration is too vast to be done justice here. One commonly cited historiographic starting point is Oscar Handlin's classic, but dated, *The Uprooted: The Epic Story of the Great Migration that Made the American People* (1951; New York: Atlantic–Little, Brown, 1990). It was supplanted as the standard text in 1985 with the publication of John Bodnar's *The Transplanted: A History of Immigrants in Urban America* (Bloomington: University of Indiana Press). The eurocentric bias of most immigration histories is corrected by Ron Takaki in *A Different Mirror: A History of Multicultural America* (Boston: Little, Brown, 1994). Some of the most recent work in the field emphasizes the degree to which American immigrants retained ties to the old country. See in particular Matthew Frye Jacobson, *Special Sorrows: The Diasporic Imagination of Irish, Polish, and Jewish Immigrants to the United States* (Cambridge: Harvard University Press, 1995). For a synthetic attempt to narrate American history from the founding through the Civil War through demographic synthesis, see Edward Countryman, *Americans: A Collision of Histories* (New York: Hill & Wang, 1996).

ACKNOWLEDGMENTS

One might wonder to what extent this particular book represents the realization of the author's own American Dream. The obvious answer is: a good deal. As is so often the case in discussions of the Dream, however—in this case, it's a Dream of Upward Mobility that took root as a child—the obvious answer is also a partial one. While I'm not sure how possible or useful it would be to provide a complete answer, it does seem worth noting here that this book feels like it has been as much a product of failure as it has success.

The immediate origins of the project can be traced to a hotel room in Long Branch, New Jersey, in June of 1997. I was on a brief tour to support my book *Born in the U.S.A.* and, amid growing certitude that it would not be a success, discharged anxious energy by making notes toward my next undertaking. It was to focus on the meanings and uses of patriotism, perhaps patterned on the book I had with me at the time, *American Politics: The Promise of Disharmony,* by political scientist Samuel Huntington. The idea was to rehabilitate a concept that had fallen into severe disfavor in recent decades and suggest that patriotism could be the refuge of reformers no less than scoundrels (who weren't always one and the same). Vestiges of this original idea survive, notably in the epigraph of this book, as well as in fragments of chapter 5.

The subsequent months and years were not particularly happy ones.

Chapters of the patriotism book got drafted, then got put aside as another project seemed to grow out of it, this one a study of Frank Sinatra and American identity. I completed the Sinatra manuscript but, after a few negative reactions, decided it was unpublishable. By the middle of 1999, I realized that my interest in questions about patriotism and identity could be most usefully focused by an exploration of the American Dream, but this inquiry was sidetracked by a detour into fiction (and an offshoot project on Catholicism and the American Dream). It was beginning to come back on track in the spring of 2001 when I first encountered Susan Ferber of Oxford University Press. Both of us had doubts this could ever be an Oxford book, but Susan showed extraordinary persistence, patience, and generosity in shepherding it through the evaluation pipeline. And so it is that I make my first acknowledgment to her, without whom, I suspect, this book would never have been finished, never mind published.¹

Most of this book, like three others, was assembled during my years as a preceptor in the Expository Writing Program at Harvard University (1994–2001). I will always be indebted to my colleagues there and particularly to Nancy Sommers, director of "Expos," and her lieutenant, Gordon Harvey. Their kindness, confidence, and flexibility were crucial in allowing me to work in an extraordinary place that I will always cherish.

For some of these years, I also taught in the Committee on Degrees in History and Literature at Harvard and had the good fortune of working with people like Dirk Killen, who taught me much of what little I know about the Puritans, and participating in a writing group from Hist & Lit and other programs that read and discussed early drafts of the book. In particular, I'd like to thank Steve Biel, now director of studies in Hist & Lit, as well as Laura Saltz, Elizabeth Abrams, Jill Lepore, Kristin Hoganson, and Cathy Cormier.

Another circle of friends clustered around Sarah Lawrence College. In recent years, I've taught insightful adult students in classes on the American Dream at the college's Center for Continuing Education, thanks to the generosity of Alice Olson, Susan Guma, and Amy Lang. A number of faculty and spouses also served as a sounding board, among them Leah Olson, Dan Greenberg, Mary LaChapelle, Pauline Watts, and Ron Afzal.

Much of the book was written during the 2000–2001 school year, when I was visiting assistant professor of American Civilization at

Brown University, my graduate school alma mater. Mari Jo and Paul Buhle and Susan Smulyan continued and deepened the support they have shown toward me for well over a decade. I also feel a particular debt to my other mentor, Jack Thomas of the History Department, who read the manuscript with his customary brio. I consider myself fortunate to be among the generations of students who have benefited from his marvelous combination of bracing honesty and paternal warmth. You've meant more than we can say, Jack.

A series of considerations—among them the arrival of twin sons Grayson and Ryland in 1999 and what had been considered the medically inconceivable arrival of daughter Nancy two years later—led me to leave academia in 2001 and take a position as a history teacher at the Ethical Culture Fieldston School in New York City. This was a change I made with some misgivings, but I have been happily surprised in many ways, among them my own capacity for vicarious pleasure in the lives of some terrific students. I'm indebted to school head Joseph Healey and principal Rachel Friis Stettler, along with some fine colleagues, among them Andrew Meyers, David Swartwout, Bethany Neubauer, Rachelle Friedman, Bob Montera, and Kate Fox Reynolds.

At Oxford University Press, Anne Rockwood ably tracked down many of the illustrations. India Cooper copy-edited the manuscript with skill and tact, saving me from countless errors. And Joellyn Ausanka skillfully shepherded the manuscript through production.

A few final words. Lydia Wills helped me believe I could write a book on the American Dream. My beloved friend Gordon Sterling has always lent a ready ear and much sage advice. Heather Winn and Lara Haggar volunteered to help with the kids and much else. My in-laws, especially Ted, Nancy, and Judy Sizer, have helped tremendously in countless ways, principally as living examples. My oldest son, Jay, has been an invaluable helpmate to his siblings and increasingly cherished company in his own right. My parents dared to pursue their dreams and allowed my sister and me to pursue our own (which, in her case, include a new husband and child).

And then there is my wife, Lyde, who has both made it possible to work toward achieving my dreams and allowed me to see their limits. To paraphrase the words of Tom Petty's soundtrack from the 1996 movie *She's the One*, she's got a heart so big it could crush a village. I can't hold out forever, Lyde. Even walls come down.

INDEX

Page numbers in **bold** indicate entire chapters.
Page numbers in *italics* indicate photographs or illustrations.